CW00392197

The Camisard

War and Religion in the Cévennes Uprising

Also by David Crackanthorpe
Marseille

The Camisard
War and Religion in the Cévennes Uprising

David Crackanthorpe

Signal

Signal Books
Oxford

First published in 2016 by
Signal Books Limited
36 Minster Road
Oxford OX4 1LY
www.signalbooks.co.uk

© David Crackanthorpe, 2016

The right of David Crackanthorpe to be identified as the author of this work has been asserted by him in accordance with the Copyright, Design and Patents Act, 1988.

All rights reserved. The whole of this work, including all text and illustrations, is protected by copyright. No parts of this work may be loaded, stored, manipulated, reproduced or transmitted in any form or by any means, electronic or mechanical, including photocopying and recording, or by any information, storage and retrieval system without prior written permission from the publisher, on behalf of the copyright owner.

A catalogue record for this book is available from the British Library

ISBN 978-1-909930-20-9 Paper

Cover Design: Tora Kelly
Typesetting: Tora Kelly
Cover Image: *Jean Cavalier, chef camisard* by Pierre-Antoine Labouchère, courtesy Le Musée du Désert, Mialet
Printed in India

For Laura

Contents

Introduction

The chief historic centre of Protestantism in France is the city of Nîmes. It was here, on the Esplanade built outside the Roman walls on the southern side, dominated by the huge masonry of the Roman amphitheatre, that the greatest number of executions of Protestants during the rising of the Cévennes were performed, to the sound of military drumbeats and church bells. Until the newly arrived maréchal de Villars, in an attempt at pacification, ordered all such equipment swept away in August 1704, the blood-stained wheels with their turning mechanism, the gibbets, the burned-out pyres of wood and human ash were left in place on this terrace built for citizens' holiday celebrations and parades. The deep hostility between Catholic and Protestant which this history left imprinted on both has only recently subsided, and can sometimes still be felt, while in the mountains of the Cévennes, visible from the topmost level of the amphitheatre, there is little pretence that it ever died away.

The uprising has been largely neglected in English historical writing, although at the time there were close connections between French Protestant (Huguenot) exiles in London and the rebels in the Languedoc. In France, however, there is a huge amount of work on the subject and it continues to attract a fascinated interest from both fiction and non-fiction writers. Histories have generally been recognizably written by Catholic or by Protestant apologists—although in recent times greater objectivity has appeared—and no early account from either side can be entirely trusted as free from bias of opinion and often from distortion of fact. The first serious study, which in the words of one of the leading modern scholars, Philippe Joutard, "can still be used as a source of reference and not merely as the expression of a mentality", was Antoine Court's *Histoire des troubles des Cévennes ou de la guerre des camisards* (the name given to the rebel fighters, first by the civil and military authorities, and then adopted by all) *sous le règne de Louis le Grand*, which appeared in 1760 but was not followed in its objectivity by nineteenth-century historians. Court was a Huguenot pastor who had been involved as a boy and young man in the last manifestations of the rebellion and his book earned the highest compliment payable in the eighteenth century by the historian acknowledged in the Encyclopédie de la Pléiade as author of "the first great modern historical work to achieve the synthesis of classical learning and the meaning of human problems": Edward Gibbon. "The Histoire des Camisards may be recommended as accurate and impartial. It requires some attention to discover the religion of the author," Gibbon wrote.

On this vital point I would claim that any partiality in my account is not due to commitment or antagonism to metaphysical or religious schemes but to empathy, after eighteen years of residence in the low Cévennes and as many more in Nîmes, with the dispossessed of their mountain land, the objectors of conscience in this tragic history, the sometimes obdurate adherents to ancestral and ethical loyalty. It was unsurprising to me to learn that the people of the Cévennes and their pastors became active resistants during the Nazi occupation of southern France after 1942, and to hear the frequently used term *camisard/maquisard* of those fighters who then sheltered, hid and stored their arms in the same caves as their Camisard predecessors 240 years earlier.

For 300 years, historians have explored the documentary evidence of the war, the few contemporary accounts, the official and military correspondence in the Archives du Ministère de la Guerre, the Antoine Court papers in Geneva, the Languedoc records in Montpellier. Henri Bosc in his monumental history published in 1985-93, *La Guerre des Cévennes 1702-1710*, gave the fruit of his lifetime of exhaustive enquiry, evaluation and judgement on all these and other sources; and more recently W. Gregory Monahan in *Let God Arise* offered his further researches. My own purpose has been to analyse and present the story supported by reference to so many versions of the evidence, to weigh them, where they or I differ, one against the other or against my own construction of events and characters, to interpret both the known facts and the readings of them by witnesses and by historians of varying tendency, and to bring to this tragic drama, with its prelude in the Saint Bartholomew massacres of 1572, and its consequences down the centuries, whatever understanding of the people and country of the Cévennes sympathy has gained by so many years spent among them.

There are two particularities of the practice of guerrilla warfare by the Camisards to which the writer's outlook is also relevant. First, the matter of revelation so often invoked, and so final, in the Huguenot mentality. Here it should be enough to rely on John Locke: "Whatever God has revealed, is certainly true; no doubt can be made of it ... but whether it be a divine revelation, or no, reason must judge." Second, the question of prophecy on which the Camisard fighters depended for their military initiatives and which deeply offended the Calvinists of the Swiss *refuge*, while it excited, in 1706, the millenarians and the London public amused by supernatural temptations. Superstition dies hard, time is a prison and prophecy still attracts, but it must be agreed that its use with self-induced convulsions and trance by the Camisard leaders to control the action in battle or flight of their followers, to identify informers, decide the fate of captives and dictate the content of their sermons and exhortations suggests an exploitation of credulity and of rhetorical influence; the fact that one of the two principal leaders, Jean Cavalier, and his ally and follower Jacques Bonbonnoux later maintained a strict silence on their own practice would seem to imply that prophecy was a technique used with such sincerity as warfare licenses, but abandoned when its usefulness was over and reality showed a different aspect. It was those former comrades, for example Élie Marion, who never returned to a shared reality after the rebellion was past, who were the most vociferous in their attacks on Cavalier for his denial of the illusions of a partisan war in which any weapon to hand was as good as its value in the field.

The term "Huguenot" is thought to derive, if distantly, from the German *Eidgenosse* signifying a confederate or, more particularly, a Swiss subject. Switzerland was the nearest country of safe exile, the *refuge*, for endangered Protestants of the Languedoc, as England was for those from Normandy after 1685; and "huguenot" was a pejorative designation given by Catholics in the sixteenth century to their Protestant enemies. By the seventeenth century the name was used of exiles of the Reformed Church living in countries of the *refuge*, and was adopted by cévenol Protestants to show allegiance to the historic Protestantism of the *désert*, and thence to the biblical story of the flight from Egypt to the "promised land". *Désert* was equally their term for the secret gathering places in the Cévennes where clandestine open air services were held in the time of persecution, of which the Musée du Désert at Mialet in the cévenol foothills is both historical museum and living shrine of memory for Huguenots of the diaspora in every hemisphere.

INTRODUCTION

The Huguenot presence in London in the years after 1685 was well advanced by 1706 when the principal uprising ended, towards integration into English religious and economic life and assimilation to English social and liberal forms. The sudden arrival in that year of a small number of escaped Camisard fighters, the "French Prophets," wild, clamorous men from the bloody fields and burnt-out mountains of the Cévennes, provoked at first sympathetic interest and amusement in a society where liberty of expression was guaranteed by the withdrawal, in 1695, of the Licensing Act of 1662; but was later followed, with the fickleness of public taste, by rejection though not expulsion. The French Prophets, whose journey and their end are recounted in the opening chapter were, by their religious exaltation, their prophesying and belief in miracles, their idealisation of martyrdom, their passionate commitment to faith under the guidance of inner voices taken as direct inspiration from god, a living illustration of the outcome of religious war, oppression, persecution, revolt and defeat that subsequent chapters relate. To the unbeliever, religious faction may seem mankind's great tragedy; to the committed such as Catholic and Protestant in this history, faction is merely the upholding of truth at whatever human cost. The divide between the two points of view seems not limited to Christianity alone, but is clearly marked in any objective sight of the relations between Catholic and Protestant in seventeenth- and early eighteenth-century France.

In our own day it is not only in the Languedoc that the Catholic/Protestant divide continues to be evidenced by ironic reference masking a still active opposition; in the Catholic Auvergne, for example, Protestantism and Protestants often evoke a reaction most plausibly explained by a sense of historic discomfort—puzzled awe, defensive mockery, disbelief in the possibility of non-conformism. But many admirers may find that the coexistence in France of differing branches of thought and behaviour stemming from a single trunk makes this great culture less monolithic than it would otherwise be, more sympathetic and better able to reach towards the state of toleration where, in Locke's words, "everyone is orthodox to himself", and where points of view, bitterly held under the dominance of sects, may merge in the light of reasonable doubt.

PILLORY DISAPOINTED,

OR, THE

Falſe PROPHETS Advancement.

To the Tune of Rotten Eggs, Turnop-Tops, Pieces of Dirt, & Brick-Batts.

'English & French Prophets Mad or Bewitched ... to terrify the Queen's people.'
Woodcuts, 1707

Chapter One

French Prophets in London

At the Sign of the Camisards

The oppressed Huguenot minority of southern France perceived the England of Queen Anne as "that happy isle where liberty and abundance reign".[1] The vision was distant, but from a land where famine was recurrent and conscience no longer free. London with half a million inhabitants was the most populous city in Europe, a centre of economic growth and site of a developing model of government and public life from which the concept of absolute monarchy had been erased. Voltaire remarked that after the Revolution and Bill of Rights of 1688, John Locke's view that a rational man will hold his opinions with some measure of doubt became increasingly dominant; in 1689, the year in which Locke's *First Letter on Toleration* and two *Treatises on Government* were printed, the Act of Toleration followed. Rational opinion superseding mere belief implied, according to Locke's formula, "not entertaining any proposition with greater assurance than the proofs it is built upon will warrant".

Even with its limits and exclusions the Act of Toleration was in great contrast to Louis XIV's revocation in 1685 of the Edict of Nantes, which a hundred years earlier had granted French Protestants security in freedom of belief and worship; gracious privileges more advanced than in any European country other than Holland, but eroded progressively through the seventeenth century and dramatically abolished by the Revocation. Queen Anne on her accession in 1702, when the persecution of French Protestants was at its height, declared, "I shall be very careful to preserve and maintain the Act of Toleration, and to set the minds of all my people at quiet." The Revocation gave formal backing to persecution of dissenters from the opinions of the Catholic majority and of the king but did not begin it, though from that moment it was intensified and grew through stages of horror to turn within a few years into a genocidal attack in the name of uniform belief and practice on the isolated and, it was thought, defenceless remaining Huguenot minority in the Cévennes mountains of the Languedoc.

Between five and six thousand French Protestants had reached London by 1593 after the Saint Bartholomew's Day massacres, but the main diaspora followed immediately on the Revocation. Numbers of emigrants are still uncertain but about three hundred and fifty thousand are believed to have left France, of whom seventy thousand came to England from Normandy, Brittany and the Atlantic provinces. At the start of the eighteenth century between forty and fifty thousand of these were settled in London and achieving gradual integration into an urban population with a literacy rate of fifty per cent and a press, uncensored since 1695, of eighteen periodicals and newspapers including the world's first daily paper, the *Daily Courant*. Huguenot immigrants entered a world more varied and generally more prosperous than they had known; but above all more intellectually liberal and moderate under the influence of Locke, later to be carried over the Channel by Voltaire's *Lettres philosophiques* (*Lettres anglaises*) which was burnt on its first appearance in France as scandalous and disrespectful, and its author arrested. Locke noted on 22 March 1676 in Montpellier that "The New philosophie (referring to Descartes) prohibited to be taught in universitys, schooles & Academies."[2]

Many of these Huguenots of the *refuge* came from the artisan class, and the weavers in particular had skills often superior to those of the English; others were from the ranks of professionals in the law, teaching or medicine; and in a few cases from the Norman gentry. Those who left France before 1685 brought much of their capital with them, but since one motive at least of the Revocation had been to drive dissidents to a forbidden emigration and confiscate their goods for the state and Church, those leaving after could bring little or nothing. Under Charles II and James II, collections of £85,000 were made and Parliament in 1696 voted £15,000 a year for Huguenot relief, but the distribution of 1705 was attacked for inequity to the disadvantage of the poor, and in 1708 accusations of fraud were brought against the French committee managing the funds. In 1706 there was still poverty among the Huguenot weavers settled in and around Spitalfields while their better off countrymen, living chiefly in the elegance of Soho where many set up as silversmiths or jewellers, were alleged to cream off the best of the subsidies to maintain the style of life they were used to, and perpetuate a hierarchical system imported from France.

Nevertheless, the Huguenot community as a whole worked towards social acceptance and integration and most of their people lived soberly under the direction of Calvinist consistories, the ruling body of each congregation consisting of minister and elected elders, worshipping in the thirty French churches, the most important of them in Threadneedle Street and the Savoy, and guided by at least a hundred exiled *pasteurs*, many without a ministry. In the same years the Anglicans of London, numbering at least half a million, were served by fewer than forty churches; this relatively non-emphatic religious practice must have increasingly spread among the Huguenot exiles, the majority of whom were absorbed into the Anglican Church by the end of the century. Further evidence of integration is found in the records of the Bank of England according to which by 1710 ten per cent of investors in Bank of England stock were Huguenot exile families.

An example of rapid assimilation to London life and to English society of a Huguenot exile of 1685 was the career of Peter Anthony Motteux from Rouen, who successfully applied in 1718 to use the coat of arms of his French forebears. Already aged 22 on his arrival, Motteux quickly mastered the language of London and by 1692 was editing and publishing the monthly *Gentleman's Journal*, considered, as forerunner to *The Tatler* and *Spectator*, to be the germ of the modern magazine. At the same time he worked as an auctioneer, had a shop in Leadenhall Street selling oriental imports, and a position in the Post Office. In 1708 he published an edition of which Book III was completed by himself and Books IV and V were his own, of Sir Thomas Urquhart's translation of Rabelais' *Gargantua and Pantagruel*, faithful to the vulgarity of Rabelais' text and reprinted six times. In 1712 he produced a new translation of Cervantes' *Don Quixote*, which remains a version of great liveliness and humour though it was criticized in the nineteenth century for its "Franco-cockney" vernacular. Motteux, described by Pope as an inveterate talker, rose in English society, married an English wife, became a Freeman of the City of London in

1712 and was the author of a number of plays successfully produced on the London stage, including the last entitled *Love's a Jest*. In 1719 he died of strangulation in a brothel near Temple Bar, apparently in the course of an erotic game; the mistress of the house and three others were tried but acquitted of his murder.[3] The moral rigour and social hold of the Calvinist consistories were evidently not uniformly felt in the life of the exiles, even of the first generation.

Even so, there was a Huguenot solidarity, and a policy of settling problems among themselves characteristic of a homogeneous community earning a place in a vital but volatile new society without attracting attention by eccentricities. These aims were dramatically put into focus and to the test by the arrival in London in 1706 of a quartet of refugees from the Cévennes mountains in the southern French province of Languedoc, where they and their fellow men and women had endured a lifetime's persecution and a savage two-year war against the armies of Louis XIV, with many atrocities on both sides. These were the battle-scarred relics of a Huguenot peasant army called the Camisards, a sobriquet soon made familiar to Londoners by the renaming of an inn near Charing Cross, *At the Sign of the Camisards*. The violence of their experience, and the lives they had led of hatred endured and repaid, separated them both from the peaceable Huguenot exile community in which they now found themselves, and from an English society in which the divisions of the Civil War had been largely closed by time, the primacy of parliament and the Bill of Rights. The events following the arrival of these men and the progress, with a growing band of followers, of their stay in England owed less to their reputation as heroes of a guerrilla war of "little people" than to their claims of prophetic powers and announcements of the approaching millennium. The accession to the throne of William and Mary foretold by Pierre Jurieu, an influential exiled pastor and historian in Rotterdam who made a study of the Apocalypse,[4] took place three years after the Revocation and was seen in the Languedoc as a portent of the coming revival of Protestantism, of the end of the reign of the "Beast" and the fulfilment of millenarian hopes in accordance with prophecies one of whose characteristics, repeatedly shown during the period of London prophesying, was to survive all failure to materialize in reality.

Prophets and the Public

Huguenots in the Cévennes often gave biblical names—Abraham, Isaac, Gédéon, Élie—to children raised on Old Testament readings by family elders, in the Protestant translation of 1588, with particular emphasis on the Apocalypse and intended to counter the Catholic indoctrination they were subjected to at school; this, in conditions of distress, fear, and anger prepared fertile ground for the seed of prophecy. The first prophets of the movement that was to become the Camisard uprising were children and young girls whose pronouncements in states of trance were taken as messages of the Holy Spirit. The four London Camisards used methods developed and exploited before and during the fighting, of apparent trance and prophecy with convulsions and vocal effects, to draw attention to their arrival in the English capital from the tragic fields of war and perhaps in the hope of recruiting fellow Protestants to continue the fight against the Catholics of France. Their behaviour alarmed the leaders of the London consistories who before long distanced themselves from a phenomenon they feared could discredit the Huguenot presence. However, there were elements in English society that still looked on prophecy with interest. In 1667 Pepys noted that in the sixteenth century Nostradamus, of whose *Centuries et prophéties* he kept a copy, had with apparent accuracy foretold the Great Fire of London of 1661, a fearsome memory still vivid in Londoners' minds. Many early Quakers believed in prophecy and miraculous cures attributed to their founder George Fox; the group of Philadelphians, followers of the alchemist John Pordage and advocates of universal love, were still more engrossed by prophecy and apocalyptic exegesis lending itself to the millenarianism shared with Fifth Monarchists, Ranters, Levellers and Muggletonians—as Voltaire pointed out in *Lettres philosophiques*, England was "a land of sects where every free Englishman can go to heaven by the path he chooses".

At the same time, philosophers and scientists pondered the problem of forces in nature, such as gravity, acting at a distance. Isaac Newton was naturally at the centre of this enquiry which set reason against revelation while leaving open every possibility including that of the Newtonian idea of universal aether[5] occupying both matter and the void, and so rendering feasible the notion of prophecy transcending time since in this scheme all is one. Newton, in common with Descartes, had been at one time the vehicle of mystical revelation which like millenarianism and alchemy would seem, in the seventeenth century, to have been felt as no obstacle in the way of reason. Millenarian speculation appears in the papers of Thomas Hobbes and Robert Boyle[6] as well as in those of Newton who, although he soon rejected the Camisards' beliefs in their own powers and avoided any direct connection, was known to be privately interested in their prophetic activities: a later contemporary wrote, "Sir Isaac Newton himself had a strong inclination to go and hear these prophets, and was restrained from it, with difficulty, by some of his friends..."[7]

Among the English supporters and emulators of the French Prophets were at least a dozen physicians and apothecaries as well as fellows of the Royal Society; on the other hand, medical books were published exploring the "disease of extreme religion". Evidently the intellectual climate of England, favourable to speculation in the spirit of doubt, accounted as much for the welcome given, at first, to the Camisard prophets and to their quick notoriety as did their reputation as persecuted rebels against the rule of the reviled Louis XIV in whom, according to the scathing observer of the king's behaviour Saint-Simon, vanity, pride and intolerance were ceaselessly fed for their own purposes by his chief dependents: priests, women and ministers.

The four prophets, destined to remain together while they lived, were of diverse origins and personality. Their leader and by far the most prominent was Élie Marion, an exception in the peasant and artisan ranks of the Camisards as coming from a family of the bourgeoisie of the important market village of Barre-des-Cévennes, owners of land and houses: he had studied in Toulouse to qualify for the bar and worked for four years as clerk to a notary in Nîmes. Marion of all the Camisards possessed the most enigmatic or ambiguous personality. His influence among his fellows and in due course over his London followers was the offspring of his self-belief or delusion. Moreover, he exemplifies a problem which from the beginning has troubled historians, especially those attempting to give an impartial account of the Camisard uprising, that is the reliability of witness both to the events of the war and to the nature of the inspiration claimed by the leaders and their ensuing use of prophecy to control and order the men in their ranks.

Marion, however, was not one of the leaders of fighting groups in the Cévennes and seems not to have joined them until at least six months after the uprising began. He moved beside the others with the same courage but perhaps with a different kind of religious vehemence, that of the educated man converted in a passionate surrender to the embrace of faith. He stated emphatically in a deposition taken and recorded in London in 1707 that at the age of 22 he had never before read the Scriptures but that from then "I retired within myself." Revolted by the "extravagant and criminal idolatries of the Roman church", he resolved to leave Toulouse and return to his native Cévennes, or "the goodness of God put these thoughts into my heart". He now found himself changed: "All that had been agreeable to me until my Creator gave me a new heart became unbearable ... now it pleased God to untie my tongue and to put his words into my mouth." This belief was the basis of the trances, ecstasies and prophecies of the band of prophets in London as it had been in the Cévennes.

Marion gave a strong description of the process which so possessed him that he abandoned his family in Switzerland to follow his inspiration to England, and then in a ten thousand kilometre mission across Europe until his death in Italy in December 1713:

> I felt suddenly a great heat that seized my heart and spread throughout my body. I felt oppressed ... after some minutes an irresistible power took hold of me and made me utter great cries and sobs, and my eyes poured out a torrent of tears. I was violently struck by the fearful sense of my sins...[8]

What sins could these have been? No moral reproach has ever been aimed at Marion who was never known to take any interest in women, the likeliest occasion of supposed sin for a Calvinist pupil at the bar of Toulouse. But his father and mother, *notables* or prosperous worthies of Barre-des-Cévennes, had abjured their faith to avoid persecution. This was, above all, the complaint of the juvenile prophets against their elders. "Repent, repent!" they cried in their trance and as they emerged from it.

7

These children of devout Protestants, raised on scriptural readings and fed with their mothers' milk a visceral hatred of the Roman Church saw their parents accept a forced conversion to Rome. Marion was only the most articulate and best recorded of many of the inspired "enthusiasts" whose utterances, explicitly or implicitly, expressed a furious rejection of their parents' apostasy and a shared guilt. Abjuration was a sin that angered God and brought down on his people the tragedies they endured in the persecution.

In 1704, Élie Marion gave himself up and benefited by an amnesty to pass the frontier into exile; in 1705 he returned to France from Switzerland to take part in a planned renewal of the revolt ending in the capture of most of the other plotters and their death by the barbaric methods of execution still practised on dissidents of conscience in France in the eighteenth century: burning at the stake and breaking on the wheel. Marion, in hiding near Saint-Jean-du-Gard, was able a second time to negotiate his departure from France. He returned to Geneva and thence to Lausanne where his family, inactive in the uprising but incriminated by association, were living in neglect and want. He remained in Lausanne for ten months while a new plot of return to the Cévennes was hatched, from which, for reasons he did not give, he was excluded or possibly withdrew. The Camisard exiles who went on this last doomed attempt were executed like the others.

By this time Marion had learned that three former Camisards, Durand Fage, Jean Cavalier of Sauve and Jean Allut, were already welcomed as inspired heroes in the English capital, their prophesying adjusted from an initial effort at recruitment to a more apocalyptic turn to suit the millenarian interests of their audience; and as he later described it, the Holy Spirit "changed in an instant the dispositions of my heart". In Lausanne on 22 July 1706, in the presence of his father, Marion was inspired "to leave worldly things and carry out the desire which God had put in my heart to go to England, and that this was the great journey he had spoken of to me..." W. Gregory Monahan in *Let God Arise* suggests that "the rationalist historian might make the case that the Spirit confirmed an already deeply felt inclination"[9] and this cautionary note could fit many occasions during the war when the Spirit's orders matched the interests, or coincided with the judgement, of the human messenger.

Marion's Camisard credentials and reputation were established and his name was already known in the London Huguenot community before his arrival, but the same was not true of the other three of the original French prophets in London. Durand Fage, at first their leader, had been a member of an armed Catholic militia engaged in attacks on Protestants at the start of the Camisard War and was not converted to the cause until 1703 on receiving his first inspiration. He was described by the historian Georges Ascoli as "ignorant, mediocre and of legendary simplicity". Fage joined a regiment in London but, it was said, enjoyed the distractions of the capital too well to leave it when the regiment sailed for Portugal.

Jean Cavalier of Sauve was a still more questionable character. He claimed on arrival in London to be a cousin of one of the two most famous of the Camisard leaders, Cavalier of Anduze or Ribaute, a claim which the latter always denied. Cavalier of Sauve, who was educated by the Jesuits but converted to Protestantism in 1701, had an uncertain record of action during the uprising and was suspected of denouncing fellow Camisards after his arrest in 1705. Worse, he was suspected of having been an agent of Lamoignon de Basville, the Intendant of Languedoc who ruled the province for more than thirty years. Unmentionable vices were also imputed to this Cavalier, evidently an opportunist who found among the London prophets a screen from suspicion and in London itself a field of unknown freedoms. He was not the first or last of the Camisards, generally men of strict standards, to be accused of debauch by those making the easy equation between religious and moral dissidence.

Jean Allut, the third of the prophets, a cousin of Cavalier of Sauve, was a cabinet maker living in Soho and, according to Ascoli, a man who had never been seen to "mutter his prayers without the help of a formulary". However, he opened his house to assemblies of the prophets' increasing number of followers, as Marion himself later noted: "His street was often full of carriages of people of quality who came for curiosity if not some better motive," Fage having on 3 September transmitted the Holy Spirit's message to him—"My child, you have but to speak openly. You must openly announce my Wonders." Marion's biographer Jean-Paul Chabrol cites the Londoners' appetite for popular theatre, especially humorous, as an explanation of the growing audience naturally more interested in the agitation of the prophets considered as actors, their "shaking, jumping, gasping, convulsions", than in their private character or the authenticity of their claim to inspiration.

Marion at 28 was the oldest and most educated of the prophets in London and soon became their leader, while his pronouncements changed the character of the prophecies being uttered. On 18 September he was inspired to declare that "Fire, Lightnings and Thunderbolts are prepared ... since there are many Persons who come only out of a Spirit of Curiosity, I will not have my Word manifested to such People..." and two days later, "Oh what Tempests are preparing for the Wicked! ... No Peace for the Wicked; He must be destroyed."[10] The same day, the consistory of the French church in Threadneedle Street, alarmed at this new aggressive tone, sent the minister Pierre Testas to interview the prophets whose vocation they judged "more than suspect". At this meeting Marion, Fage and Cavalier were accompanied by the first of their London adherents, Nicolas Fatio de Duillier, a Huguenot mathematician from Geneva and a Fellow of the Royal Society and associate of Isaac Newton with whom he had experimented in alchemy, until their friendship ended abruptly in 1693 when Newton accused him of "fansies". Fatio, a dandy, was said to have rid the original prophets of their rebarbative aspect "like unwashed bears" and made them more presentable, and from 10 September he began to record their prophetic words and soon to receive inspiration himself.

Most London Huguenots were still after twenty years more or less precariously placed as immigrants for whom no laws of naturalization yet existed, and this was reflected in the attitude of the consistories towards any disturbing element suspected in their midst. Moreover, many of the exiled pastors manning the consistories were criticized both in the *refuge* and among the remains of the persecuted population in the Languedoc for deserting their flocks and leaving them leaderless rather than face martyrdom in France as their more sacrificial or unlucky colleagues had done. Hostility to the prophets on account of their uncontrolled language could be fed by residual feelings of guilt over this supposed failure in sacred duty. The meeting of 20 September included a display of inspiration by Cavalier in which he accused the exiled ministers of this; an inauspicious start to the relations between prophets and the French Protestant Churches. Cavalier's inspiration, according to Testas, was "nothing but very violent and convulsive movements of the chest and head, with general prophecies of the destruction of Babylon and Antichrist ... spoken in a manner very unworthy of the Spirit."[11] The presence of a number of apothecaries among the followers has been taken to suggest the use of hallucinogenic substances inducing trance and an ecstatic sense of divine effusion. One former supporter, the physician Henry Nicholson, spoke of the power of a "separate agent" to explain actions by the inspired beyond that of "meer Nature", and Marion is recorded as ordering prolonged fasts whose effects could include hallucination.

The exiles' hostility to this was soon expressed from the pulpits in a scathing analysis: "the agitations of these pretended Prophets are only the Effect of a voluntary Habit, of which they are entirely Masters, though in their Fits they seem to be agitated by a Superior Cause ... But the way in which they make the Spirit speak, is still more unworthy of him ... by childish Repetitions, unintelligible Stuff ... Predictions convicted of Falsehood by the Event ..."[12] The last of these charges was eventually the one that most hurt the prophets' credibility as the English turned their allegiance, sunflower-like, from revelation towards the light of reason.[13] "Enthusiasm laying by reason ... substitutes in the room of it the ungrounded fancies of a man's own brain," Locke had declared.

Enthusiasm

This state, in the Orphic sense of intoxication through union with the god and the mystic knowledge resulting, was out of favour in England by the early eighteenth century, enough of it having been seen in the seventeenth. Locke defined enthusiasm as "a strong and firm persuasion of any proposition relating to religion for which a man hath either no or not sufficient proofs from reason, but receives them as truths wrought in the mind extraordinarily by influence coming immediately from God himself". Shaftesbury described the French Prophets as subject to "enthusiastic panic", and Ronald Knox, writing from a Catholic point of view in his historical study *Enthusiasm*, referred to Ranters, "who may consult the light within ... and mistake some psychological urge for a

11

divine guidance", and to "ultrasupernaturalists" who believed that the solution to problems was given to them directly by the voice of God. An ironic parallel can be drawn with Michelet's remark on Louis XIV that he calmly presumed God to be in him—not as the mouthpiece of the divinity but its incarnation. Daniel Defoe described the prophets as "these poor Deluded People", and a Huguenot minister writing of their ecstasies asked, "Can't all this proceed from Natural Causes? May it not be performed by art? And may it not be affected?"

Locke ascribed enthusiasm to melancholy inducing the enthusiast to do "violence to his own faculties", to which Shaftesbury proposed ridicule as the antidote, though separating enthusiasm from fanaticism which were often taken as the same. He called the former a spiritual faculty of which love, joy and imagination were other manifestations: "The poet, the philosopher, the madman, the prophet are capable of the same frenzy."[14] The humane breadth to this understanding of the strange phenomenon of inspiration may have been shared by many in the London population attending the prophetic assemblies whether from curiosity or sympathy; it was certainly an element in their attraction for some among the educated English, and together with an interest in millenarianism perhaps accounted for Isaac Newton's early enquiries into the activities and claims of the French Prophets.

The Swiss mathematician Nicolas Fatio became convinced of the sincerity of the French Prophets' inspiration and a believer in the validity of their prophecies as he recorded and later published them. The prophets' followers were further reinforced by the arrival among them at the end of 1706 of two English gentlemen of means, a justice of the peace John Lacy, and Sir Richard Bulkeley, baronet and Irish landowner, and by the adherence for a time of Thomas Cotton, a Scottish Presbyterian minister who had witnessed the sufferings of Huguenots in northern France. This swelling of the ranks of followers and rise in their prestige and in the volume and tone of their predictions caused alarm among the leaders of the Huguenot community. On 4 November Marion prophesied the "Burning of a great City within a few days" and that soon there would be "Overturnings of whole States. I tell thee ... I will overturn them upside down." The message was ill received by the consistories whose hostile criticism accusing the prophets of imposture, and described to Marion by the Holy Spirit as "mischievous contrivances plotting against you", grew more public and less restrained. At this time Marion was visited by François-Maximilien Misson, who came to examine the prophets for signs of imposture but claimed to find none. He went on to seek out witnesses of prophecies and miracles during the Cévennes war among the refugees and to record their accounts, which he published in April 1707 as *Le Théatre sacré des Cévennes*, at the same time as its translation by John Lacy, *A Cry from the Desert*. Both books had an immediate success, firmly identifying in the public mind the French Prophets and their followers with a heroic uprising, and associating popular millenarianism with Camisard inspiration, a combination which further outraged the leaders of the Huguenot consistories who began to campaign in earnest against the "so-called prophets of the Cévennes (and their) counterfeit Inspirations".

At the beginning of January 1707 the Savoy consistory issued a formal condemnation, the *Acte Noire*, as testimony "to the nation in which we have the good fortune to live that we have done all we can to remedy so great a scandal". But scandal was Marion's aim: "I wish thee to give scandal in the world; I wish the world to be scandalised by thee," the Spirit told him, and he obeyed by announcing that "the earth must be drunk on the impure blood of the world", and adding that the eyes of the Spirit would "rejoice at the carnage".[15]

Not every remedy had yet been tried. At the end of March the Church in the Savoy, soon followed by the others and citing the authority of the Bishop of London, excommunicated Marion, Cavalier and Fage. Dogmatic hostilities turned violent with the first attacks by angry London Huguenots on 3 May 1707 and with a riot the next day forcing Cavalier and Allut to quit their lodgings and retire along the Thames, accompanied by Marion, to Northfleet. On their return on the 10th there was another riot and Marion, Fage and Cavalier took refuge in the house of a magistrate who received them with ironic mockery while the crowd hurled stones at windows from which Marion cried "may God bless you" while the others sang the Psalm 34, "I will bless the lord at all times: his praise shall continually be in my mouth." With a growing mob outside his house the magistrate, finding no charge to bring against them, asked the prophets to leave by a ladder to a garden providentially owned by

Sir Richard Bulkeley. The next day they left London a second time to Northfleet and the Savoy consistory began legal process against them for disturbance of the peace.

The divorce between the Camisards and the Huguenot community was complete but many of the prophets' English followers remained as committed to inspiration as the prophets themselves despite the wide difference in education between them. Bulkeley was an Oxford graduate from Christ Church and Lacy, though not from the university, was of a family long associated with Cambridge. Some, such as the clergyman Richard Roach from Saint John's, Oxford, found the language of the prophets under inspiration and their rural values refreshing; allowance must be made for the fact that the prophets' language was French strongly marked by the accent and vocabulary of Languedoc, and that the followers were ten or twenty years senior to the Camisards, none of whom were yet thirty years old. Taste for the unfamiliar with a subversive flavour probably made some appeal to palates used to a metropolitan intellectual and emotional diet, or in some cases to minds revolted by a libertine and atheistic London they felt unable to combat. In a society where the nature of the relation of man to God or even its existence was questioned, the new enthusiasm ran like a fever and inspiration to prophecy; with the inspired, both French and English, mouthing the messages of the Spirit, it had the allure of revelation to a chosen sect allowing escape from reason's discipline. Defoe wrote of his astonishment at seeing men reputed for judgement and intelligence embroiled with prophecy. But the certainty of God within the believer cured all doubt, as Louis XIV in Michelet's account was relieved, for the same reason, of humane compunction.

Sir Isaac Newton had already drawn back from his early interest in the activities of the prophets. Nicolas Fatio's growing support of the prophetic movement and his public adoption of a millenarian programme led to Newton's retreat from any connection with the Camisards' supporters. Newton's enemies referred to Fatio as "Newton's ape", while his friends feared that he "might become infected by the prophets as Fatio had been".[16] It has often been suggested that there was more between Fatio, commonly suspected of secret homosexuality, and Newton than mathematical interests, and certainly Fatio was an ardent disciple to whom Newton in a letter of November 1692 signed himself, "Your most affectionate and faithfull friend to serve you"; but speculative gossip seems to spring more from well-meaning efforts by psychologists to provide a genius with emotional life than from evidence. Locke appears to have tried to do this in his own way since Newton, temporarily ending their friendship in 1693, accused Locke of attempting to "embroil him with women".

By 1706 the terms of Newton's connection to Fatio were distant as the latter's involvement with the French Prophets went far beyond mere scientific interest in the possibilities of true prediction. Meanwhile, Élie Marion's prophecies were becoming more violent and immoderate and combining advocacy of enthusiasm with calls to social reform, including an attack on the Bank of England and the naming of London as the New Jerusalem. "You will see in a few days the burning of the great city," he predicted on 21 December 1706, and in the New Year announced an imminent deluge of fire and sulphur to fall on the unrepentant. Fatio was the recorder of these messages and published them in April 1707 as *Avertissements prophétiques* which had, according to Ascoli, a resounding success in London; his continuing adhesion to the group shows the degree of his abandonment of judgement as Defoe had remarked, and his name was accordingly joined with those of Marion and Jean Daudé, exiled doctor of law and son of a Nîmois advocate, in the prosecution initiated by the Huguenot consistories.

On 5 May the trio appeared for a first time in the court of the Lord Chief Justice Sir John Holt; it was lucky for the prophets that while the hostility of the Huguenot community began to catch on among the native population, with riot and stone throwing, the trial was held before a judge who had played a part in the composition of the Bill of Rights, was noted for tolerance and credited with putting an end to witch trials by a series of acquittals in his court: he did not believe that to "acquit a witch was to undermine the constitution or deny revealed religion". The charge was publication of prophecies filled with blasphemy and sedition, disturbance of the peace and terrifying the Queen's subjects. Giving evidence for the defence, Fatio warned the Lord Chief Justice of the danger of rejecting a message which came from God, and reminded him of the fate of the Jews who rejected Jesus. The judge let this warning

15

pass and is given credit for avoiding any religious issue in the trial beyond asking Fatio whether he considered the prophets divinely inspired. There was laughter in the court when Fatio answered that he saw no reason why the same Spirit that had made Balaam's ass speak should not equally speak from the mouths of the accused. The jury brought in a verdict of guilty of publishing the book and of holding illegal assemblies at the Barbican; the prophets were "forbid their Tumultuous and Disorderly Assemblies", but not condemned for imposture.[17] Sentence was delayed to November and the prophets released on bail to follow their inspirations; as they left the Guildhall they were threatened by the waiting crowd and took refuge in an inn.

At this time the question of miracles and the problem of non-fulfilment of prophecies came to the fore with a promise by John Lacy to cure blindness in one of the female supporters, Elizabeth "Betty" Gray. Many accusations of immorality and both heterosexual and homosexual slanders were made against the prophets and their supporters—Swift noted the marked amorous propensities of visionaries—but few were corroborated by evidence; the relationship of Lacy and Gray, however, was well documented and made for later scandal since Lacy had a wife and child. The miracle cure failed to materialize and the explanation for this, a standby for repetition when other predicted miracles also failed, was offered by an English follower: "Although God might intend in the Morning to work a Miracle ... yet there coming in a Medley sort of People, with Obdurate Hearts ... God might withdraw his Spirit for a time ... because of the Want of Faith in these People." In a familiar dichotomy, what appears specious to a sceptic may seem to a believer too self-evident for apology. The same conviction led to the growing belief among the supporters, expressed between the two hearings, that "the lord Jesus will soon come to purify his Church and to reign a thousand years on Earth with the faithful". And six days before the second hearing on 22 November, an inspired woman stripped naked outside a Catholic church in Duke Street and ran up to the altar after mass where she "appeared in several strange and indecent Postures ... and (announced) that she had come to Reform the People".

At the second hearing, again presided over by Sir John Holt, sentence was given that the three men stand on a scaffold and pillory for two hours, once at Charing Cross and on the second day before the Royal Exchange, wearing paper notices of their offence. "We testified", they later wrote, "that we esteemed ourselves honoured by what Christ found us worthy to suffer in his Name."[18] It can be added that the leniency of this sentence, for which Defoe had publicly pleaded, brought an infinitesimal part of the suffering they would have endured in France for dissident opinions, as one Huguenot pamphleteer pointed out—death on the wheel, the stake, or by the rope—and that they must have been well aware of this, perhaps accounting for the "pleasure with which we received it". The London Huguenots, disappointed by English clemency, declared that "We, the French, have had enough of this farce," and abandoned the prophets who would, they hoped, soon depart and take their mission with them.

The great apologist and historian of the Camisards, Henri Bosc, reminded readers that these men (though not Fatio) had seen their homeland destroyed by fire and the sword, their companions killed fighting or by barbaric methods of execution if captured, their starving families herded into camps. "Far from their beloved Cévennes they lost, in a sense, their roots, their soul, even their religious equilibrium ... but there in the Cévennes, had not their vehemence, their spectacular immoderation and their faith been the only arm against that implacable persecutor, their king?" The Huguenots of the *refuge* who excommunicated them had by contrast escaped with their families and in some cases their wealth, and none had seen the fighting. Respectability and observance, which meant nothing to the Camisards, were the key to the exiles' entry into English society whose liberal eccentricities were not for Huguenots obedient to their consistories to follow; whereas the Camisards, said Bosc following Michelet, were History's witnesses and infinitely greater than those who mocked or condemned them in the name of propriety.[19]

Doctor Emes

When Defoe was condemned to the pillory in July 1703 the crowd pelted him with flowers. The Camisards became unpopular with the fickle London public once the novelty of their fits and convulsions and the humour they gave rise to wore off; the illustration to a contemporary

17

broadside showed them serving their sentence "To the Tune of Rotten Eggs, Turnup-Tops, Pieces of Dirt, &Brick-Batts." Marion was wounded in the face and Fatio in the left eye, while some of the French in the crowd called out, "Prophesy who hit you!" The scaffold was cordoned off and protection given to the condemned as they finally walked away from the scene with the paper pinned to their hats denouncing "wicked and counterfeit Prophecies" to "terrify the Queen's people". On 6 December a newspaper announcement made it known "to all the world" that Marion, Daudé and Fatio had been prosecuted at the expense of the London Huguenot churches.

Prophecies by the London Camisard leaders or their acolytes had so far been unspecific enough that non-fulfilment may have seemed to the public watching them, usually in a sporting spirit, as disappointments to be taken in their stride while odds shortened on the coming millennium. The case of Doctor Thomas Emes was more radical in the character of the prophecy and its verifiability and so strengthened the opinion of those like Defoe who was surprised by the "Prevalency of this new Delusion". Sin, repentance, an implacable God had no part in the promised raising from the dead of Doctor Emes. There seems to have been no religious element in the prophecy as though the promise of a miracle was its own justification.

Emes, whose earlier life is unknown, described himself in 1698 as "chirurgo-medicus" practising as surgeon, possibly unqualified, among the poor of London in an age of medical revolution dominated by the great discoverers William Harvey and Thomas Sydenham, when physicians aspired to cure even old age; the resurrection of Emes was to be a demonstration of the ultimate therapeutic exploit, that of restoring life. Emes' religious position was delicate as he appears to have moved from atheism to membership of the Baptist Church from which he was expelled in 1698 for denying the divinity of Christ. In 1706 he became a follower of the French Prophets after publication of his *Atheist turned Deist, and Deist turned Christian.* But his medical and religious careers were cut short by sudden death, the first among the prophets' supporters to go, following a violent migraine on 22 December 1707.

This contretemps was unacceptable to a movement believing that its members would participate in the coming Kingdom and a process of denial began with Emes' remains being kept in a heated bed in hope of revival, "till he stunk so there was scarce any enduring it". He was then buried on Christmas day in Bunhill Fields where Bunyan, and later both Defoe and William Blake were put to rest, but in the view of the prophets this interment was to be temporary. One of the English supporters, the caster out of evil spirits John Potter, foretold the resurrection of Emes to take place on the 25 May, "one Month above the Number of Days that Lazarus was in his Grave" by the agency of John Lacy who may have found himself nominated and enrolled without his full consent. Other followers seemed to have doubts as the day approached: Richard Roach heard voices warning that the resurrection would not take place, Thomas Dutton believed that the irregularities in God's work were due to incomplete human knowledge, and Lacy himself withdrew from the project and decided not to attend in Bunhill Fields on the appointed day while another prophet, John Glover, asked "Who can find out the Almighty to Perfection?" thus preparing for the new occasion the shelter of an excuse that had served on an earlier one.

On 25 May, the Whitsun public holiday, only the wealthy Abraham Whitrow among the English inspired attended at the graveside. But there was a festival, jocular and potentially turbulent crowd of twenty thousand at Bunhill Fields to enjoy what promised to be the best of "all the shows and wonders that are usually seen on holiday-time".[20] Defoe had suggested that the prophets be protected from violence likely to follow failure of the miracle and by order of the Queen's Bench two regiments of soldiers were posted about the cemetery. Marion and Cavalier of Sauve had been commanded to attend by Whitrow, who was to be the presiding *inspiré*; it is an indication of the selectiveness of Marion's *Mémoires* that they made no allusion at all to the occasion of Emes' announced resurrection. One of the prophets later explained to Voltaire that no miracle had taken place on 25 May because on that day one of the others had been in a state of mortal sin; but for which, said Voltaire, "this resurrection was infallible!" Ascoli quoted Voltaire's account of the event:

> The magistrates took their place, the clerk of the court recorded everything on the pages of the public register since one cannot be too careful about new miracles; a corpse was dug up, the saint

in charge prayed, cast himself on his knees, went into pious
contortions and was imitated by his companions. The dead man
giving no sign of life, he was pushed back into his hole.[21]

And Defoe, taking the matter more seriously than the satirists who
invented speeches uttered by Emes as he arose promising that the
Thames would flow with ale, addressed the prophets:

> The Charm is now over, the Snare is broken, and if ye please you
> are escaped ... not to abandon these pretences now, would ...
> court the Delusion ...[22]

Defoe's choice of the word "pretences" evokes the varying responses
to prophesy of other contemporaries who took the prophets seriously
enough to attack or occasionally defend them. Claude Groteste de la
Mothe, minister of the Savoy church, published an attack entitled *An
Account of the Lives and Behaviour of the Three French Prophets Lately
come out of the Cévennes and Languedoc* in which he described the
prophetic performance as a product of disease and delusion. He was
followed by Richard Kingston, an Anglican clergyman who wrote a
careful study, *Enthusiastic Impostors no Divinely-inspired Prophets*.
A large number of polemical broadsides flew back and forth, strongly
critical for the most part, even those by observers sympathetic at first
sight, such as John Humfrey who wrote about the French Prophets
and their "Pretended Inspirations ... by a Lover of Truth and a Hater of
Persecution". Some Anglicans, including at least two bishops, aligned
themselves with Shaftesbury and the theory of Enthusiasm as explaining
a phenomenon of inspiration which fascinated while alerting the
suspicions of both Christian and medical or scientific onlookers. Henri
Bosc, himself a minister in the Cévennes, by his passionate defence of
the prophets and an attack on the Huguenot exiles who had not shared
the experience of persecution sidestepped the difficulty of unrealised
miracles:

> Was it not the true miracle that these men resisted the armies
> of Louis XIV and maintained the protestant faith at risk of
> their lives? From their mouths spoke the thousands of known
> or anonymous fighters who died for liberty of conscience ...

What is most surprising is less the exaggerated and admittedly sometimes ridiculous character of the prophecies ... explicable by suffering, misery and isolation, as the attitude of the émigrés hounding three unhappy survivors of the cévenol hell.[23]

Cavalier of Anduze

Despite the Emes fiasco the numbers of the prophets' followers increased in the next months so that by the end of 1708 more than four hundred adherents could be counted. But the consequences of the failed resurrection were more subtle than this suggests. Polemic turned on the question of the loss or retention of intellectual faculty during prophecy. If consciousness was lost, then reason slept and what certainty could there then be that the prophet spoke with the voice of God? It began to be claimed by Lacy and Bulkeley that reasoning and memory continued to function during prophetic inspiration, a change in the nature of the prophets' claims that left doubt as to whether the message spoken at one moment or at another was of human or divine origin. Naming and expulsion of "false prophets" and progressive splitting into tribes or sects followed, with a consequent worsening of relations between them. Whitrow, accused by Lacy of being an "imposter", and his wife Deborah were shut out of the gatherings of the faithful after Whitrow's criticism of those who had stayed away on the day of resurrection, and they were followed by Sir Richard Bulkeley, the supplier of financial support; Cavalier of Sauve was excluded from the group led by Marion on account of his involvement in the Emes prophecies from which Marion had dissociated himself. And meanwhile, detractors fastened in the usual way on alleged sexual irregularities of individuals or entire gatherings accused of becoming less prayer meeting than orgy.

The only substantiated sexual straying from the narrow path set by these moral ascetics was John Lacy's adultery with one of a number of female prophets, the aforementioned Betty Gray, who was satirized as Betty Plotwell in Thomas D'Urfey's "serious and moral" play *The Modern Prophets*, performed at Drury Lane with songs by Blow and Purcell. "To be plain with you," says one character to Betty, "I fancy you deal more in the Flesh than the Spirit." D'Urfey may have known of the "Meeting at Sir Richard Bulkeley's Chamber ... when Betty Gray, under violent

Agitations, personated the great Whore of Antichrist ... laid aside her night-clothes, tyed up her hair ... and for about an Hour together, thump'd and beat with her fist every one in the Room ... except Mr Lacy ..." (Durfey, like Peter Anthony Motteux, was of Huguenot origin and produced a dramatization of Motteux's *Don Quixote* with music by Purcell.) *The Modern Prophets* was banned by the Lord Chamberlain after a number of performances but not before its message that the prophecies were an imposture had been popularly broadcast. Lacy defended himself by declaring that the Lord had commanded him to leave his wife and lie with Elizabeth Gray and threatened him with eternal destruction and hell-fire if he disobeyed. Although Lacy and Gray were not expelled, and there was a gradual reconciliation, in 1711 they retired to Lancashire to carry on their millenarian proselytizing far from the disputes of the capital.

Although ridicule kills, in the well-worn formula of seventeenth-century French theatre, the French Prophets' movement still had the impetus of its curiosity value. But an initiative taken by the Huguenot consistories was to have an indirect but deep effect on historical evaluation of the Camisard War and its principal actors, and opened a wound in both legend and memory that has never healed. This was the enrolment of the survivor of the two great Camisard leaders, Jean Cavalier of Anduze or of Ribaute (where he was born in 1681) in the consistories' campaign to discredit the prophets' leader Élie Marion. At the start of the uprising Cavalier, then aged 21, worked as assistant to a baker of Anduze, the once fortified town guarding the principal entry to the Cévennes. He was a small man but sturdy and apparently a charismatic leader; within days of the first acts of revolt he had gathered followers from the borderline of the Mediterranean plain and taken them into the mountains to join the fighting.

Cavalier's band became the largest of the guerrilla groups, the most highly organized, the only one to include cavalry in any numbers and was later to operate far into the plain around and beyond Nîmes as much as in the cévenol hills and valleys. His lieutenant Jacques Bonbonnoux wrote that Cavalier's men obeyed him blindly in all the speed and boldness of his exploits "almost like God himself". But few of them followed him in his negotiation with the royal authorities in 1704, which led to an amnesty and his exile. To the intransigent among the Camisards, and notably Élie Marion, this was a betrayal of the cause and Cavalier was a contested and, to some, a reviled figure especially after he accepted a commission as colonel in the English army at the age of twenty-five, raised a Huguenot regiment in Holland and fought against the French in Italy and Spain.

Despite an undeniably heroic record, and the opinion of Voltaire who praised him as the only Camisard chieftain deserving to be named, Cavalier has been disdainfully treated by many historians—by the Protestants among them ostensibly for his negotiation and surrender; by others, including Michelet, as a man of humble origin aspiring to military and social rank. Derogatory references to the "Colonel" come from all sides; the convert Ronald Knox, after complaining of Cavalier's "sustained invective against the Catholic Church", concluded, "I do not find it easy to admire Colonel Cavalier."

Cavalier was in Holland in 1707 and it was there that the consistories sent an emissary to obtain from him, as one supposed to know intimately the prophetic and inspirational manifestations of the Camisard War, a sworn statement discrediting Marion, Cavalier of Sauve and Fage in their prophecies of miracles. Cavalier obliged with a declaration which laid him open to the accusation of denigrating his companions in the fight for freedom of conscience, and thereby repudiating it; when he arrived in London in February 1708 he repeated and swore to his declaration. The hub of the dispute that followed was the Emes débacle, Cavalier's claim being that no such miracle had ever been predicted in the Cévennes and that the London prophecy of Emes' resurrection was both blasphemous and absurd. But he went much further in attacking the record of the three men for their part in, or absence from the fighting in the Cévennes. Marion, he said, had been deprived of command of a small group of men on the ground of complaints against his conduct and no more had been heard of him until his arrival in Switzerland; Fage was a coward and vagabond who, in common with Cavalier of Sauve (with whom the colonel denied any family relationship) had never remained more than two days together in his troop.

The three alleged prophets were described in the declaration as "idiots, blasphemers and imposters" and Cavalier, denying their claim to inspiration and refusing to recognize any connection between the London prophecies and the miracles, military or otherwise, of the Cévennes (notably the often repeated story of the Camisard leader Claris walking unharmed over a burning brazier which Cavalier described as a "miracle without fraud or affectation"), remained silent about his own well-attested past as the most "inspired" of the Camisard leaders, while continuing to enjoy the admiration that surrounded him in London as a resistance hero. The result of these accusations was exactly what the consistories had sought—the purported link between the French Prophets and the religious experience of the *désert* was weakened and, for any waverers among the London Huguenot community, broken.

Cavalier later modified some of his account, perhaps in defence against the attack on him by Marion whose animosity, though certainly enflamed by Cavalier's references to him, dated from the negotiation and amnesty of 1704; Marion, a diehard intransigent *enfant de Dieu* who had wept tears of blood as his companions burned Catholic churches, never saw the amnesty as anything but a betrayal although he himself in the same year had benefited by an amnesty to leave France for Switzerland. "This poor wretch," he wrote of Cavalier, "puffed up with pride, speaks gibberish and has lost his reason since the Spirit of the Lord departed from him." On his return to the Hague Cavalier wrote more temperately of his companions without withdrawing his earlier version: "It is not ... that I wish either to approve or condemn (without further proofs) these alleged prophets ... although I have said, and repeat, that if what I have been told is true, they were imposters and fanatics ..."

Before the dispute broke into the open the French Prophets had invited Cavalier to a meeting where they warned him against the suspect flattery of the Huguenot community of London which had received him, according to Marion's account, as "great captain, chief of the Protestants of France, defender and protector of the religion..." That Cavalier was manipulated and perhaps deceived by this flattering reception there seems no doubt; he later described the ministers of the Savoy as "jesuitical" or hypocritical. That he also exploited his reputation as a fighting hero is equally certain, and these failings were severely charged against him both by his contemporaries and by later historians sympathetic to the Camisard cause. Bosc accused him of lying, of *arrivisme* or opportunistic ambition and of a taste for power and honours, though allowing him his indignation over the prophets' announcement of the end of the world for London and its unbelievers. Marion's contempt, coloured by envy and expressed with his usual incontinent vehemence in the *Mémoires* of 1710, has left a legacy of prejudice which can be felt today in that any defence of Cavalier must start by apologizing for him. The excesses and, it may sometimes seem, the self-indulgent absurdities of the prophets are ascribed, with the sympathy that excuses all, to their sufferings. Cavalier with his successful career in the English army, but whose experience of the horrors of persecution and war was the same, has not usually benefited by that exonerating sympathy. His biographer Marcel Pin explained in 1936:

> He was the most famous of the *inspirés* ... but for several years had understood that his fits (of prophecy) did not have a divine origin ... the revolt which had glorified him owed its successes to the enthusiasm created by prophecies, and he would have been happy to forget it.[24]

Pin added that to Cavalier the three or four London Camisards who were tireless shakers seemed retarded and compromising—potentially compromising in the easy sense that connection with them in the minds of patrons and military superiors could harm his professional interest. But Pin's use of the term retarded suggests, though he did not pursue the idea, that Cavalier had progressed in his relationship with reality as shown by his emphasis on proof; in that case the change in his outlook was evidence not of lying but of the unusual intelligence which his record in the field had shown in action.

Prophets in Decline

The English now outnumbered Huguenots among the French Prophets—in 1709 by two hundred and forty to a hundred and twenty-five—and the separation into sects with differing aims and religious views was accelerated. Whitrow began to preach social levelling and the sharing by the rich of their fortunes with the poor, a programme from which the majority of supporters took their distance and which was refuted by Lacy "on the order of God". Bulkeley, on the other hand, accepted the doctrine, followed Whitrow to Ireland and began the process of stripping himself of his wealth so that on his death in April 1710 his heirs found him to be penniless.

The assemblies fragmented as the differences grew; some groups left London for Oxford, "with the sure instinct of the foreign adventurer and a lost cause," said Ronald Knox; others to Cambridge, Coventry, Worcester, Bristol, Wales and Scotland. At Oxford "six of the pretended prophets, called Camisars, namely, two men, three women, and a girl ... put up at the Greyhound. They continued three or four days in the town without any discovery; but at last the women had agitations, and abundance of people went to see them."[25] After this meeting the group was expelled by order of the Vice-Chancellor who, Knox claimed, "had formed an unfavourable opinion of their morals." At Bristol the movement took some root since John Wesley later met a representative of the Camisards in the town where the first violent paroxysms occurred in Wesley's audience, and in alarm he preached an anti-Camisard sermon. At Colchester the missionaries were chased by a mob accusing them of being traitors and at Ipswich no innkeeper would give them a room. A number of prophets were briefly imprisoned in Monmouth and Edinburgh as well as in various London jails. Londoners grew angry when they learned of the warning of the Spirit that "A horrible Tempest is to be poured upon thee, O London ... God Almighty will plant his Battering-pieces against this City..."[26]

The French Prophets had become missionaries; their message, for delivery as widely as possible to the world, was millenarian and redemptive through repentance. From his first arrival in London Marion had received orders from the Spirit urging him ever further on his journey as though unsure of welcome in any one place. In September 1706 he was warned, "Prepare thyself soon to quit this land and go with thy brothers to fight more than ever"; in April 1707 the Spirit gave the order to leave London, but only as far as beyond the Thames; then in mid-1711 the formal command was issued to the Camisard prophets to set sail for Holland. They left at once to the profound relief of the population at all levels, having created, according to Bosc, grave divisions as much in the aristocratic quarters of the city as the popular.[27] Marion, Allut, Charles Portalès, another lawyer in exile who later became secretary to the last Protestant Bourbon the marquis de Miremont, and

Fatio, the Spirit's nominees, embarked for Rotterdam on 22 June. Fatio returned to London the following year but Marion and his companions pursued their grandiose and tragically unreal mission, which included the project of converting Rome, over the face of Europe until Marion's death far from the Cévennes in Livorno in November 1713, a moving demonstration of the power of intense and prolonged suffering to induce a state of monomaniac delusion with no way back. But the story, in no sense delusory, of the Huguenots' persecution and martyrdom is still commemorated in the diaspora and told in France where its effects are alive, run deep and can be recognized.

Notes

1 François-Maximilien Misson, *Le Théatre sacré des Cévennes*: 142
2 *Locke's Travels in France*, (ed.) John Lough: 60 & footnote 2
3 R. N. Cunningham, *Peter Anthony Motteux, 1663-1718*
4 R. A. Knox, *Enthusiasm*: 357
5 Hillel Schwartz, *Knaves, Fools, Madmen*: 33
6 Hillel Schwartz: *The French Prophets*: 8
7 Joseph Spence, *Observations, Anecdotes and Characters*: 63
8 Élie Marion; *Avertissements prophétiques*: VI
9 W. Gregory Monahan, *Let God Arise*: 119
10 Schwartz, *Prophets*: 76
11 Threadneedle Street Church, *Livre des actes*: 499, 501
12 Schwartz, *The French Prophets*: 80; John Blanc; *Anathema of the False Prophets in a Sermon*
13 In *Le Siècle de Louis XIV,* Voltaire stated that in England "philosophy was becoming dominant".
14 Shaftesbury; *Letter on Enthusiasm*
15 Jean-Paul Chabrol, *Élie Marion le vagabond de Dieu*: 123
16 Schwartz, *Prophets*: 8
17 Schwartz, *The French Prophets*: 94; Henri Bosc: *La Guerre des Cévennes 1702-1710*, vol. V: 847
18 Schwartz, *The French Prophets*: 109
19 Bosc, vol. 5: 822
20 Schwartz, *The French Prophets*: 121
21 Chabrol: 164
22 Daniel Defoe, *Review of the State of the English Nation*: 131
23 Bosc, vol. 5: 857
24 Ibid: 865
25 Knox: 371
26 Ibid: 369
27 Bosc, vol. 5: 878

The *crime d'état* of St. Bartholomew's day: François Dubois, *Le massacre de la Saint-Barthélemy* (Wikimedia Commons)

Chapter Two
The Edict of Nantes

Saint Bartholomew

Fernand Braudel remarked in *The Identity of France* that while all nations are divided, France illustrates the rule rather too well; another historian, Marc Ferro, alleged in *La Grande Guerre* that his country was gifted not so much for battle as for civil war; and Jules Michelet's judgement was that France, essentially divisible, strained ever towards disunion. In 1562 the Protestant scholar Sébastien Castellio wrote from his exile in Basle in *Conseil à la France désolée*:

> It is not foreigners who make war on you ... your own children desolate and afflict you ... your towns and villages, fields and roads are covered with dead bodies, your rivers run red and your air reeks of the dead...

Perhaps no event in French history so demonstrated this essential division as the state massacre of Saint Bartholomew's Day begun on Sunday 24 August 1572—*albescente jam die*, in the whitening dawn between 4 and 5am—when, at first in Paris and then in towns across France, about ten thousand Protestants were slaughtered in a frenzy of hatred directed at what Catholics called the Huguenot stain (*souillure*).

In the sixteenth century more than a tenth of the French population was Protestant. From 1562 fierce religious wars were continuous and atrocities on both sides frequent. Although Calvinist Protestants were said to act with cold rather than panic violence there were exceptions when they were physically dominant and moved by fear; in Nîmes, often described as the capital of a Protestant republic within France or said to have been to French Protestantism what Manchester was to the industrial revolution, on the night of 30 September 1567 forty priests and nuns and leading members of the Catholic minority were thrown into wells, sometimes alive, during the course of the *Michelade* commencing on the feast of Saint Michael and lasting several days.

A recent historian has suggested that Protestants massacred fewer than Catholics only because they were seldom numerically superior; whether the speculation is valid or not, the historical certainty is that Protestants were overwhelmingly the victims. Catholic Provence was the site of the greatest number of massacres, savage in execution and with all imaginable sexual atrocity against women. A contemporary calculation of the number of victims of massacre, as opposed to those killed in fighting, prior to Saint Bartholomew gave a figure for the whole of France of thirty thousand on a hundred and fifty occasions. Patrick Cabanel, the historian of French Protestantism, asks if it is unreasonable to compare the extreme violence of French Catholics against the Huguenots in a period of European brutalization attributable to religious difference, with that of Germans against Jews in the twentieth century, and this parallel has often been drawn—with the corollary that some Protestants, like Jews, survived to return.

A massacre may be the work of undisciplined or covertly ordered military groups, of an uncontrolled mob, or of plotted personal revenge. It was the exceptional character of the massacre of Saint Bartholomew's Day to be a *crime d'état*, authorized by the king himself, and a crime against hospitality and the laws of truce which debased the memory of French civility. The occasion that made the massacre possible and presented itself as uniquely opportune for the extermination of the leading Protestant nobles and their followers was their presence in the Louvre as guests of King Charles IX to celebrate the marriage on 18 August of his sister Marguerite to the Protestant Henri of Navarre, later Henri IV. The marriage was detested by the more extreme Catholics and in particular by the Guise family, a branch of the sovereign house of Lorraine with their fathomless ambitions and close connection to many of the ruling dynasties of Europe including that of France. What was apparently offered to the Huguenots as a day of ecumenical epiphany when guard would be lowered and hatred put in abeyance was to turn during the period of celebration into a pogrom for which no one was ever judged except by history, and doubtfully even then.

Nevertheless, it is now known that the decision to eliminate the leading Huguenots was taken by the *Conseil du roi* on 23 August, and it is thought well enough established that Charles IX was present at the

Council and sanctioned the decision. The long held belief that the Queen Mother, Catherine de Medici, had secretly planned the attack is generally discredited, though she certainly endorsed it.[1] The first murder at dawn was of Gaspard de Coligny, Admiral of France, Protestant leader, hero to many but enemy of the Guise family, while still in his bed: "Would I were killed by a man and not by this boor," he said of the bodyguard of the duc de Guise who was also present. Coligny's body was pitched into the courtyard of the Louvre where it was dismembered, decapitated and castrated before being thrown into the Seine, soon followed by those of his companions and other leading Protestant nobles expelled at the express order of the king from their lodgings in the palace and into the courtyard where the assassins awaited them. "Coligny ... was better obeyed than I by those of the new religion, so that I could no longer call myself absolute king ... but king of only part of my realm," Charles wrote to the German princes.[2]

Catholic joy at the massacre was expressed in both poetry and drama of the aftermath, and Catholic historians from the first advanced extenuating arguments similar to the king's while disparaging the accounts of opposite tendency given at the time and later by Protestants, such as that of François Hotman, professor of law at Bourges in *De furoribus Gallicis, A True and Plaine Report of the Furious Outrages of France* on which Marlowe based his drama *The Massacre at Paris*. Patrick Cabanel points out that the king was seen by Huguenots as their only protector against Catholic violence and that Charles and Catherine betrayed this trust. "The man with the dagger was followed by the man with the sponge," wrote Lord Acton, himself a Catholic, of the Catholic apologists.[3]

As the news of the first murders of the Protestant élite was spread, the city gates were closed, shipping guarded, cannon posted at the *hôtel de ville*.[4] By full daylight the people of Paris hunted out Huguenots in hiding and continued the massacre on their own account. Between two and three thousand Protestants were murdered, most of them passively accepting death as a fatality in a Catholic city. It has been claimed that the killers were a minority and that the majority of Parisians stayed behind closed doors as death was dealt outside; also that the authorities in the Louvre followed the development with alarm and tried unsuccessfully to control it as bourgeois and plebeians and their militias, forerunners of the private armies that have often reappeared in French history, carried out "the pogrom of the century"[5] after the duc de Guise entered into contact with the militia on the evening of the 23rd.

However, enough written evidence survives of the complicity, or even the initiative, of the court in extending the killing beyond Paris in the days following the assassination of Coligny to make it unlikely that the king or his advisers either believed or wished that the extermination should be stopped until the destruction of the Huguenots was so complete that the chance of their revival could be written off. The pope wished to see the king "purge the kingdom of France of the Huguenot pestilence" and emissaries of the court took to the provinces the king's permission to "complete the extermination of those of 'the religion'".[6] The principal cities of France with sufficient numbers of Huguenots to ignite prejudice produced their own massacres within days; Michelet declared that the Saint Bartholomew was not a day, it was a season. The Guise and their supporters pursued the Huguenots with the war cry, "It is the king's wish, his express command."[7] Forty-six eruptions of murderous violence have been identified in which the order to get rid first of the principal among those of the reformed church and so more easily do away with the rest was obeyed by Catholics believing themselves part of a crusade and wearing a white cross to their hats.[8] The pope ordered a commemorative medal struck.

Saint Bartholomew was a turning point in the history of French Protestantism, a "*rupture terrible*".[9] Huguenots were now no longer so much the military adversaries of the Catholics as a defensive minority subject to the fury of the Gallican Church supported, with the shining exception of Henri IV, by the royal rulers. Braudel, writing in the first version of La Méditerranée of a similar attack on a minority in Spain described it as "the surgical operation ... as radical as it could be, the same as that adopted by Hitler himself to resolve the problems of minority". Patrick Cabanel preferred the comparison with the Armenian genocide of 1915 combining mass murder with conversion as the alternative for survivors. He saw the Saint Bartholomew as an unfinished enterprise of ethnic cleansing in Paris and the provincial cities.[10]

Throughout France a considerable number of more or less insincere conversions followed among those most exposed in towns or with most to lose professionally or financially; in Rouen, for example, at least three thousand abjured, in Orléans a collective abjuration was watched by a mocking Catholic crowd. But many others took refuge in neighbouring countries promising Protestant shelter; again as an example, from Rouen alone two thousand crossed the Channel to England. In 1560 Calvin wrote that "we see today that many leave their country of birth on account of the horrible captivity which is there." In some cities such as Lyon the known Huguenot element of the population disappeared; in a few such as Nîmes, a secure town with a large Protestant majority, and in parts of the mountain country of which the Cévennes was the chief example, remote, almost inaccessible by road and peopled by a peasant race imbued with the beliefs and inspired with the biblical visions of the Reformed Church, the force of the attack was still to come. And for this, the Saint Bartholomew massacres prepared the way. From 1572, French disunion in Braudel's sense became fixed, since Bartholomew's Day was the expression of the Catholic will to conformity whose traces are still evident in social and cultural life, and sometimes in the thought process of intellectuals passing for agnostic or atheist.[11]

Henri IV and the Edict of Nantes

The former Huguenot Henri IV exemplified in himself the division of France. The sincerity of his conversion to Catholicism cannot be known but pragmatism of the kind that saves lives was one among many of his qualities admired perhaps more outside France than within. In 1599 he addressed the Paris *parlement*:

> I am a Catholic king, a Roman Catholic, not a Jesuit Catholic ... there must be no more distinction between Catholics and Huguenots ... they cannot be converted by violence. I am the shepherd king not wanting to spill the blood of my sheep with the force of a tyrant.

Huguenots, formerly his companions in arms and shocked by the apostasy, still knew that Henri was their protector. Nevertheless, the Jesuits were allowed to return by the Edict of Rouen of 1603 with fateful consequences and the king when speaking of the Protestant form of faith pleased his Catholic subjects with the phrase, still in use, "the so-called reformed religion". The Huguenots, partisans of royal absolutism,[12] had overly high expectations on Henri's accession and fears too raw for quietude after the Bartholomew massacres. They now felt deserted, and they increased what pressure they could on the king for a guarantee of their safety by edict. Their elected representatives assembled in November 1593 and remained in session in one city after another until May 1601, sending petition after remonstrance. The king's need of Huguenot soldiers eventually made him give ground, and by 1597 a text of eighty-five articles was broadly agreed. In April 1598 Henri signed, at Nantes, the edict that became famous in that name and brought relative peace for at least a generation of Huguenots.

Advanced though it was for its time in respect of religious tolerance, its parchment sealed by green wax hung on ribbons of green and red, colours reserved for the most solemn royal edicts *perpétuels et irrévocables*, this text included the phrase which over the next eighty-seven years gladdened the hearts of Catholics greedy for religious monopoly and weighted those of Huguenots with menace: "If it has not pleased God to allow as yet (*pour encore*) that all our subjects adore him in the same form and religion, let it be at least with the same intention." But the edict attempted to calm and mollify all parties; "that the memory of all that has passed since 1585, and during the preceding troubles, be lulled and extinguished as if it had never happened." A clean sweep of the last years of the nation's history was made by enactment, but as usual with history's clean sweeps, not effected in reality. The Catholic effort to whittle down and weaken the Protestant position under the Edict of Nantes began at once with the delays of registration and amendments of *parlements*, dominated without exception by Catholics, throughout the country. The "as yet" phrase was taken from the first as an encouragement to the Catholic Church to work at reducing or undermining the applicability of an edict which it regarded as creating a state within the Catholic state. The clergy and universities immediately condemned the edict, and "It is the worst edict that could possibly be imagined" was the verdict of the pope. It took the king's eloquence two years to extract, by prayers and threats, the consent of all the *parlements* to an edict which Voltaire rather airily described as "at bottom only a confirmation of the privileges that the Protestants of France, weapons in hand, had won from previous kings".

These advantages, though Huguenots only grudgingly accepted them as the last word, were considerable and with theological adversaries less adamant on both sides in their claims and hatreds, could have brought into being a more tolerant society in the most populous country of Europe than in any other except Holland, and saved by the way thousands of Christian lives squandered in years of fratricide. The division of France regretted by Braudel might have healed; it is certain that the prime but not sole responsibility for the tragedies that followed lay on the Catholic clergy, relentless in detestation of heresy and as careless of life as the early Christian fathers. Bishop Bossuet, leading light in the canon of funerary oration, preached of "extermination"[13] and the right to persecute.[14] For the moment, the great gain for the Huguenots was "liberty of conscience", the freedom to believe and worship according to their rites, both in churches (*temples*) which they were now again authorized to build, in their homes, and in the chapels of manor houses permitted to hold services. The Huguenots were industrious, frugal, many of them educated, and relatively rich. Hundreds of temples were erected in all parts of France, the only one now surviving from this time of creative freedom being that at Le Collet-de-Dèze in the Cévennes.

Huguenots were again allowed to enter schools and universities, to create academies of their own, to hold public office even in *parlements*, to practise professions, particularly in teaching and the law, and to hold their synods and assemblies so fertile in remonstrances, proof of the continual war of attrition between co-existing schools of Christianity over the next thirty years. Courts composed, ideally, in equal parts of Catholic and Protestant judges were created, though never, in a state so increasingly oriented to uniformity, uniformly brought into action.[15] Contest was ceaseless but from 1599 the Huguenot destiny, according to Cabanel, was of a gentle downward slope growing steeper and less gentle. But he adds that for several decades the happiness of the Protestant minority, granted peace at last, grew and spread,[16] their security ensured in eighty defended, often walled, towns designated as havens (*places de sûreté*), principally in the south and west, manned by garrisons either Huguenot or royal and administered by Huguenots.

Until the eve of the 1680s many Huguenots lived well in the shelter of the Edict of Nantes and thereafter "attached themselves desperately to the now vanished edict and the hope of its reestablishment".[17] Despite this, under the guidance of Protestant intellectuals such as the king's friend and adviser Philippe Duplessis-Mornay, or Sébastien Castellio who thirty years earlier had pleaded for tolerance of theological differences—leaders more supple and learned than their Catholic counterparts still fixed on the abstruse formulae of the last Council of Trent of 1563—the edict was seen as enclosing French Protestantism within a wall of bronze, protective but constraining and with no hope of enlargement.[18] Already it was claimed that the existence of these eighty safe towns created a state within the state and an "equilibrium of fear".[19] The only movement now possible was tightening of the constraint, and this was not long in coming.

Under the Edict

Hopes of tolerant co-existence, and even the impulse towards reunion of faiths favoured by some Protestants, met the immoveable hostility of the Catholic Church and clergy. Pope Clement XV proposed that Protestantism in France be "extirpated to the root and to the point, if possible, of abolishing its name and memory", and the Gallican Church needed no urging. How did the Huguenots earn such single-minded hatred? One obvious conclusion would be that the strength of the fissiparous tendency noted by Michelet was deliberately countered by the Catholic Church with greater pressure to the conformity and centralization so markedly imprinted on French society since the seventeenth century. A theological element reinforced the social one: the central article of Catholic practice and of faith in the Church and its works, underlying the authority of the priesthood and the power and wealth of the episcopate, was belief in the miracle of transubstantiation in the Eucharist of the mass. This idea was explicitly refused by the Huguenots: "bread at the moment of communion remains bread, as iron reddened in the fire remains iron."[20] Such a challenge to a fundamental belief diametrically the opposite of Locke's advice that opinion be based on necessary proofs resembled too much the iconoclasm of Protestants in the religious wars and was inevitably felt as threatening. The Church hierarchy responded with violence in proportion to their increasing influence on state policy. Yet not every Catholic believed the miracle: Locke tells the story of the Huguenot Marquis de Bordage attending mass in Rome "where the Pope was present, not being above a yard or two from him, a very considerable cardinall who was just by him, asked him after the Elevation: 'Che dice vostra signoria di tutta questa fanfanteria?'"[21]

If the supposed strictness of Calvinist ethics and the suspected claim to consequent moral superiority were other reasons for Catholic hostility, the registers of the independent Huguenot consistory courts tend to contradict the supposition. Sexual laxity among the faithful was reproved but no more frequently charged than appears in the records of other courts. Locke gives this account of the process: "If any one live scandalously, they first reprouv him in private. If he mends not, he is called before the Consistory & admonished there. If that works not, the same is done in the publique congregation, & if after that he stands incorrigible, he is excluded from the Eucarist. This is the utmost of their power."[22] Most cases brought before the consistories involved violence, physical or verbal, between men and men or women and men equally. The behaviour of Huguenots apparently reflected that of the more or less brutal society around them, though in the Catholic population much would go unrecorded or be redeemed in the pardon of the confessional firmly placed at the centre of Catholic lives by the Council of Trent in 1551. The Calvinist discipline, by contrast, imposed an individual responsibility on those belonging to a community of the elect.[23] It is true, however, that by the records of the Nîmes consistory, exceptionally complete, in sixty per cent of cases of sexual misconduct women are cited as the accused, another reflection of a customary bias from which the Protestants were not free.

The existence of consistories with authority within their own communities underlines the state within the state exceptions so much resented by the majority, and the relatively high social provenance of the deacons who were the chief members may have aggravated them. At Nîmes between 1581 and 1685, thirty-five per cent of deacons were from the nobility and fifty-one per cent were doctors of law and advocates. In the last quarter of the sixteenth century the pastors in the south came predominantly from the nobility and the magistrature; the consistories, manned by officials of similar social origins, saw themselves as teachers of peace among their own people.

All these features supplemented the separateness and difference against which Paris and the powerful *parlements* of Paris angrily set their face, while at the Catholic popular and bourgeois levels there was the readily exploited jealousy of Protestant wealth: "Already in the seventeenth century the jealousy of poor against rich, of lesser against greater merchants, of small industry against large, of land against money can be seen contributing to Catholic hatred."[24] And this greater wealth had been created, in the opinion of some officials such as d'Aguesseau, the governor (*intendant*) of the Languedoc before the arrival of Basville, by use of greater intelligence: "The prosperity of Nîmes was owed to the industry of the Protestants, richer, more intelligent, more credited than Catholic merchants who, jealous of their success, planned to take away this advantage as if heresy must exclude the right to work and talent."[25]

For as long as the peace following the Edict of Nantes endured, Huguenot schools flourished even in small villages of the Cévennes as evidenced by the comparative rates of literacy between Protestants and Catholics. At Millau in mid-seventeenth century forty-four per cent of Protestant men against ten per cent of Catholics could sign their name, while for their wives the comparison was seventeen against four. Alongside schools and colleges for children of both sexes the construction of temples authorized by the edict, many of them of great magnificence, emphasized, especially in southern cities, the economic difference between the communities and provoked a destructive envy which would before long be let loose.

Two particular influences have been suggested for the design of the *temples*: Serlio's *Libro quinto d'architettura* of 1547, which illustrated the antique circular temple design on the model of the Roman Pantheon, and the Elizabethan galleried theatres, polygonal cylinders open to the sky. A series of churches across France were built on the circular, oval or polygonal plan. The great church of Charenton, built to hold three or four thousand Protestant Parisians and destroyed in 1621 in an anti-

Protestant riot, was credited with influencing Wren's design for some of the City of London's churches and of Saint James's in Piccadilly.[26] The particularity of the chief southern centres of Nîmes and Montpellier was their strong Huguenot majorities both within the city and in their hinterland. Cabanel points out that they were the only Protestant towns in Europe to correspond to Braudel's model of a close relationship between the Mediterranean corridor and the wall of mountains enclosing but not nourishing them. In Nîmes, where *temples* were built on the site of churches, they kept to the rectangular basilical plan. At Montpellier a new scheme was used, which Locke noted during his stay in 1676: "There are two protestant churches; one of them ... is a pretty construction, a single stone arch, like a bridge, embracing the full length of the church," and this was repeated in at least fifteen other churches in the Languedoc. The Grand Temple of Montpellier was demolished on 1 December 1682 on the personal order of the king to be executed within twelve hours, but before then the unravelling of the edict, though not yet its revocation, was almost accomplished.

The Duc de Rohan

If the assassination of Henri IV in 1610 was a sorrow for France, it was a tragedy for the Huguenots. Louis XIII was nine at his father's death and France was then ruled for the second time by a Queen Mother from the Medici family, Marie, until her counsellor Richelieu—already the most powerful priest in France—became first minister in 1624. In 1615, addressing the Estates-General at their last meeting before the French Revolution, Richelieu spoke of the Huguenots in peaceable terms: "We ... desire their conversion by example and prayer, the only arms we will combat them with." But in 1625 his policy had changed: "As long as the Huguenot party subsists the king will not be absolute in his realm ... therefore ... the first and foremost of his plans must be to ruin them." By then, the renewal of the Huguenot wars had presented the central power and the Catholic Church with the occasion to pursue the grinding down, relentless as a millstone, of the protection promised by the *édit perpétuel et irrévocable*.

Not for the last time a sense of abandonment and injustice, fear and hardship drove the Huguenots to arm themselves and fight. It is at least arguable that in the interests of their descendants and the hopes of Protestantism in France they made a fearful mistake. Their leader Henri duc de Rohan had been a favourite with Henri IV of whom he wrote that "France was so happy during his lifetime that for 1200 years she had never known such fortune." Rohan, who was described as "a great lord, frugal and modest, accessible to all and loved by all", although by a less sympathetic observer as affecting an exaggerated religious devotion, wrote to the king in 1621 that the Protestants had shown the patience which they had for too long "chewed on and borne". It was perhaps the first mention of Protestant patience which like many collective virtues often fell short of the demands made on it. But as strength and numbers and protection diminished, impatience would take the tragic turn to desperation.

The Estates-General, dominated by the clergy and by elements of the Catholic nobility demanded, in spite of the Edict of Nantes, that "the exercise of the so-called reformed religion be banned and forbidden in this kingdom"; and a resulting process of bending the articles of the edict in an ever more restrictive sense was set in motion. The Béarn, a personal fief of the Crown and a Huguenot enclave since Henri IV, was forcibly annexed to the kingdom and Catholic practice imposed in 1620. Huguenot representatives from the rest of France assembled at La Rochelle at the summons of the duc de Rohan, champion of intransigence, in defiance of royal prohibition, and by progressive stages with popular Catholic riots in Paris and the formation of a Huguenot army, revolt became war.

In 1627, representatives of thirteen towns of the Cévennes and of the plain toward the sea met at Uzès, recognized Rohan as their commander-in- chief and swore an oath to "have the infractions of the Edict repaired ... and our Church restored to the liberties the Edict granted". After the siege of La Rochelle, whose fall in 1628 was seen as a disastrous blow to French Protestantism, the Huguenots were left isolated for want of any of the expected effective English help. Rohan, with many of the Huguenot gentry, concentrated military activity in the Languedoc, recruiting chiefly in the Cévennes where the men, as the governor Basville later noted, were "by nature suited to war, good under arms, and apt for service as infantry," and deployed his force of eight thousand in fast-moving actions from the hills and mountains while the royal armies attacked Montpellier. "Whoever holds the Cévennes," claims Cabanel in his comparison of Rohan's guerrilla movement with that of Afghanistan, "controls the spine of southern Protestantism."

But forces were unequal, Montpellier fell and the Huguenot defeat was inevitable. A truce was followed by amnesty and by the terms of the peace of Alais, followed by the Edict of Nîmes, of 1629. Protestants were assured, by "the king's grace" and not by treaty, of their continued freedom of worship and of the social gains under the edict but the walls and fortifications of their towns were demolished, garrisons disbanded and assemblies forbidden. The sole relic of the stout fortifications of Anduze, "gateway to the Cévennes", is the clock tower which stood at one corner of the quadrilateral nearest to the River Gardon.

The particular denomination of safe havens disappeared and Huguenots were henceforth dependent on the king's protection only. "The faction is extinct ... they will look for no other security than my goodwill," wrote the king to his mother, and this is said to have been at the origin of their commitment to royal absolutism which was still evident in loyalty to Louis XIV through the persecutions of his reign—"our lord the king disposes of our lives and land, but not our consciences"—and their refusal to take part in the Fronde rebellions after 1648. Safety lay in quiescence, or so it was hoped, and so it was, for a generation more.

The peace of Alais pardoned the duc de Rohan, who was exiled to Venice where he remained until 1635. Historians have taken differing views of him as the man incarnating the ultimate Huguenot defeat. Was he an actor imbued with the sense of his own rank and prestige who endangered his followers, or a great magnate hobnobbing with cévenol peasants whose distance from him might seem immeasurable, and leading them to fight when their best hope lay in reassuring the king? Michelet described him as one of those "ambitious great lords who exploited the last passions of the protestant party to sell their submission to the Court at a high price," perhaps implying that the exploitation was cynical. Or was he rather the last faithful soldier in his Church's cause, a war lord cut off from the aristocratic world, preaching like a pastor and fighting side by side with his men and in the same danger, and who believed the protection of the minority depended on their nuisance value and power of retaliation?[27] He returned to France in 1635 and was given command of an army which fought successfully in Switzerland, but his presence was still considered dangerous and he went into exile again in Geneva, dying in 1638 of a wound in battle six weeks earlier. It seems likely that to Richelieu and his successors, and even more to Louis XIV, the Huguenots of Languedoc and the Cévenols in particular were suspect, distrusted and always fit for punishment in consequence of the military adventures and devout enthusiasm of this uncorrupted, self-promoting nobleman.

Prelude to Revocation

The royal absolutism in which Huguenots put their trust was the weapon that brought them down step by step once absolutism's slogan—one king, one law, one faith—turned from exhortation to enforcement, and to its logical effect of including conformity of opinion. During the long reign of Louis XIV the protection given to Huguenots by the king shrank in proportion to his growing piety, as an English agent reported in 1655: "Things did daily grow worse for them on all sides."[28] Analogy with the Jewish experience in twentieth-century Germany is inescapable. Early in the century, Protestants filled many important positions in the financial administration and the military establishment and were prominent in the scientific and medical faculties of the University of Paris. The king's architect who, among other projects, joined the Louvre to the Tuileries where artisan workshops largely manned by Huguenots flourished under Henri's patronage was a Huguenot himself, as was the king's physician-in-chief.[29] Voltaire pointed out that Cardinal Mazarin, principal minister until the inauguration of Louis XIV's personal rule, made no difficulty about appointing a Calvinist as comptroller general of the finances of the state, and that Colbert "who reanimated the nation's industry and can be seen as the founder of French commerce employed many Huguenots in the arts, in manufacture, and in the navy." However, the deaths of Mazarin and of Cromwell, from whom the Huguenots had hoped for support in their developing confrontation with the Catholic clergy, accelerated the pace of unravelling of the Edict of Nantes and its promises, under the eye of the young king overseeing all.

The king's personality and political views were to have as determining an effect on this process as the religious influences. The public beheading of Charles I and the eviction of Louis' cousin James II in favour of William of Orange were naturally seen as the work of Protestants, as was the Republic of the United Provinces and its "bad example of liberty"[30] which France would not follow, particularly as regards the press and the printed word. But most important in the developing rule of conformity of conscience was the king's view of himself: "It is possible," Ernest Lavisse wrote, "that Louis XIV was no greater an egoist than anyone else in his time ... but he was unprepared to resist the temptation which others, in adoring him, gave him to adore himself ... he was only just and fair in business where neither his authority nor his pride ... were concerned."[31] Adoration, said Michelet, can create a fool and engender a cult of the self; this would be particularly so in a society such as that surrounding Louis, a milling cast whose members combined servility with narcissism since in adoring a king seen as incarnation of the glory of France they adored themselves at a remove. In discussing the genesis of the king's vanity historians agree (since the evidence is compelling) that his education, though not neglected, was both narrow and superficial and that the influence of his mother Anne of Austria, a devout Catholic, did nothing to broaden his mind. The duc de Saint-Simon, a close but not detached observer, spoke of his mediocre intelligence and stated that care was taken to bring him up in greater ignorance than his role required, both criticisms repeated with emphasis (*forte médiocrité*) by Michelet. Lavisse described the king's intelligence as "almost entirely passive, incurious and without initiative ... and very poorly furnished by an education which was deplorable for both mind and character," and added that the education life gave destroyed in him, if it existed, the faculty of sympathy. Louis' great capacity for work seems to be almost the only quality found in him to admire by these writers, though Saint-Simon, often so scathing, praised his charm and the natural and invariable politeness of his manners. Eugène Bonnemère, admittedly a Protestant writer, stated that Louis "in the naivety of his spirit, believed himself God's representative ... a fourth person in the Trinity," and Lavisse also was astonished by the intellectual naivety of the same belief repeatedly shown in the king's *Mémoires* of 1666 to 1672. After the defeat at Ramillies the king cried out, "Has God forgotten all that I have done for him?"

The fault in the king's character was manifest in his religiosity and obedience to his confessors, increasing as he became older and happier to "be led in safety by the priest legally responsible before God for his salvation".[32] The Jesuit order understood better than any other the power of the confessional and its exonerating function depending on a lightly taken promise of amendment. Michelet, whose thought on this aspect of the king's life must be respected though weighed for bias, stated that the Jesuits always kept a priest carefully chosen for the king's confessor, supple but tenacious and native of the ultra-Catholic Massif Central; the marquis de Dangeau in his *Journal* added to this information that the king chose Jesuit confessors for his family and shared one with his eldest son, the dauphin, in order "to know what he was thinking". Michelet makes the accusation that these directors of the king's conscience allowed him to expiate his unamended private life and tolerated the pretension expressed in his *Mémoires* that God was within him, thanks to his acceptance of the approaching ruin of the Protestant cause and faith. And Saint-Simon added in his turn that the Jesuits worked to convince Louis, in the new devoutness of his middle age, that any divergence from their teaching was an attack on his authority and proof of a republican spirit; this was repeated by Voltaire who spoke of the "insinuations of the Jesuits".

The Huguenots were thus painted, for the king's eye, in the blackest colours. His confessor La Chaise, from the mountains of the Forez, brought him to the fold, and while Saint-Simon claimed that the king revelled in making his penitence on the back of the Huguenots, Madame de Maintenon, the secret wife, wrote, "the king is thinking seriously of his salvation, and if God preserves him for us there will soon be only one religion in his kingdom." In 1678 Locke was present at the king's *levée*: "There is nothing so remarkable as his great devotion ... for as soon as ever he is dressed, he goes to his bed's side where he kneels downe to his prayers, severall priests kneeling by him, in which posture he continues for a pretty while, not being disturbed by the noise and buz of the rest of the chamber..." Locke's praise was perhaps in part ironical; after inspecting the tapestries that were to hang in Versailles he wrote that "In every piece Lewis le Grand was the hero ... In one was his making a league with the Swisse where he lays his hand on the booke to swear the articles with his hat on & the Swiss Ambassador in a submissive posture with his hat off." Lavisse in his summing up of Louis' character set off against his beauty, vigour and grace, his just and true sense and noble idea of duty, the danger of his being perverted by religion as much as by pride. Bishop Bossuet wrote that the royal throne was "the very throne of God". Since the religion of the man who sat on it, son of a pious Spanish-Austrian mother, was more and more devoutly Catholic, the Huguenots had all to fear, despite their loyalty, by conscientious dissidence.

At the death of Mazarin and the start of the young king's personal rule, his unfriendly disposition towards the Protestants and the Edict of Nantes was immediately evident. In 1661, of thirty-eight decisions taken by the royal Council involving the guarantees of the edict, thirty-five were unfavourable to the Protestants. In December of that year Louis refused to receive a Protestant deputation from the Languedoc to congratulate him on the birth of the dauphin. Cabanel observes that one of the first acts of the personal rule showed the king's attitude toward the Huguenots as that of malevolent solicitude; "The face of the theatre changes," he announced to his Council on the morning after Mazarin's death. The king's Council functioned as a court of last resort in matters arising from the edict and throughout the 1660s pronounced systematically against the Protestant party, driving through its early stages the process of destroying the Huguenot cultural landscape, and of abrogating the articles of the edict one by one in the service of the "patient, persistent, eloquent" hatred of it felt by *parlements* and clergy.[33] Emmanuel Le Roy Ladurie in his study of the peasants of the Languedoc wrote of a forced "deculturation" carried through by stages and rising to climax in the Revocation: "We all know of the traumatic shock and bloody consequences that normally result from similar undertakings, especially in the twentieth century."[34] The king wrote in his *Mémoires* intended for the instruction of the dauphin, "I believed, my son, that the best means of reducing the Huguenots of my kingdom little by little ... was to accord them nothing more and to enclose the execution of what they had obtained under previous reigns within the narrowest boundaries ... I took care to have closed down the undertakings of those of that religion," an apparent reference to the policy of silencing Protestant intellectual centres, including in April 1664 the historic academy of Nîmes founded by François I. A series of histories and interpretations with titles such as P. Bernard's *L'Explication de l'Edit de Nantes* of 1666 worked with more or less openness towards a redefinition of the *perpétuel et irrévocable* nature of the edict so precious to Huguenots, while "tireless militias" of the Catholic Church strove to undermine its content.[35]

The next step was the destruction, on one pretext or another, of a great number of both ancient and recently constructed *temples* without which public worship by Protestants became impossible or dangerous. Cabanel states that by 1685 and the Revocation which ordered the immediate demolition of every remaining *temple* in France, the major part of the work had already been done, with more than four hundred destroyed. In 1676 Locke noted that in the region of Montpellier "they have had within these 10 years at least 160 churches pulled down", and gave as an example of the pretexts used the destruction of the only church left to the Protestants of Uzès who were three-quarters of the population: "The pretence given is that their Temple being too near the papist church, their singing of the psalms disturbed the service."[36]

The demolitions were minutely regulated and the details recorded; Cabanel points out that it was not, except in a few cases, the work of crowd iconoclasm but of judicial and administrative violence in cold blood, the application of rules and regulations framed with this purpose in view and entirely characteristic of the French bureaucratic model. *Temples* and Catholic churches were to stand at least a hundred paces apart; if not, the former were to be demolished. The intendant of Béarn, Foucault, had an audience with the king in 1684 and convinced him that five *temples* to be left standing in his region was enough; he then nominated five whose pastors were accused of contraventions for which demolition was the penalty. Thus within the space of six weeks the Protestant majority whose leader had been Henri IV lost all its *temples* and pastors in a successful civil service operation.

The destruction of *temples* entailed the virtual if gradual disappearance of the right granted by the Edict of Nantes to public exercise of the religion. In the period of twenty years before the unleashing of full-scale violence against the Protestants, oppression grew and took many forms, often the most bureaucratically petty. At marriages and baptisms no more than twenty persons could be present, at funerals no more than thirty, and the hours at which these ceremonies could be held were severely restricted. From 1664 no more than twelve Protestants could walk together at any time in the public streets, thus indicating to them that they "made an ugly stain in the kingdom of France".[37] Protestant schools were forbidden to teach any subject but reading, writing and counting. Protestants were increasingly prevented from exercising the profession of artisan in trades or industries. After the national Synod of the Protestant Church in 1659-60 it was determined that there should be no more and their organization should be destroyed. From 1679 the holding of local synods required the king's permission. All these measures and more were carried through in accordance with the forms of centralized bureaucracy, except where a bishop or intendant had some special axe to grind and could reach the king in person, when a decision could be expedited. If violence has been endemic in the history of Christian belief and its propagation, it cannot anywhere have been more chillingly organized than in France in the years before and after the Revocation of the Edict of Nantes.

The treaty of Nijmegen in 1679 which left Louis XIV apparently master of Europe allowed greater attention to be turned to the presence in his kingdom of a non-conforming minority obstinately persisting in error, and till now living quietly while the king and his ministers concentrated on war. The Assembly of the Gallican clergy had recognized that while war lasted, the king's zeal was retained by state considerations; now in 1682 they composed a "paternal warning" to the Protestants in which there occurred twice, in capital letters, the question, "Why have you separated yourselves from us?" This document was passed by the king to the intendants to be read to consistories throughout France. Its conclusion was menacing: "If you refuse to be won by our prayers ... know that this final error will be more criminal than all the others ... and you must expect misfortunes incomparably more dreadful..." Cabanel refers to the official reading of this *Avertissement* as a "high moment of *soft* totalitarianism" combining violent threats with expressions of tenderness, and describes the series of new legislation of the 1680s as

47

creating a form of "apartheid" in which the population played their part, as outlined by a historian in 1698: "the Roman Catholics got used little by little to watching the Protestants suffer, and then to making them suffer."

The king's orders accompanying the *Avertissement*, on the other hand, were to treat gently those of "the religion" and to prevent anything that might prejudice what had been given them by the edict. This moderation has been interpreted, given the violence of the warning itself, as an attempt to dissuade Huguenots from leaving the kingdom and to soothe Protestant opinion in Europe while the machinery of oppression speeded up; but a less devious explanation could be that in the royal mind the two aspects of the paternal role as then understood, stern authority and sheltering guidance, were in their usual alternation. Before long the shelter would be withdrawn and the king's sheep, as Henri IV had called them, would be not guided, but herded to the fatal end.

Meanwhile, the Huguenot community, driven from offices of every kind under the Crown by a series of exclusions since 1679 and active in the liberal professions in numbers out of proportion to its share of the population, was to be further weakened. In early 1685 the practice of law, medicine, printing and publishing became forbidden occupations. The special courts set up by the edict to ensure its just application, the *Chambres de l'Edit*, were suppressed in 1679 on the pretext that "the animosities which could exist between our subjects of either religion are extinguished," while the Archbishop of Arles explained the true reason in a letter to a secretary of State: "Our great king by his suppression of the *Chambres de l'Edit* will force more conversions than all our preaching and missions could in a century." An anonymous writer asked in 1684, "Isn't it that they want to make these poor Protestants die of starvation, since they take away all their means of subsistence ... and prevent them working with their hands at the craft they learned in youth to earn their living and that of their families?" Considering the statutes against the Jews of 1940-41, a member of the French Resistance against the Nazis wrote, "I have looked at the old ordinances of the revocation of the edict of Nantes: the similarities with the present are striking."[38]

In these years of prelude to Revocation, voluntary conversion to Catholicism for motives not strictly religious was encouraged by soft methods compared with those that followed. Missions were sent to various parts of the kingdom but propaganda made little impact on the committed Protestants it was directed at. Not much more effective was the financial incentive held out to the less committed or the destitute. Six *livres* was the cash price of a conversion first offered by the *Caisse des conversions*, an office funded directly from the king's pocket into which poured for this purpose the surplus revenues of the great Abbeys of Cluny and Saint-Germain-des-Prés. Cabanel argues objectively that it was not so very immoral for the monarchy to help refugees from the Huguenot camp who cut themselves off from their community. Statistics of the conversions obtained in this way between 1676 and 1681 give a figure of ten thousand and forty, or one and a quarter per cent of the Huguenot population of eight hundred thousand[39] for an outlay varying between the six *livres* of the opening offer and a maximum of sixteen in the Protestant stronghold of Nîmes. And it was calculated that at such a rate it would take more than three centuries to reach the final end of Protestantism. In Paris the apostasy of a number of aristocrats and influential figures was better paid: Marshal de Turenne, grandson of William the Silent Prince of Orange and author of the maxim "God is always on the side of the big battalions", was awarded a state pension on joining them. An advocate of Montpellier writing in 1698 spoke for those who were troubled by this traffic of consciences: "The buyer tries to get the lowest price he can and the seller the highest. The broker runs between them until the bargain is agreed ... if the future convert has problems with the law, he is promised to win; if he has no job, he is promised one of the best; if he is a rebellious son, he is assured that his father will have to make him an allowance ... or be ruined in the process."

A method of inducing conversion wholly accordant with Jesuit practice in education and for which no excusing formula has ever been found, was the government policy regarding children. In June 1681 the age when a child could convert to Catholicism against its parents' wishes or be taken from them and put at their expense in a Catholic school was lowered to seven; from 1685 it was reduced to five. After 1677 the intendants practised a policy of systematic abduction of children to place them in specialized Catholic establishments which, especially in the case of girls, were often no better than prison convents.[40] Protestant historians, who are often criticized for *misérabilisme* or concentration on the pitiable details of the Huguenot experience, have pointed out that by an ordinance of 1942 seven was also the age at which Jewish children could be taken from their parents in Germany, and Cabanel again refers to the genocide of Armenians in 1915 with the same system of abduction of children. By a historic irony, it was from the visionary inspiration, or overwrought delusions of children, mostly girls, that the impetus towards the fury of the Camisard uprising first sprang.

Until the Revocation was implemented by pressures violent enough to yield a nationwide flood of abjurations, the Protestant party included many leading figures in French life whose families had survived the Saint Bartholomew massacres. It is often questioned what effort these well placed leaders made to delay the approach of Revocation, or to shelter their co-religionists from the fearful consequences that had already been seen in 1655 in the canton of Vaud in the Alps where an early programme of extermination, described in gruesome detail by Michelet, an impassioned historian scrupulous about his references, was put into practice. Bossuet declaimed in praise of Louis after the success of this experiment and the extinction of the small dissentient community of these mountain valleys: "You have affirmed the faith, you have exterminated the heretics. King of heaven, preserve this king of the earth!"

Fear, as each tightening of the knot brought closer the strangulation of Protestantism in France, perhaps kept many under cover and preparing for flight. Many more, including famous names such as Sully, Coligny and La Rochefoucauld, converted to Catholicism to keep their places at court. An exception was the Marquis de Ruvigny, named by Louis in 1653 as deputy general of the Reformed Church. Now in 1681 at the age of seventy, watching the king's war minister Louvois set about the work of suppression with no quarter given to strong or weak, he obtained an audience of the king who listened to him in icy silence. The scene was reported by Gilbert Burnet, an exile who became Bishop of Salisbury in 1689: Ruvigny expounded the merits, skills and riches of the Huguenots and advised the king that the pursuit of his policy of oppression would drive them to other countries with their talents and wealth; he warned of possible civil war. Louis XIV answered curtly that it was his sacred duty to extirpate the heresy, that he would finish the work if it cost him his own arm, and that in any case he "stood higher than the Edict". Ruvigny preferred exile to apostasy, sacrificed his estates in France and with his sons settled in England in 1688.

1685: Revocation

Giving his account of the events of 1675 Michelet asked whether it was true that France deluded itself in "its frenzy of royal idolatry ... It seemed settled that the king did everything. All the world believed it, and he believed it himself." If so, the responsibility for the sufferings that preceded and followed the Revocation must fall on the king, and apologists' efforts to lighten the moral load by suggesting that others acted in his name and without his approval will not convince readers of Michelet who as Keeper of the National Archives had almost a lifetime's access to the records. The personal rule was as absolute as the divine right. Every order despatched to the intendants by the king's ministers passed across his table and many carried notes in his hand, the obvious exception being word of mouth instructions from ministers; the proven existence of these may occasionally be taken as diluting the king's personal involvement. "It is certain that the king did not know of every act of violence committed ... but if he had really wanted to prevent them ... he would have spoken a public word to stop these excesses of zeal."[41] Louvois wrote to the intendant of the Poitou that "his Majesty desires by use of violence (*violenter*) to convert the Huguenots."

The euphemism "excess of zeal" would cover, in the years before Revocation, the system of coerced conversions obtained by *dragonnades* and first tried against Huguenots in 1681 in the Béarn and Poitou. Regiments of dragoons, often mercenaries of varying nationalities and with brutal experience of war, particularly in Holland, were lodged in towns and villages as in an occupied country, and housed in the homes of Huguenots known for devotion to their faith, at their expense and in growing numbers in case of obduracy. More than a hundred of these often sadistic marauders were posted in one Nîmes household. The royal confessor called them "booted missionaries", and Madame de Sévigné believed they had been "very good missionaries up to now; the preachers being sent at present will perfect the work." The orders given to the officers of these men were to "make them live (in Protestant houses) very licentiously ... you may allow them whatever disorder is necessary to bring these people to heel."

Horrifying accounts are given by historians of all periods of the activities of these soldiers whose pay was usually in arrears or unsettled. Rape was frequent, deprivation of sleep and torture by burning usual, in the best cases humiliation, looting, impoverishment and fear were enough. No official or unofficial refutation of these accounts was ever made; Lavisse, more generous to Louis than most, claimed after reciting the horrors at length that "it was certain the king ordered none of these atrocities; he may not have known much about them; probably he didn't want to know anything." Nevertheless, Madame de Maintenon wrote that "God used every means." And the academician Georges Duby in his *History of France from 1348 to 1852* questioned how Louis explained to himself the extraordinary number of conversions presented to him in so short a time other than by violence; thirty thousand in the Poitou almost overnight, fifty thousand in the Dauphiné, the great Protestant centre of Nîmes converted within twenty-four hours of the dragoons' arrival, twenty two thousand in the Béarn of which the king's confessor La Chaise wrote to the intendant "that his Majesty took pleasure in reading"; the papal nuncio Ranuzzi wrote to the Vatican of four hundred thousand conversions obtained in two months and predicted the total prohibition of the Huguenot cult.

The king's own conversion to piety took place under Jesuit eyes in 1679; "exercises of devotion, sermons, adorations, rosaries were multiplied." Madame de Maintenon wrote that "the king is full of good sentiments ... he recognizes his weaknesses ... He thinks seriously of conversion of the heretics and will soon set to work on it for good and all." The influence of Françoise de Maintenon, three years older than the king and granddaughter of the Protestant poet Agrippa d'Aubigné is probably impossible to measure, but Lavisse wrote of the continual interference, during thirty years, of the government in matters of faith and piety, and vice versa; the bishops certified to the king that "God asks Madame de Maintenon to speak to his majesty about everything," and she in return protected their interests at court. Maintenon was born in the prison at Niort where her father Constant d'Aubigné was held;

abducted by Catholic relations and placed in an Ursuline convent, she converted to Catholicism at thirteen. Her hold on the king depended on her beauty, respectability, devoutness and sexually undemanding character. Michelet described her as unwomanly and spoke of arrested development; she remained, he said, at the age when a girl is partly a boy, "she had no sex, or she had both." Saint-Simon made the accusation that she bought Jesuit acceptance of her marriage to the king with the promise to urge him to Revocation. Under her aegis, he said, the pleasures of the table (to which the king was always addicted) replaced those of the bed. The royal digestion was systematically overloaded for years by enormous meals and the king drank profusely. Bloating and stomach pains were his daily lot, and to make matters much worse, nature, in the words of Michelet, humbled him in the quarter where she humbles all alike, the anus. Ulceration of a *fistula-in-ano*, an unnatural passage opened between the rectum and the exterior, led to surgery which the king was said to have borne with great courage. But these sufferings affected his temper as well as his appearance. He became *colérique* and ever more egocentric. He lost his teeth, his jaw decayed, the morose face was "furrowed by disdain" and the look of his eyes, as represented in the famous portrait by Hyacinthe Rigaud intended as a monument to the glory of the reign, was "sombre, sharp and full of pettiness".[42] It was in this state that he ordered the shelling from the sea of defenceless Genoa, and that the Revocation of the Edict of Nantes was finally promulgated.

The applause that greeted the Revocation by the Edict of Fontainebleau on 18 October was almost universal, while no one yet foresaw the results. "Let us say to this new Constantine ... this new Charlemagne ... You have exterminated the heretic ... thanks to you heresy is dead," thundered Bossuet, beyond reach of contradiction in the pulpit; and Madame de Sévigné, beyond that of empathy in Catholic Provence, wrote, "Nothing is more beautiful than what it (the Edict of Fontainebleau) contains, and no king has ever done anything more memorable." Lavisse, however, makes the contrast between the humanity of Henri IV—evident in the wording of the Edict of Nantes that urged his subjects to "live peacefully together as brothers, friends and fellow citizens"—with the icy, haughty and impersonal tone of Fontainebleau. Saint-Simon claimed that from mistrust, idleness and pride Louis, like many kings, communicated with only two or three people—confessor, first minister, new wife—putting an insurmountable barrier between him and his subjects. In a passage which somewhat exaggerates the depopulation yet rises by degrees to an impassioned eloquence, Saint-Simon's humanity, and his underlying relative freedom from disabling preconceptions of religion and caste become evident, contrasting with the tone he used when writing of the life of the court, its ribbons and its minutiae, and giving a résumé unmatched by any other historian of the disastrous consequences of the Revocation:

> The revocation, without the least pretext or need, of the edict of Nantes and the proscriptions that followed were the fruit of this scheming which depopulated a quarter of France, ruined her commerce, enfeebled her in every part ... which left her prey so long to the public pillage of the dragoons, authorised the torture and executions whereby thousands of innocent people of both sexes were made to die, ruined a numerous population, tore to pieces a world of families, armed relation against relation, stealing property and leaving the robbed to die of starvation; which drove our manufactures abroad to enrich other states whence they could watch the spectacle of so prodigious a people proscribed, bare, fugitive for no crime, in search of shelter far from the homeland; which chained to the oar of the galley old men or young, people highly regarded for piety, knowledge and virtue, delicate and weak people placed under the boatswain's efficacious lash uniquely for their religion ... and which at the height of horror filled the provinces of the realm, where everything rang with the cries of these unhappy victims, with the perjury and sacrilege of those who bought their peace by pretended abjurations ... The bishops wrote panegyrics to the king and the Jesuits made the pulpits resound with them. All France was filled with horror, but never had there been so many triumphs of joy, such profusion of praise...

"Let our acclamations soar to heaven," Bossuet urged, and the Gallican Church, having much to gain, joined in. But the mentality of the Catholic clergy, so active against the Huguenot heresy and so potent through the

Jesuit influence on the court, was not an admirable one. Financial greed and envy of Calvinist intellectual superiority reigned together in the minds of country priests and of their senior hierarchy; in the southern and western crescent of France where the Huguenot presence was strongest, the powerful intendants Noailles, d'Aguesseau and Foucauld unanimously complained of the ignorance and shameful lives of priests in the territories under their control and most especially in the mountains of the Cévennes where the population was predominantly peasant and obstinately Protestant. The pastors of the Languedoc with their learning and moral austerity were a standing reproach felt as a humiliation by the clergy whose zeal, according to Noailles, was not so much zealous as inspired by hatred and vengeance.[43] The influence, and the privileges, of the upper clergy and the everyday prerogatives of ministers were sometimes at variance in an unsettled balance of power where all depended on the king, his health and his mood. The war minister Louvois' part in the coming persecutions was the principal one after that of the king himself. It has been argued that Louvois attempted to urge moderation and that the king was moved to Revocation irresistibly by the Jesuit clergy; if so, the king's responsibility was greater than his apologists would admit. Voltaire described the cry of joy uttered by Louvois' father the ex-chancellor Le Tellier as he signed the Edict of Fontainebleau "not realising that he was putting his signature to one of the great misfortunes of France"; and the son who succeeded him wrote, "the king judged in the present state of affairs that it would be best to banish the pastors as soon as possible."

Lavisse states that the banishment of pastors was the chief object of the Revocation, but banishment is a lenient term for what was to follow in the lives of the pastors and their parishioners, for which most but not all of the accounts that history must rely on came from Protestants, literate, anguished and dispersed. Michelet as Keeper of the National Archive evaluated the worth of these accounts: "Is it unwise to believe victims in their own cause? No, these documents are confirmed by the best authority, that of their enemies." He gave three reasons for crediting the Protestant account: first, that the persecutions were confirmed by demands of the assemblies of the clergy which granted the king money for his wars at this price; second, that they were established by a series of ordinances and by administrative correspondence; and third, that far from being exaggerated the Protestant accounts were silent about *circonstances odieuses* well known from other sources.

Banishment, destruction of *temples* and the impact of *dragonnades* were probably judged by civil servants to be enough; "my realm is being purged of bad and troublesome subjects," the king wrote and those who believed they could exterminate Protestantism in France hoped to do as much for Europe, as Louis informed his ambassadors in England and Spain with "superb self-complacency."[44] But Protestantism survived in France and if the king at first hoped that moderate methods would ensure a single religion in his kingdom he, and those acting in his name, turned inevitably to violence as the policy failed.

Article XII of the Edict of Fontainebleau guaranteed civil rights and freedom of conscience and it was necessary to correct this benevolence rapidly by a series of declarations and ordinances. At the end of 1685 Louvois, ignoring the wise advice of Marshal Vauban who fortified the frontiers of France that "kings are masters of the lives and goods of their subjects but never of their opinions", sent formal orders to the intendants: "his Majesty desires that the greatest severity be used ... not a single Huguenot should be left." Nevertheless, no way was found to retract Article XII from the edict and to the end of the reign and beyond, discreet Protestants were still found who had never abjured though living permanently in isolation and under the threat of terror.[45] Pastors permitted to emigrate were prevented from taking with them their children older than seven who were placed in Catholic schools and convents; good offers of pensions and tax advantages were made to pastors who abjured, the few who stayed and attempted to continue their mission were arrested and executed since the first articles of the edict forbade all practice of the Protestant cult whether in public or private.

Huguenots, and particularly those in the Cévennes who never saw a wider world than their own magnificent landscape and that imagined from the Bible they were raised on, felt themselves orphaned by the loss of their leaders; pastors who returned clandestinely from exile to their flocks, as some did, risked death by the barbaric method of breaking on the wheel, still practised in France in the following century. Abjuring

Huguenots became known as the "new converted" and were subject to supervision by the Catholic clergy of their parishes whom they despised and to humiliating religious observance in a discipline rejected by their beliefs. The Edict of Fontainebleau and a royal declaration of April 1686 were explicit on the penalties of relapse: women were imprisoned and men sent as galley slaves for life, and their property confiscated. Meanwhile the *dragonnades*, temporarily suspended at the beginning of the year, were resumed and intensified in the spring of 1685 and intendants freed from constraint; with the frontiers tightly guarded against exit "it was a kind of hunt within a great enclosure," said Voltaire, and the order went out that "it is mistaken to believe the king forbids that Protestants be mistreated"—though with the circumspect rider that "his Majesty recommends that you are accommodating to the bankers and manufacturers."[46]

Property confiscations interested the Catholic Church in general and its satellites both individual and collective, and the Revocation brought rich pickings, though not on the scale of monastery lands sold in England under Henry VIII. The sites of six hundred destroyed *temples* and the funds held by consistories to finance the welfare of the poor in their area were to pass to Catholic hospitals; the Jesuits, however, obtained a decision in 1688 that these proceeds should instead accrue to the king and from him to those he favoured. To this was soon added the value of property confiscated from individuals who chose forbidden emigration and became refugees from the law, although the sale or exploitation of these gains turned out more difficult and more often caught in legal snares than was foreseen. Those already in exile called to fellow Huguenots left behind to join them in prosperous communities where they were making good; the numbers leaving France clandestinely by any means on land or sea has been exaggeratedly estimated at a million between the years before the Revocation and the end of the century, despite all attempts of the government to put the country under lock and key.[47] But for the new converted under suspicion and still more the obdurate Protestants who continued their practices in secret, the full force of persecution was about to follow. In November 1685 Louvois ordered the intendants to hang without pretence of trial half of those caught attempting to emigrate and to chain the rest and send them to the galleys. "The barbarous treatment of the Huguenots after the revocation of the edict of Nantes became the model for the treatment of whoever would not bend his conscience to the new yoke," Saint-Simon declared.

Basville and the Languedoc

Michelet described the intendants as *commis souverains*, dictator-bureaucrats. First created by Richelieu, their powers were greatly increased under Colbert, particularly the judicial powers they had previously lacked; the only flaw in their sovereignty was subjection to the minister's will in moving them, and their exposure to pressure at court by the clergy. Michelet states that their one means of calming the bishops in their province was to attack the Protestants and in this they were supported by the orders of Louvois, in his own hand, that the intransigent among the Huguenots "must be pushed to the last extremity". Voltaire drew attention to the "strange contrast that from the bosom of a voluptuous court where gentleness of manners and the charms of society reigned, there could issue such hard and pitiless orders".

The most important post of intendant to rule over the remaining Huguenots was in the Languedoc, where Protestantism was most deeply rooted and resistance to conformity most feasible thanks to the vast cévenol hinterland, forested, inaccessible, precipitous and peopled, then as now, by a population intensely devoted to family, history, custom and belief. The man chosen was the son of a judge and president of the Paris *parlement*, typical of the new nobility created to honour civil servants and lawyers who, unlike many of the older sort of whom Saint-Simon was a talented example, would be unenvious of the king and obedient to his wishes. This was Nicolas de Lamoignon de Basville, advocate and counsel to the Council of State, aged 37 at the date of his appointment to become virtual sovereign of Languedoc, the largest and possibly most troublesome province of France.

Basville, an early friend of Madame de Maintenon but said to have opposed the Revocation of the Edict of Nantes probably because he thought it unnecessary, was believed to know the mind of the king and he remained intendant of the Languedoc until 1718. He was a ready viceroy to stand between Versailles and the hard reality of ordinances devised in the royal cabinet but executed in the Midi, a land to which he and other members of the council of state were alien but where he developed an authority that made him feared at court and, by the appointment of his friend and supporter Esprit Fléchier as Bishop of Nîmes, respected by the Church whose priests he used as spies on the concealed faith and practices of Protestants.[48] His policy, for which he had carte blanche, was based on his opinion that the Inquisition had had the "happy effect" of striking down heresy; the Protestant dissidence would be disintegrated by slow and relentless persecution, exhausting the survivors as their numbers were reduced by death and their children taken for indoctrination in Catholic schools. "Children who have never seen a temple or a pastor will be the more disposed to receive the good impressions they will be given..." Basville seems to have made the mistaken judgement that the greater the disintegration, the less strenuous the reaction of the Huguenots would be, and Bosc alleged that his activity in the region he ruled with such control and autonomy impregnated the distant court with a spirit of the violence he believed to be the only resource.

He was left by the government to form a regular army in the province of eight infantry regiments, and a huge and less controlled Catholic militia of 52 regiments. Saint-Simon referred to his "tyranny", and the hatred felt towards him by Huguenot historians has masked whatever may have been more humane in a character described by one of them as naturally inclined to cruelty. His correspondence claims that he several times granted amnesties on his own authority and that the work of persecution, torture and capital punishment which he carried out so ruthlessly exhausted and depressed him, as he wrote to Bishop Fléchier in 1701.[49] But these details cannot erase the long record of domination by methods usually so harsh that resistance would either break, as Saint-Simon wrongly believed would happen, or explode in a matching violence and bloodshed. Voltaire analysed the process clearly: "persecution inspired terror as it strengthened obstinacy; it is only too well known that men love their religion more, the more they have to suffer for it." This was the outcome in the Cévennes in what was to become, from unplanned and spontaneous beginnings, the audacious epic of the Camisard uprising.

The disappearance of the pastors did not have the desired effect of starving the Huguenot spirit of its last nourishment. Preachers took the place of pastors and theologians and distributed, by hand or post, tracts to hearten and encourage resistance and urge the continuation of secret assemblies for prayer and worship. This endurance of Protestantism against the odds was recognized by an official pronouncement in 1715 a few months before Louis XIV's death; it has led one historian to refer to the "fiasco of the revocation" failing to achieve its ends and another to describe the policy of attack on the Huguenots as a "calamity for France".[50] Credit is given by many historians to Claude Brousson as saviour of the reformed religion in France. Brousson was an advocate in Nîmes who emigrated but returned "in remorse for encouraging at a safe distance the constancy of the faithful living under persecution". He installed a propaganda press in Languedoc to print and distribute his sermons, and Basville put a price on his head. "The danger in forcing two million people to abjure the religion which they are convinced is the only one true to the word of God has never been understood," he wrote, clearly pointing towards active resistance even at the price of life, as persecution intensified and between two and three thousand Huguenot men were sent to the king's galleys, part of the great fleet envisaged by the minister Colbert and in need of a constant supply of slaves.

Brousson himself was eventually captured and broken on the wheel at Montpellier in 1698, by which time the remaining preachers had been taken or had fled. At the end of the century it could have seemed that the state had finally defeated the Huguenots; but the distribution of Brousson's sermons continued, some were learned by heart and repeated in clandestine assemblies by spokesmen who saw themselves as leading their people into the *désert*, as the cévenol forests came to be called in conscious biblical emulation. "Take very few prisoners, and put those few on the wheel," were the orders from Louvois when any of these meetings were discovered. Voltaire's dictum was to be put to the proof.

The text by Brousson which had the most lasting emotional and symbolic influence and bearing on the events that followed in the Cévennes, the "Mystic Dove", adapted from the Song of Solomon, illustrates the lyrical ardour and prophetic leaning of the Huguenot faith and the freshness of its vitality relative to a Christian world grown grey:

"My dove," spoke the Lord, "that hide yourself in the clefts of the rock and the mountain caves ... my dove, show me your face and let me hear your voice, for your voice is sweet and your face is comely. Rise up, my love, and come away, for the winter is past and the flowers are budding and the time for singing is at hand. Don't you hear the turtledove? Rise up my love, my fair one, and come away with me."

The extraordinary and sometimes hardly believable, yet well attested, courage of the Huguenot martyrs under torture and at the terrible end awaiting them can be better understood as passionate immolation to a love transporting mind and soul to an ideal union beyond pain.

Another, equally symbolic but far more earthy text whose original unwritten content, flying by word of mouth, put the spark to the touch-paper of the Camisard War was Abraham Mazel's account of a dream that became famous. Mazel was the first of the Camisard leaders though not militarily the most important, and he was the last to die, campaigning to the end in October 1710; his primacy is due to his prophesying in 1701 the destruction of the Empire of the Beast, combining apocalyptic menace with emotional appeal to the "Beast's" victims. His dream occurred in the spring of 1702 and was regarded by him and all those he imparted it to as a portent to be interpreted: a herd of fat black bullocks was devouring, with impunity, the cabbages growing in a garden. Analysis of the dream symbolism was made easier by a vision Mazel experienced a few days later. The garden was the church of Christ, the bullocks were the black-clad priesthood whose rule of celibacy made them, or should make them neutered as bullocks, and he, Mazel, was the chosen of God to drive them forth. Magic is the most potent and elastic vehicle of hope for the non-sceptical and the long-suffering. The symbolic power of the dream lay naturally in its interpretative effects, and the first would be the unleashing of a storm of hatred against the Huguenots' main enemy, the Catholic priesthood and its chief representative in the Cévennes, a powerful friend of Basville and of Bishop Fléchier, the Abbé du Chayla—"*ce prêtre terrible*" in Michelet's description. His murder at Le Pont-de-Montvert on 25 July 1702 was the opening signal to the Camisard uprising.

Notes

1 Arlette Jouanna, *Le Temps des guerres de religion en France*: 196-7
2 Ibid: 199
3 Patrick Cabanel, *Histoire des protestants en France XVIe-XXIe siècle*: 278-82
4 Geoffrey Treasure, *The Huguenots*: 172-3
5 Cabanel: 264-5
6 Ibid: 277
7 Denis Crouzet, *La nuit de la Saint-Barthélemy*: 401
8 Jouanna: 202
9 Ibid: 203
10 Cabanel: 288-9
11 An example is Emmanuel LeRoy Ladurie's assumption that an English art critic, stemming from a Protestant culture, could not empathize with the baroque art of the Counter-Reformation.
12 Cabanel: 314
13 Yves Charles Zarka, *Les Fondements philosophiques de la tolérance: Textes et documents*: 296
14 Jules Michelet, *Louis XIV et la Révocation de de l'Edit de Nantes*: 277-8
15 Cabanel: 354
16 Ibid: 391
17 Ibid: 351
18 Ibid: 350
19 Agrippa d'Aubigné, *Ecrits politiques*: 44
20 Cabanel: 446
21 *Locke's Travels in France*, ed. John Lough: 257. May be best translated as "What says your lordship to all this flummery?"
22 Ibid: 43
23 Treasure: 297
24 Ernest Lavisse, *Louis XIV*: 400
25 Eugène Bonnemère, *Les Dragonnades:* 37-8
26 Cabanel: 469-70
27 Ibid: 528-9
28 *State Papers of John Thurloe*: II, 443
29 Treasure: 240-1
30 Lavisse: 403
31 Ibid: 112-13
32 Ibid: 988
33 Cabanel: 553
34 Emmanuel Le Roy Ladurie, *The Peasants of Languedoc*: 272
35 Cabanel: 538
36 Locke: 23, 27
37 Lavisse: 408-9
38 Cabanel: 580
39 Ibid: 585

40 Ibid: 583; Michelet: 179
41 Lavisse: 429
42 Ibid: 731; Michelet: 202
43 Michelet: 200; Lavisse: 431
44 Lavisse: 434
45 Ibid: 1048-9
46 Treasure: 355
47 Lavisse: 1041
48 Henri Bosc, *La Guerre des Cévennes*, vol. 1: 15
49 Cabanel: 682
50 Treasure: 366

'… narrows where a hundred will defeat a thousand or ten thousand': Gorges de la Jonte (David Hughes/Shutterstock)

Chapter Three

The Sacred Theatre of the Cévennes

The Cévenols

At the moment in *Travels with a Donkey* when Robert Louis Stevenson's route through the cévenol uplands crossed the Atlantic and Mediterranean watershed on the summit of Mont Lozère, he found himself in possession of "a new quarter of the world":

> For behold, instead of the gross turf rampart I had been mounting for so long, a view into the hazy air of heaven, and a land of intricate blue hills below my feet ... Speaking largely, I was in the Cévennes ... during all my journey; but there is a strict and local sense in which only this confused and shaggy country ... has any title to the name ... In that undecipherable labyrinth of hills, a war of bandits, a war of wild beasts, raged for two years between the Grand Monarch with all his troops and marshals on the one hand, and a few thousand Protestant mountaineers upon the other.

Mont Lozère stands at the geographic centre of the Camisard history, "a seminary from which came the most famous pastors of the *désert*," said the Huguenot historian and pastor Napoléon Peyrat, friend and mentor of Michelet. In the singular, *la Cévenne* designates that lozenge of forested hills, gorges and valleys, fifty kilometres by forty-five between the rivers Ardèche, Cèze, Gardon and Hérault, likened by the new prefect of the department in 1813 to "an extremely agitated sea deeply furrowed by a furious wind", and by Peyrat to "a gigantic stairway whose steep flight falls constantly southward ... and merges at last with the sand of the beach and the stormy waves of the gulf." This country of the Camisards, said Stevenson, was the "scene of a romantic chapter—or, better, a romantic footnote—in the history of the world."[1]

The image of the stairway, less fitting now that this monumental scenery has for the most part fallen from creation to disrepair and then into neglect, would have been inspired in Peyrat's time by the view of descending steps of man-built terraces embracing in an amphitheatre the flanks of hills, from the bare high grassland to the plain of vine and wheat, sustained by dry stone walls, drained and watered from cisterns and canals, each terrace banked with earth from the excavation above it, disciplined, logical, economic and as austere as the interior of a *temple*; a landscape where goats and sheep fed and vine, chestnut and fruit trees were the staple cultivation. The walls ran for thousands of kilometres around the contours, and the chestnut forest, which provided a great part of the diet of the Cévenols, was tended and replanted, the trees often numbered in deeds of sale of land, and grew from earth grazed clean to facilitate the gathering of fruit. From the plain to the summit and beyond, the forests and clearings which were to become the Huguenot *désert* were threaded with tracks believed to have been first created by the instinctive seasonal transhumance of sheep and goats, followed but not guided by shepherds, since at least the seventh millennium BC. These mule pathways were used throughout the period of cévenol cultivation for the transport of goods and haulage of materials and, being often hidden in forest undergrowth but well known to people of the country, served both the Camisard groups in their rapid displacements from ambush to confrontation or tactical flight by night or day, and the Protestant faithful making their secret way to forbidden assemblies of prayer for which the most merciful punishment on discovery was death. "The mountains were impassable," announced Basville "and nothing contributed more to making these people mutinous and seditious ... a few men could stop an entire army."[2]

La Cévenne, then as now, was the cradle of a tribe and with its isolation and rigour a constituent part of the character of the inhabitants; a refuge where the peasant was first of all a builder and architect in a wilderness sought and found by fleeing Albigensians, by Protestants in the sixteenth century, by anti-Nazi Germans, Jews and resistants in the 1940s, and by hippy rebels, the *soixante-huitards*, in the 1960s and 1970s, who remained to make less conformist lives in "the labyrinth of hills". Patrick Cabanel, pointing to the identification of this territory with French Protestantism, asks whether without it the Cévennes would exist as such or be only

The Theatre of Conflict: From the Cévennes t Mediterranean (Sebastian Ballard)

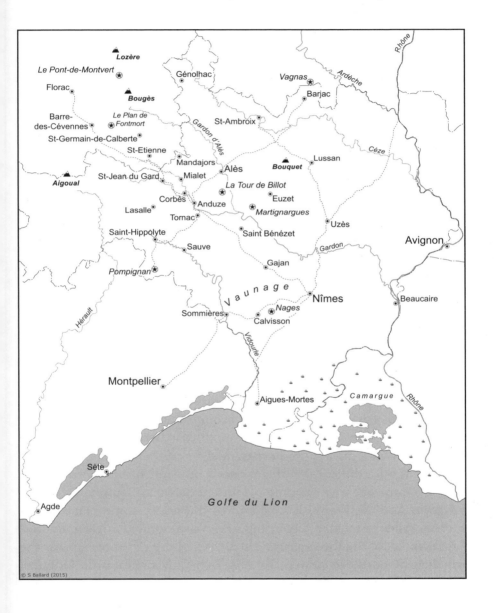

© S Ballard (2015)

another Mediterranean hinterland like those behind Nice or Perpignan. But the historic identification exists and is taken to have acted as a magnet to the disaffected during the three centuries since the Camisards rose in revolt for what they most prized, freedom of religious conscience. "It was to the spirit of god alone that the Cévenol, individualist, recalcitrant, deliberately insubordinate and argumentative, owed obedience."[3]

The name *Cévenne* is derived, said Napoléon Peyrat, from the Hebrew *Giben* or the Celtic *Keben*, both signifying mountain; a double etymology appropriately both religious and racial, and with a probable root in ancient Indian idiom. Peyrat, though ten years younger than Michelet, so influenced *De la Révocation de l'Edit de Nantes à la Guerre des Cévennes* that echoes of his *Histoire des pasteurs du Désert* can be clearly heard in it. For example, Peyrat's "assuredly unique episode in the history of France" becomes Michelet's less sober "nothing resembling the affair of the Cévennes in the whole history of the world"; and the passionate rhetorical empathy of Michelet writing in 1860 of the Esplanade du Peyrou at Montpellier where the terrible deaths by breaking on the wheel were inflicted — "those who at evening in the last rays of the sun follow the luminous avenue of the Peyrou towards the sea and the sky will still see the souls of the martyrs on the *via sacra*" — derives from the grave sentence of Peyrat writing in 1842 of his own people: "a magnificent horizon which stretched without limit toward the sea and sky like a road illuminated for the flight of their souls."

At the Roman conquest the Cévennes were found to be divided among four semi-independent Celtic tribes, made subservient but prosperous in the age of the Roman peace; a number of large Roman farming estates have been identified around the slopes of Mont Lozère, and the patrician poet Sidonius Apollinaris wrote approvingly in the fifth century, during the Roman decline, of the civilized life in the villas of the foothills. After the Visigoth invasion of southern France the Cévennes became a frontier country between Septimanie of the Visigoths and the Frankish kingdom of the north, some place-names such as Vallée Française suggesting a Frankish outpost in Visigoth land. Peyrat spoke of the three gigantic struggles of the Cévenols against the wielders of northern power; the Frankish Clovis, Simon de Montfort the crusader who destroyed the Albigensian heresy, and finally Louis XIV. "As Arians, Albigensians, Protestants, they have always rejected the

Catholic rule which brought them first barbarism, then feudality, and finally despotism, all three orthodox."

If this claim offers a possible background to the seemingly innate anti-conformism of the Huguenots of the Cévennes, Patrick Cabanel denies the existence in them of any predisposition to heresy, arguing that few regions of France have so many *communes* whose name indicates dedication to a saint, and pointing to the great wealth and quality of Romanesque church architecture in the Languedoc and particularly in the department of the Gard comprising the greatest part of the Huguenot resistants' territory. On the other hand, most chapels and churches were erected and owned until the Revolution of 1789 by the great landowning monasteries and their existence is in itself no proof of the religious disposition of the cévenol population, whether peasant or noble. At all events, Nîmes and its cévenol hinterland at the heart of the Languedoc where the Albigensian heresy took root were evidently fertile ground for Calvinist Reform and among the earliest Calvinist consistories was that of Nîmes, set up in 1561.

The apparent contradiction between traditional Catholic practice and the new attachment to a passionately held Protestantism may be partially explained as the academician and cévenol novelist André Chamson accounted for it: he saw mountains running to the sea with its coming and going, its coastal shipping, its philosopher merchants exchanging ideas and copies of the biblical translation of 1535 from Hebrew and Greek against the raw material of the western lands and their mines; and the resulting creation of a mentality from the mixture of landsmen going down to the sea with maritime adventurers exploring the foothills and mountains. By 1550 the Reform, though widespread throughout France with the exception of Brittany, was densest in the Béarn near the Spanish frontier, and in the Languedoc zone of Mediterranean transfusion where the arrival of proselytizing Calvinist ministers from Geneva was easiest and most frequent. Cabanel shows from examination of wills that the demand for masses and the presence of priests at deathbeds in the Cévennes fell from eighty-three per cent of testators in 1530 to none after 1565,[4] and gives some credit for the rapid growth of the reformed religion to the Seneschal of Nîmes, Charles de Crussol vicomte and later duc d'Uzès (whose descendants are still in place), who although perhaps not Huguenot himself showed tolerance toward those who were, and attachment to the reformed ideas.

André Chamson claimed that the spread of the Reform was carried not only by travelling salesmen at the annual or biennial fairs but particularly through the artisan class—tanners, textile workers and tradesmen—and he originated the phrase repeated by Emmanuel Le Roy Ladurie that "wool oozed heresy" or that heresy was the "daughter of wool". Rich Calvinist businessmen and landowners came to dominate the economic scene from mountains to sea, particularly in the region of Nîmes, and in the period of expropriation of Church wealth between 1563 and 1576 were often the purchasers of monastic and episcopal lands, thus earning the permanent hatred of the priesthood[5] which, more than its counterpart in England after the distribution among the gentry of Church lands, remained a dominant force. A later duc d'Uzès was one among many of the noblemen who by abjuring kept their acquired lordships and sheltered from the king's anger and the Church's vengeance. Almost none, when the time came, were to join the Camisards in their revolt although the conversion to Protestantism of the country gentry had often been followed by that of their dependents, employees and tenants.[6] These were the principal victims of the fall in profits from land in the second half of the seventeenth century, while industry benefited largely from the building of the great Languedoc canal, Louis XIV's endowment to the province. On 1 May 1676 Locke wrote, "The rents of Lands in France fallen above ½ in these few years by reason of the poverty of the people & want of mony," and Ladurie refers to the suffering of the two hundred thousand Protestant peasants in the Languedoc from the depression "so deadly in the Cévennes" where ninety per cent of the Cévenols were reduced to subsisting on acorns and grass while faced with a "concerted campaign of unlimited oppression engineered by the central authorities and the local clergy".[7] This centred on the compulsory attendance at mass by devoted or, as some writers accused them, fanatically Protestant peasants driven by violence to abjuration and to whom the mass was a sacrilegious reminder of their apostasy. A dramatically moving representation of this violence to faith was given in the marseillais René Allio's film *Les Camisards* of 1972, proof of the living resonance of the mystic revolt[8] in the Cévennes three hundred years earlier.

Philippe Joutard, introducing texts by active witnesses of the uprising, corrects Michelet's suggestion that it was in some way a forerunner of the Revolution: "its social programme was inexistent ...there was no 'biblical communism' such as proclaimed by Levellers and Diggers in Cromwell's time ... the aims of the insurrection were purely religious." Jean Cavalier wrote in his memoirs that "to avoid attending at mass, to escape persecution, to win the right to serve God as he commanded us—such were the principal reasons for our taking up arms." Contrary to much popular belief, the men who served under Cavalier and other leaders were not only from the rural proletariat, shepherds or artisans, but were often owners of the land they worked and sometimes, as in the case of Élie Marion, from families of substance. In the Cévennes, it was said, and with particular bitterness by the Catholics, that all the levers of power—the land, the wealth, the consular authority—were in Protestant hands. Moreover, though the upland *Cévenols* were poor the land in the lower valleys and foothills where the revolt was equally violent was fertile and life relatively secure. Basville noted in 1698,

> It is remarkable to see, every Thursday, the Nîmes merchants at the Anduze market bringing 25,000 or even 30,000 *Livres* in cash. They distribute this sum to the rural dealers who in their turn spread it among the work people, making this countryside the richest in all Languedoc.[9]

Joutard points out that the Camisards had access to enough regular provisions to accumulate stores and to survive the systematic devastations in the months of fighting to come. In the mountains the dragoons had been present since 1683 and many of the remote *communes* were ruined; mass abjurations and the permitted flight of the pastors left cévenol Protestantism apparently moribund. But the forests of the Cévennes have always sheltered fugitives, sometimes for years on end; after the fall of Montpellier to royal forces in 1622 the Huguenot population of the city evaporated, fleeing to the high valleys, and never returned in significant numbers. Montpellier became a Catholic city. Between 1685 and 1699 the high forested diocese of Mende alone sheltered in hiding at least nine hundred and sixty fugitives who found the means to stay alive; and in this way the mountain became the paradigm of the *désert* where the migrant faithful followed the paths of transhumance to their places of assembly or, in the case of discovery, fled to the caves and forest darkness.

The first recorded clandestine assembly was held near Anduze ten days after the Revocation; these prayer meetings, led by untrained lay preachers repeating by heart sermons learned from the originals of Claude Brousson, were attended by fugitives and by newly converted Catholics regretting their abjuration and were multiplied in the months following, accompanied sometimes as at Saint-Jean-du-Gard, where by 1686 five or six preachers were at work, by early examples of mysterious manifestations heard or seen. Cabanel remarks that henceforward "patient preaching and miraculous enthusiasm nourished by Old Testament culture went together"[10] in assemblies that were often armed for self-defence, numbered sometimes between two and three thousand faithful and included groups organized for occasional action long before the Camisard uprising began. A significant example was the rescue in May 1699 of the itinerant preacher Jean Roman by a group formed at the fair of Lédignan and led by a gardener from nearby Anduze. Roman, betrayed and badly wounded during his arrest, was kidnapped by his rescuers, taken into hiding and nursed for three months before being carried over the Swiss border to safety. This bold exploit, said Bosc, made a strong impression on the authorities of the province and was the first occasion since 1682 when armed Protestants went into action. "The liberation of Roman clearly showed a mentality of resistance and revolt in the oppressed masses which later events confirmed."[11]

The growth of the assemblies was the outward show of inner resistance which left four or five secretly practising Huguenots in the country for every one departing into exile after the policy of coercion had been long tried; the belief in coercion and its failure are taken as proof of misunderstanding by the authorities and by the Catholic Church itself of the nature of the Protestant community, of its teaching of individual salvation and its support to its own people crying their distress as they moved gradually towards revolt.[12] But not all Protestants approved of this "church of the desert". The social background of the majority of courageous, or as Catholics saw it, fanatical participants has been identified from judicial records (admittedly concerning only those arrested, "questioned" and condemned) as nine-tenths of rural artisans and peasants; the bourgeois from the cities of the plain, and still more the nobility, looked askance at a movement threatening their security, while the leaders of the Huguenots in exile, whether in Switzerland, Holland or England, believed that the king should be obeyed and that the only hope for Huguenots in the Languedoc lay in persuading the royal mind, a hope by now delusory and showing a lack of grasp of the absolute Catholic mentality equal to that of Catholics towards Protestantism.

There was therefore a great gulf between the exiles led by and largely made up of cultivated pastors and their families, theologians living in safe Protestant lands, ruled among themselves by consistories and usually supported, as was the case in England, by public subsidy, and the remaining Huguenots alert to constant danger in woods and valleys of the Cévennes. The more these threatened people formed themselves in armed groups and let themselves be led by uninstructed preachers not subject to Calvinist discipline the greater was the disapproval of the exiles fearful of the taint of democracy in cévenol turbulence. Few of the exiles originated from the Cévennes; it is calculated that among the total of recorded Huguenot exiles fewer than 1.4 per cent were cévenol.[13] But the population of the Cévennes was so massively Protestant that the men and women who would form the Camisard army and their supporters and suppliers felt themselves encapsulated and stayed rooted in their own lands to risk or invite martyrdom among their own people. From other parts of France the diaspora, according to Voltaire, dispersed the Huguenots further than the Jews, but from 1686 the frontiers of France were closed and policed by an army of sentries on land and water; rewards were offered, and claimed, for denunciation of Huguenots in flight and of those attempting, or even thinking of attempting to leave the kingdom. An official "Project for capturing fugitives and preachers" foresaw the transformation of the Languedoc, in Voltaire's words, into a hunting ground in which the quarry would be run down like wild boar, yet the exodus continued for those lucky enough to reach the Swiss frontier and cross it.

By the end of the century many at court, and particularly the king himself, appeared to believe that the poison of heresy had been effectively drained. Bossuet wrote, "I adore the design of God who wished to reveal, by the dispersal of our Protestants, the mystery of iniquity and to purge France of these monsters." It was to be within this small world of oppression, hatred and terror that there first arose among the least schooled of an unprivileged population, children and young girls at first, the greatly disputed phenomenon of prophesying.

The Enigma of *Prophétisme*

The hunting down and slaughter of the preachers left Protestants of the Cévennes leaderless. Only three exiled pastors returned to their flock, left languishing for guidance and hungry for communion. These men were captured like Claude Brousson and executed in the same way in 1690 and 1693. The Bible, and in particular the Old Testament, usually in the first French translation by Olivétan of 1535, was now the cévenol people's emotional and theological mainstay, the narrative that created them and in which they felt themselves living actors with salvation after suffering as their due. Side by side with the Bible on the single bookshelf in Huguenot mountain households stood *L'Histoire des martyrs* of Jean Crespin, called by Cabanel a tragic Old Testament of their people, and these works were read out in the evenings by the head of the family, male or female, to all the others. French translations of the Bible were made in narrower language than the English, using a vocabulary free from demotic speech and poetic image. In the mouths of visionaries whose mother tongue of everyday was Occitan the use of a formal French learned from Bible translations, which was thought of as the language of officialdom and of the court, astonished hearers whose upbringing had not included intimate familiarity with the Bible or the text of the psalms by Clément Marot, constantly recited in cévenol assemblies public and private, and which were later to be ritually sung by Camisard soldiers going into battle. But if the French Bible lacked the richness of language of the English, Cabanel nevertheless demonstrates that the Huguenot self-image was imprinted with a fateful sense of victimhood and martyrdom based on the reading of books whose clandestine possession was at times punished by death, and that this small library of works was to the identity of French Protestantism as the ghetto and the observance of the Law were to the dispersed Jews.[14] And neither quality of language nor resonance of imagery was what counted for Huguenots in that part of the New Testament they read most, the Apocalypse or Book of Revelations. Relentless persecution naturally creates hope of an ending and a reliance on prediction of when this will come about. Readings of the Book of Daniel and of the Apocalypse gave Huguenots the promise that "finally the world would bloom again, more beautiful than before".[15] This promise watered the parched soul of the cévenol people whose Celtic element was perhaps attracted with fervour to a culture of mysteries of the imagination.

The line between prophecy and dream is a fine one; on each side the relation to time and reality is dramatically present but arbitrarily distorted and in the same way—convincing, disturbing, urgent. Dreams may be construed to predict the future, especially if this is predestined, and prophecies to interpret both past and future, representation being the vehicle in either case. The dream of black bullocks and Mazel's later visionary reading of it which took him and his fellows into action are examples of the interaction of these two faculties of the mind, supposed or real; and since dreaming is universal, the belief in and exploitation of supposed powers of prophecy as practised by the few should seem less outlandish. Moreover, failure of prophecy to materialize can be seen as not so disabling after all since universal dreaming is not disqualified only by its apparent disjointedness from the supposed facts of reality.

This, however, did not shield the *prophétisme* of the Cévennes from the disapproval of Calvinist theologians exiled in Geneva or in London, as the French Prophets would discover after 1706. Patrick Cabanel, referring to "the prophetic disorder submerging all like an autumn flood", describes it as the most disturbing moment in the history of French Protestantism,[16] and Antoine Court, who is credited with the rehabilitation of Protestantism in France in the eighteenth century from its loss of reputation due to the prophets' excesses, wrote from Geneva in 1713 that his work was to "make known the source and the abuses of inspiration". The Huguenots remaining in the Cévennes were neither theologians nor familiar with the life of cities which they had never seen; a possible element in their mentality which would not appeal to Protestant exiles in Geneva was a romanticism naturally connected to the vast, wild and rugged landscape that was the master of their imagination and their economy and in which God was immanent and everywhere.

This pantheistic "romanticism" became apparent in a veneration for the first prophets who were children, regarded as closer to God and to acquaintance with the sublime than adults could be, and whose inspirations were soon followed by those of their elders and sometimes of parents themselves. Veneration for children's proximity to God is familiar in eighteenth-century romantic poets: "Thou best Philosopher ... thou Eye among the blind ... Mighty Prophet! Blest Seer! ... Thou little Child ..." With lyricism subtracted, the words could have been spoken by onlookers in the Languedoc of the first transports of inspiration in children "trailing clouds of glory ... from God". The wave of trance-like visions, sleep-walking, convulsions, glossolalia and biblically worded prophecy quickly reached into the Huguenot community, male and female. Some of the more coherent young prophets were boys, notably Daniel Raoul who spread the cult of prophecy in the Cévennes and was in 1701 the youngest victim, not long out of childhood, to be broken on the wheel, but most were female and this distinction of gender led naturally to the supposition that prophecy was a product of hysteria. Doctors from the famous medical faculty of Montpellier, the academy of Nostradamus whose prophetic quatrains were still studied by the curious and the apprehensive, were ordered to examine some of the imprisoned adolescents and concluded that a contagion had crossed the Rhône from the eastern side where a school of prophecy had allegedly been set up.[17] From an early stage, future leaders of the Camisards, and in particular Jean Cavalier, were known to have attended prophetic sessions and observed the expressive forms, physical, verbal and often provocative, used by female visionaries.

No convincing explanation can be given of the phenomenon which permeated the uprising with at least fifty of the Camisards claiming in their ecstasies to be the voice and instrument of God, and their inspired announcements being followed, in the words of Élie Marion, "as our law, our guide and our military discipline". Ladurie adopts the "convulsive hysteria" or neurotic diagnosis and offers the explicitly Freudian suggestion that sexual repression, "taken very far by the Huguenots", was the cause. Michelet, who thanks to his deep empathy with the people, and with the events set out in the London publication *le Théâtre sacré des Cévennes* (1707) preserving and making known the spiritual experience of the Camisards and their families and which strongly influenced him, proposed that *prophétisme*, so troubling and controversial, was a "somnambulism aggravated by the horror of a unique situation, by ceaseless anxiety, and which had become a racial condition ... the true reason is easy to find ... it was despair that produced these facts, well established, indubitable, astonishing, natural, and ... unmiraculous." And their Hebraic source and power of spiritual infusion were traced by Antoine Court to a familiar passage from one of the Twelve Minor Prophets, the *Book of Joel* "I will pour out my spirit upon all flesh; and your sons and daughters shall prophesy, your old men shall dream dreams, your young men shall see visions." Ladurie explains the Huguenot acceptance of suffering and particularly the rebels' transcendence of torture and the horrors of execution by the "apocalyptic mentality which transforms the worst misfortunes into an antechamber of supreme joy". This was the martyr's self-immolation whereby Claude Brousson, on the wheel, saw "the heavens all aflame" against the persecuting king; though the vision must have come to him before the executioner's iron bar struck the first blow since Basville had given secret instructions that the victim be strangled in advance, not from compassion but in order to "finish the show promptly".

If not in its beginnings, certainly as it ran its violent course the Camisard revolt was a conscious challenge to unlimited authority imposing uniformity of Christian practice, and of the articles of faith of which the miracle of transubstantiation was an important example. So great was the Huguenot respect for and dependence on the word of the pastors that the people of the Cévennes would probably never have risen against authority without the incitement of one of these exiled theologians, and this came to them from Rotterdam where Pierre Jurieu, a Norman pastor who had been professor of Hebrew and theology at Sedan, took refuge in 1681 and from where he exercised a growing influence that spread throughout the Huguenot community. Michelet credited him with the audacity to proclaim that God was under contract with man not to abuse power without limit. What monstrosity is it then, he asked, that attributes to a king a power not attributed to himself by the king of kings? This incendiary doctrine, certainly owing something to the execution of Charles I in 1649, was promulgated in a series of pastoral letters by Jurieu, smuggled into France and passed from hand to hand in the Languedoc, giving hope by announcing the forthcoming end of the reign of the oppressor.

Jurieu is a contested figure on account of his reading of the Apocalypse and consequent encouragement of prophecy. Ladurie accuses him of humbug on the ground that as a fanatic who was also a bourgeois he announced that the coming millennium would institute community of goods but also respect private property.[18] With perhaps more serious intentions Jurieu "placed a great hope in the year 1689" as the end of Louis XIV and prophesied the end of papism between 1710 and 1720 to be followed by the Second Coming and "a thousand years of peace and righteousness on earth". Copies of Jurieu's prophecies were seized by militiamen in remote cévenol farmhouses. Cabanel blames Jurieu for fanning the embers of revolt and lighting the flame in the Huguenot south by his *Lettres pastorales* but goes on to question whether French Protestantism would have survived the Revocation without his violence, his excesses and the freshness of his piety which surpassed social barriers. "It was his gift to put himself in unison with simple people."[19] Inevitably, some simple people in the Cévennes took the word and the apocalyptic readings of the "prophet of Rotterdam" to their heart in a world of daily persecution and, believing that action was prerequisite to the millennium, the law eventually into their own hands.

The "Disagreeable Adventure" of the Abbé du Chayla

In assessing the quality of the senior Catholic clergy it must be remembered that the priesthood was one of the usual destinations for younger sons of the nobility of all ranks. Lack of priestly vocation could go with appetite for power and an aristocratic tendency to float free of the moral restraints it was the clergy's role to preach. The most famous and brazen instance of this combination was the diplomat, foreign minister, Bishop of Autun from 1788, Charles-Maurice de Talleyrand sometimes called the "bishop of the Revolution". At a humbler level of the hierarchy François de Langlade du Chayla, Archpriest of the Cévennes and Inspector of Missions from 1686, was a younger son of one of the leading noble families of the Gévaudan, now corresponding to the department of the Lozère, and was therefore by birth a Cévenol with an atavistic sense of lordship over the peasantry, if not the gentry, in his charge.[20] The degree of his sincerity as a man of the Church can only be estimated from Eugène Bonnemère's description: "aged fifty-five ... with a sombre and exalted piety, tall and of an austere and bellicose appearance, everything about him announced ... the priest of the church militant," while the known history of his activities makes it certain that he considered himself author of his own ethical responsibility and that a sadistic element of omnipotence entered into the exercise of powers delegated to him by both ecclesiastic and civil authorities. Because he was to be the catalyst by his death for the Camisard revolt, conflicting versions of du Chayla's character have been given by Catholic and Protestant camps. He has been demonized as tyrant-torturer, and only in 1914 fell short of papal canonization as heroic martyr. The conflict of accounts epitomizes the split which at least until the mid-twentieth century kept Catholic and Protestant historians not merely apart, but often diametrically opposed in treating the same material though seldom from the same stock of evidence, and usually ruled by passionate bias one way or the other.

At his own request, du Chayla had accompanied the embassy sent by Louis XIV in 1685 in an abortive attempt to convert the King of Siam to Christianity from Buddhism; this was seen by Catholic commentators as showing a missionary vocation later to be exercised in the Cévennes. An apparently mythical tale was added of capture and near-martyrdom foreshadowing his death at Huguenot hands: "as a missionary in Siam he was condemned to torture ... returned to France ... he met a glorious death, assassinated for hatred of his faith," wrote a Catholic apologist in 1942. Cabanel deflates the myth with irony: "what he was not, in fact, in Siam, the abbé intended to become in the intimate Tropics of the Cévennes—missionary and ethnologist, anxious to learn the strange Huguenot tribe." His mission from the Church hierarchy was to propagate the true faith among the "new converted" who had abjured to save themselves and their families but about whose sincerity in the new faith no one was under any illusion.

Du Chayla produced a "Project for the sincere conversion of the people of the Cévennes" describing the harshness of the mountains, the snares laid for priests by the leaders of the Huguenot community, the people's passion for learning, the strong biblical attachment of the population and hence the need for solid training of missionaries if they were not to be despised. In pursuit of this programme he founded in 1687 a seminary in the hills at Saint-Germain-de-Calberte to train under Jesuit guidance up to eighty young men of better character and more enthusiasm than the average country curé for this work, and while the seminary sowed the missionary seed Du Chayla travelled tirelessly through the parishes of the region, often on foot according to Catholic accounts but driven by horses in a two-wheeled vehicle according to Protestants, pursuing men and women suspected of illegal prayer assembly and ensuring that compulsory attendance at mass and acknowledgement of the miracle of transubstantiation by partaking of the sacraments were imposed. Priests were given powers of compulsion and of report over intransigent absentees and non-communicants, but in

1700 hardly a tenth of the new converted performed their Easter duty in the diocese of Mende at the centre of the archpriest's territory. "Everywhere, in the hollow of valleys, in the remotest parts of the mountains as in the depth of the forests, ever more numerous assemblies were secretly convoked and held at night. Entire villages went to hear the preachers..."[21]

Du Chayla's zeal was enough to earn him Protestant hatred, but it was his work as Inspector of Missions with additional powers under Basville that created in the Cévennes that anger which testifies to the likely truth of witness to the archpriest's methods: the Catholic version of pure martyrdom would only be plausible if there were no evidence that he was an active enforcer of persecution. Among many other accounts, convincing evidence of the character of the archpriest's enforcement comes from a report to the war minister Michel de Chamillart by the comte de Peyre, lieutenant general, or lord lieutenant, of the Languedoc: "the abbé du Cheyla was holding seven prisoners in his house at the time (of his death) whom he personally flogged daily and invented tortures for them..."[22] Peyre wrote later to the king's bastard the duc du Maine that "if only the bishops and priests had stuck to preaching and never meddled with being in command there would have been no uprising in the Cévennes," though this was possibly intended to take some of the burden of responsibility for the long disaster that was the war in the Cévennes off the political and military authority of which he was part.

Michelet suggested that du Chayla, "this fearsome priest", took advantage of his powers to abuse female prisoners for his own gratification, but Bosc claimed that from childhood he had shown a constant and growing antipathy to women. He used the police and judiciary powers delegated to him by Basville to hang the young prophetess Françoise Brès and her companion Catherine Martin, first publicly whipped at every crossroad in Le Pont-de-Montvert, who warned him from the gallows that his own time would come; but he spared the lives, while exploring the pain threshold, of young male captives. Du Chayla's biographer Marcel Pin asked if this revulsion towards women was not the symptom of so-called abnormal sexual preferences which found a tortured expression in well attested incidents of flagellation of boys. Pin claimed that du Chayla's deviant sexual orientation and frustrated religious continence strongly affected his character and actions, echoing Le Roy Ladurie's allegation of sexual repression influencing the Huguenot character but based, in Pin's work, on witnesses' accounts. Even Basville had occasion to recommend that du Chayla moderate his zeal in treatment of prisoners,[23] and it may be that some distaste lay behind the intendant's seemingly ironic description of the archpriest's murder as "the disagreeable adventure".

Among the powers delegated by Basville to du Chayla were supervision of the building of cross-country roads to remote hamlets and farmhouses, previously reached only by goat tracks, to improve control of a scattered population and ease the capture of "fanatical" Huguenots in hiding; and the command of local *milices* and even regular army units with officers made answerable to him. He became ruler of the Cévennes and lightning conductor for the rage of the oppressed, and seems to have been aware of the danger he ran in travelling comparatively unguarded from village to village.[24] "I really fear that you will become the victim of your own zeal," wrote his cousin the comte de Morangiez. In this sense, and in refusing to moderate the ferocity of the methods he believed in, du Chayla's courage was undoubted. It was by spying and policing methods and the advantage given by the new strategic royal highways constructed by Basville from 1687, "wide enough to allow the passage of cannon and explosives", and interconnected by the minor roads that his last captives were taken on 20 July 1702, by which time he had been the principal oppressor of the cévenol Huguenots for sixteen years. These young people, boys and girls of the Huguenot bourgeoisie, were being secretly conducted by a practised guide in the direction of the Swiss frontier when a suspicious Catholic alerted the authorities in hope of a reward. The group was arrested by a detachment of the bourgeois militia and taken to du Chayla's "château" at Le Pont-de-Montvert, a large house of three floors with a garden overlooking the Tarn and a single entry close to the bridge, which had been confiscated from a Protestant family in 1685. Here he kept and "questioned" prisoners in a cellar, locked upright night and day in heavy wooden stocks, before either sending them to Basville with the results of his interrogation or using his own powers to settle their fate. On 22 July the captured girls were sent to a convent in Mende to be kept at the discretion of the bishop after payment of a heavy fine by their families; the males, whatever their age, would go to the galleys at Marseille, chained and on foot, all except for the guide who was to be hanged.

The presence of these captives in du Chayla's house was quickly known throughout the region and he was approached with supplication by their friends and family at the great fair of Barre-des-Cévennes on 22 July. But the archpriest was implacable as a priest of the church militant must be and unwisely made known his inflexibility and the punishments in store for his prisoners while he was still two days' journey away from home. There was thus time, before his return to house and prison on 24 July, for the people's fury to swell and overflow the patient, humiliated temper of their usual subjection to superior power; the fuse was lit and from seventeen and more years of government contempt and brutality, la Cévenne in the heat of July was tinder ready to ignite.

The First Camisards

In 1700, in the archpriest's home diocese of Mende, the proportion of new converted carrying out the prescribed Catholic Easter duties was one in ten, and in some outlying parishes, where Huguenots were a hundred per cent of the inhabitants, down to one in thirty. Withdrawal of the dragoons and their return to the depleted armies engaged in the war of the Spanish Succession had removed immediate fear of brutal consequences and the new converted across the region flooded to nocturnal assemblies with relative impunity. Although Bishop Bossuet opposed the use of force to compel attendance at mass on former Protestants, the reaction of Basville to this evidence of Huguenot recidivist nonconformity was to ignore Bossuet and increase the authority of du Chayla in the system of terror supported by spying and by the Catholic bourgeois militia that he commanded, so that he became more and more the intendant's ecclesiastic sub-delegate.[25] This aggressive policy had the counter-productive effects that have seldom deterred an authoritarian power, public or private, from relying on it. The first was to drive more reluctant Catholic converts further into the camp of secretly practised Protestantism; the numbers attending assemblies in the forest clearings grew in proportion to the threats, fines, confiscations of property and of children, and executions carried out against them. The second was to focus a light of resentment rising to murderous hatred on the figure of the archpriest so that he "became himself the dreaded inquisitor ... finally the cause of his downfall".[26]

On Saturday 22 July a group of men organized an assembly in a forest some three and a half kilometres as the crow flies from Le Pont-de-Montvert, though much further on the ground by goat track, high in the Massif du Bougès rising between the foothills of the plain and the Mont Lozère, a country of thin grassland pasture with beech, chestnut and birch trees scattered among stone outcrops. The presence of large numbers at the cattle fair, the *foire de la Madeleine*, at Barre-des-Cévennes and on the roads leading to it, many of them believed to have been present on account of rumours about du Chayla's captives, simplified the announcement of an assembly and made the work of spies more difficult. Du Chayla circulated among hostile crowds and delivered sermons at which attendance was compulsory, accompanied only by two bodyguards.

The moving spirits behind the historic assembly and its aftermath were Abraham Mazel, Salomon Couderc, Pierre Séguier, David Mazauric and the brothers Rampon, men who received and acted on "inspiration" which they passively awaited but which undoubtedly had in each case after the first an element of mimesis not wholly spontaneous. The first of the inspired was Mazel, the dreamer of bullocks in the sacred garden who later wrote that he had repeated inspirations ordering him to take up arms for the *cause de Dieu* and that his companions each received the same command from the Spirit. Evidently the idea of insurgency was already present in the minds of these men: "All the inspired who were present had the same warning confirming this order of the Spirit, with more or less detail but always the same."[27] Bosc adds that "the conspirators were therefore agreed that the hour had come to launch a counter-attack and to raise the standard of revolt."[28] This determination was entirely new, although the grief and anger that fed it had been long fermenting, and in the following days it spread across villages, farms and valleys like smoke on the wind.

On the night of the 22nd a large number of Cévenols assembled in the forest close to the village of Saint-Julien-d'Arpaon where du Chayla was lodged in the priest's house, still standing today but in ruins. At this meeting the leaders were guaranteed recruits and arms and on the following day, a Sunday, another assembly was held higher in the mountain in a shepherd's stone shelter where Mazel was again inspired: "The Spirit came on me with such violence that all present were afraid." The order given through his mouth was to free the prisoners at Le Pont-de-Montvert and "all the inspired

83

received the same order." Some of the men present appear to have had doubts or fears. Witnesses to the cruel practices of du Chayla were called to convince them, and the families of the young captives were heard; perhaps most important, the meeting was joined by two former soldiers whose military experience convinced the waverers. One of these was Gédéon Laporte, aged forty and older than most of the others, tall and with a strident voice fit for issuing commands. It was agreed to rest for a night, and then gather on the 24th at a place in the high beech forest above Le Pont-de-Montvert called the *trois fayards* after three enormous beeches eventually felled in 1909 but whose coppiced remains have recently been identified.

Forty-seven men gathered, all peasant labourers, shepherds or textile workers, armed with twenty guns and pistols between them, with swords and halberds, axes, iron-tipped staves, scythes and stones, clothed in the hard-wearing cloth of their own manufacture and above all shod in leather kept repaired for long rough marches through forests, rivers and ravines. The supply of boots to Camisard fighters was later to be among their vulnerable points and great efforts were made by the authorities to cut it off and immobilize the guerrilla force that when well shod could evaporate so swiftly. Apart from Mazel the chief visionary among the forty-seven was "Esprit" or Pierre Séguier, a wool comber who had been living as a refugee in the forest, sought by the authorities as the most dangerous of the inspired prophets. It was alleged with no substantiating reference in 1705 by the Catholic Charles-Joseph de La Baume, a counsellor of the tribunal at Nîmes, that Séguier had been condemned in absence to be hanged for the rape of a young girl. This accusation, one of many charges and counter-charges surrounding the conduct of both sides that have shadowed and blurred the demarcation line between myth and history in the story of the uprising, is not advanced by Bosc or Cabanel, the principal authorities, but is repeated by Ladurie. Whatever the truth, Séguier later showed perhaps more than any other the resistance to torture and defiance of the horrors of execution that became legendary and astonished the world. At the *trois fayards* a detailed plan of attack on du Chayla's house in Le Pont-de-Montvert was made under the leadership of Laporte and Séguier. At 8.30pm as night began to fall the troop of men, marching four by four, began the descent by the most direct path toward the valley of the green-watered Tarn; Psalm 51, known to all by heart, was chosen for singing in the darkness to the sound of drumming when the troop approached the town an hour and a half later, both to alert inhabitants and hearten prisoners. "Let no one move! Close your windows!" was the shouted order accompanied by several gun shots, and a patrol was sent round to post guards at all the entrances and exits of the town. The drama was beginning, the "sheep had been maddened".[29]

Le Pont-de-Montvert, a grey-stone, slate-roofed upland town, distant in feeling from the fertile Mediterranean-oriented slopes of the southern Cévennes but surrounded by steep bare hills marked with repeated horizontal rock strata and threaded by deep winding river valleys, had a population between seven hundred and a thousand of whom only thirty or forty were Catholic. Du Chayla, who believed the old Protestants too longsuffering to be capable of violent reaction—as they themselves till now may also have believed—was thus again surrounded, with his prisoners, by a hostile people from whom no help could be expected. Du Chayla's companions were three Capuchin Friars, Franciscan missionaries particularly rejected by the Huguenots, two secular missionaries, a choirboy, apparently and in the view of some historians dubiously attached as page to du Chayla, the cook Michel, and a soldier-servant nicknamed la Violette. Permanently in the household were the local schoolteacher Roux, the farm tenant of the property, and two militiamen to guard the prisoners.

At ten, du Chayla retired to his bedroom where the only usual sound was the running of the Tarn over stones below his windows, but he was almost at once disturbed by the noise of shots and of drumming and singing from the direction of the bridge; he sent Roux to discover the cause of this commotion in the nominally obedient town where he was sole master with full powers. "What do you want? Roux called out to the troop of men massed with their weapons in the darkness of the street and on the bridge. "The prisoners! The prisoners!" Roux, startled by the roar of voices, turned back to run toward the house and was at once pierced through the body by a pitchfork, ran a few paces more and collapsed. Some accounts claim that du Chayla ordered the militiamen to charge the crowd with bayonets fixed but that they, seeing the numbers and the determination of the men facing them, dropped their arms and vanished. During this time the Capuchins escaped over

85

the garden wall and took refuge in a strong Catholic house outside the town; the farm tenant imprudently came out to enquire in his turn and was shot dead; the choirboy jumped from a window and hid in a tree trunk from where he witnessed the events that followed.

Du Chayla was now alone but for the two domestics, Michel and la Violette, and a militiaman. Mazel and another of the insurgents attacked the door of the house with axes while the rest shouted for the release of prisoners "in the name of God". As no answer came from within, the massive chestnut timber held fast and no prisoners emerged, a group armed with a beam as battering ram charged the door. Du Chayla, appearing now to choose the line of least resistance in the probable expectation that once the prisoners were let out the crowd would melt away and he could later revenge himself, sent la Violette to release them, even offering the keys of the door while the battering continued. As the captives emerged to join the crowd outside it was seen that Massip the guide, chained upright in stocks in a cell underground, was not among them. The insurgents now invaded the building and still calling for the release of Massip started up the stair towards the rooms where du Chayla lived, interrogated his captives and decided their fate. From the first floor turn of the stair the two domestics on guard opened fire on the men as they mounted; one of these was wounded in the face, the bullet passing out near his ear, and all withdrew to the street as the firing continued from the windows. Mazel, Séguier and others went aside to pray for divine instructions on the next steps to take. The inspiration came, as usual, to Mazel: "I was seized by the Spirit with the same violence as before ... Here is the order given to us ... 'that thy brethren light a fire at the foot of the staircase, and that the house and those in it be condemned'." (mis à l'interdit according to Bosc, a biblical expression signifying doomed to extermination.) If this account given later in his exile in Geneva by Jean-Antoine Rampon is exact, it would follow that the decision to kill du Chayla was taken while he was still in the house."[30]

The fire was lit with a candle held by Gédéon Laporte to a pyre built of straw from the prisoners' cells, dry faggots of broom, broken-up wooden benches, ornaments, hangings and tables from the chapel which all went up in a moment—"so prompt a flame had never been seen" in Mazel's words—and soon spread from the stair well to the floors and ceilings of the rooms above. Du Chayla took refuge with his two servants in a vaulted closet on the second floor where they would before long certainly be asphyxiated or burned to death under the collapsing roof. Du Chayla took the confessions of the two men and promised them salvation while from the cellar desperate cries were heard from Massip, chained and forgotten as the heat rose. From the outside, a small opening in the cellar wall was enlarged by removal of enough stones to allow the unhurt though sweltering Massip to be rescued. La Violette meanwhile wrapped himself in rags for protection, jumped over the flaming staircase and fell among the insurgents who spared him on reports of his reputation for kindness to prisoners and on his easily given promise to renounce papism. The cook Michel was less lucky after leaping from a window; he was seen in the half-darkness by the light of flames and shot as he ran, dying from a wound in the liver seven days later.

The remaining militiaman helped du Chayla to make a rope of sheets tied to the mullion of a window above the garden, and descended first; he was captured, tried by the visionaries on the bridge, and pardoned as a former Protestant. Du Chayla was the last man in the house and must have known what to expect, probably looking on it as a martyrdom thanks to which his sentence in purgatory would be remitted. The rope of sheets was too short to reach the ground and as he slid down in his nightshirt and fustian nightcap and barefooted, he was seen, fired on and fell heavily, landing on a stone. Despite a leg broken in the fall he crawled to shelter behind a cherry tree and out of the light of flames. At half past ten the roof timbers with their great weight of slate collapsed into the burning building and the sky was lit up by blazing sparks. Mazel, once more inspired, picked out in the dark shadows the white-clothed figure of du Chayla huddled behind the tree; he was dragged or lifted over the garden wall and onto the bridge across the Tarn where his judges awaited with a verdict inspired and therefore preordained. Unable to stand, he knelt by the light of flames before the tribunal made up of men recently his helpless subjects.

The dialogue that followed is differently rendered by witnesses but the gist is clear. "You know, gentlemen, that God forbids murder," said du Chayla. "The time left to you would be better spent in prayer" was the answer; and as captured Huguenots could win a quicker end to the tortures of their execution by abjuring, so at the Spirit's command Séguier offered the archpriest his life in exchange for a renunciation of Catholicism. Du Chayla promised to leave the Cévennes and never return but refused to deny his faith. "It is the time of retribution" called out one of the judges, "your sins are against you." Séguier with all his force brought down his sabre on the priest's head where it broke in two, a natural consequence of the fragility of a blade tempered in the siliceous waters of the Lozère.[31] Many of the others followed with knives, halberds and bayonets, each naming a victim to be avenged by the blow and inflicting, according to the surgeons, fifty-two wounds of which twenty-four would have been fatal. Mazel later explained the savagery of the execution with the claim that it was necessary to make sure of the archpriest's death as he was believed to be a magician capable of rising unharmed. By eleven o'clock they were satisfied.

Opposite accounts of the character of du Chayla and of the narrative of his murder are driven by passionate faith and fanatical intolerance equally. The worth of the accounts on either side is affected by the fact that no Catholic witness was present except la Violette, whose alacrity in abjuring and rapid return to Catholicism once the Huguenot danger seemed less than the Catholic must affect his credibility. Moreover, this crucial historical event produced versions that were heavily weighted by later history. For example, both Jean Cavalier of Anduze and Élie Marion suggest by implication that they had been among those present though it seems from other accounts that neither of them was. Cavalier was baker's assistant in Anduze, a full day's ride or two days' fast walk from Le Pont-de-Montvert for a man with no horse, and Marion, though a native of Barre-des-Cévennes, was elusive on details and equivocal about his own whereabouts on the day and night of this action which, as all agreed then as now, was the starting point of the Camisard War. In the words of his biographer Jean-Paul Chabrol, Marion's *mutisme* on the subject and on his actions during the first six months of the uprising poses a problem which he makes no attempt to elucidate. The last and best words on du Chayla are those of Henri Bosc who, though he was Protestant, a pastor and descendant of Huguenots who had suffered the persecution, recognized a scholar's responsibility to his readers:

One must be just. Du Chayla remains the victim of an outdated idea of religion: "He was the brave and fanatical servant of Basville and of his king, and of the God he saw through his king, the God of unity." (Pierre Poujol.) What is certain (and all agree on this) is that the Archpriest's inquisitorial activities carried on for so many years in the diocese of Mende, finally led to this explosion of anger in the remaining Protestant population which started the war of the Cévennes.

The war that was beginning was a war of modest agricultural people unbalanced by desperation; it was waged, with whatever excesses, for what they believed was the justice owed to their conscience.

The Immediate Aftermath

The insurgents, aware of the gravity of the night's work, had by dawn split into two groups. One, including the released prisoners and their guide and twenty of the Camisards who refused to take part in further attacks, notably on the priest Joseph Reversat considered as du Chayla's lieutenant, left at first light to take advantage of the few hours before a general alert; the other, consisting of thirty resolute Camisards whose thirst for vengeance had not been slaked by a single murder, left for the high ground equipped with a list of "bad priests" to be executed in priority.[32] Now the population began to emerge from their shuttered, narrow houses to make sure the magician was truly dead. The Capuchin Friars were among the first on the bridge and took charge of du Chayla's remains which after his death, according to only one of many Catholic sources, had been "sacrilegiously profaned from hatred of his sacerdotal state". Urgent messengers were sent to Mende, Barre-des-Cévennes and Florac to inform the local authorities, warn the clergy and have news of the crisis forwarded to Basville in Montpellier, a task undertaken by du Chayla's secretary Salomon Gardès, the apostate charged with collection of fines imposed on the village after the murder. At midday, by when the guards posted about the town had withdrawn and returned to their everyday life—though from now on no day would be like another—a first militia force of twenty-six men arrived from Florac, their unimpressive approach watched from the summit of the Lozère by Séguier, Mazel and their companions.

On the 26th the body of du Chayla was carried on a bier to Saint-Germain-de-Calberte where he was to be buried after the preaching of panegyrics fit for a martyr and numbering his charitable works, natural qualities and saintly practices, including the well-known distance he kept from "the conversation of women". Before the end of the ceremony, attended largely by priests from surrounding parishes, a cry went up from outside the church: "The insurgents! The insurgents! War! Fire and blood at Frutgères! Fire and blood at Saint-André-de-Lancize!" The corpse was quickly buried in the tomb du Chayla had prepared for himself, while the clergy scattered to safety, some in Catholic-owned fortified châteaux, others in the larger towns with an armed military presence. An exception was the priest of Saint-André-de Lancize, Jean Boissonnade, particularly loathed by his new-converted parishioners, who went home to his village and his presbytery despite fears expressed to some of his colleagues.[33]

The Camisard troop meanwhile had marched on the village of Frutgères and its church served by Reversat whose name headed the list of "bad priests". Warned barely in advance, Reversat leaped from a window of his presbytery in his nightshirt and was shot like a hare as he ran across a field of barley towards the river where he was finished off by Séguier, surprising his executioners by the bass profundity of his last cries likened to the bellowing of a cow. The church and presbytery were burned after altar, font and ornaments had been destroyed and a list allegedly found of Reversat's parishioners about to be denounced to du Chayla for disobedience. From Frutgères the avenging marchers continued into the mountain forests under the leadership of Séguier and there passed the night of the 25th. The leadership of this group of thirty-five armed men at this point by Séguier was the determining factor that changed a murderous assault on one hated figure into a war involving thousands. Were it not for his fanaticism, his blindness to danger and fearless contempt for all the possibilities of violent pain, the insurgents might have melted into the forest without further harm and returned to a life of angry, humiliated subservience. But Séguier carried his seer's inspiration into that hallucinatory region where visionary leaders may conduct the led. "There are men made for revolutions," said Peyrat, "the storms that overwhelm nations obey their voice ... they appear in the morning to disappear in the evening, and destroy a whole world ... such was Séguier, the wild Danton of the Cévennes." He was tall and lean and of wild appearance with a thin, dark face, few teeth and long hair and at fifty a good deal older than any of his followers. "He came out of his forests as the lightning comes out of the clouds," wrote the advocate, historian and playwright David-Augustin Brueys, a former Huguenot converted to Catholicism by Bossuet.

On the 26th the group descended to the Catholic village of Concoules for supplies, passing themselves off as militia in search of the assassins, then returned into hiding on the Mont Lozère for the night. There, the Spirit speaking through Mazel commanded them to put Boissonnade to death and burn his church. As the Huguenot pastors and preachers had been hunted down throughout the Languedoc like driven animals, so now the priests of the Cévennes, principal local agents of persecution, were the quarry, and this reversal of roles evoked in Catholic historians and clergy an indignation so fierce that its cause was forgotten. Ronald Knox, Catholic chaplain at Oxford writing in 1950, put almost the whole weight of blame for the atrocities of the Camisard War onto the Huguenot side,[34] and was especially outraged by the stories of priests being subjected to "the shameful operation of Origen" (Peyrat), or in another circumlocution, of Marcel Pin, "the reductive operation that professional gelders inflict on lambs and young pigs".

On the 27th in the early morning the troop reached Saint-André-de-Lancize where they found the presbytery empty, took whatever arms and supplies they could find and set fire to the house. Boissonnade and his acolyte Jean-François Parant, who was also the village school master and was reported to share a concubine with the priest, were hidden at the top of the church bell-tower with arms and provisions. At the moment when the Camisards were leaving the village, Boissonnade made the mistake of putting his head over the parapet to watch and possibly identify them. They returned to the church, destroyed the ornaments, images, vestments and furniture as they had done at Frutgères and would continue to do in any Catholic church attacked, and removed the ladder leading to the bell tower before setting the building alight. Boissonade was shot on sight as smoke and flames reached the upper part of the tower, and fell wounded to the ground where he was finished off; Parant was captured and castrated, dying from the wound a fortnight later.[35] The concubine was sought but not found.

As the group withdrew to the forest of the Bougès where they would spend the night, Séguier received an inspiration commanding "that we go to the château de la Devèze after sunrise to exterminate all those there except the servants, and set it alight". Devèze, hardly more than a large farmhouse with corner turrets, high, isolated and simply constructed into the side of the hill behind it, was the property of the d'Arnal, a Huguenot gentry family converted in 1610 and turned zealous Catholics. Priests found hospitality and, when necessary, refuge in the château; the stable served as a prison, the chapel as parish church, weapons forcibly taken from the new converted were stored there and there were tales in the country of bad treatment of captives. Arms were now vital to the Camisard group in their forest retreat, so the Spirit's inspiration had a practical side. At the end of the same day du Chayla's secretary, Salomon Gardès, reached Montpellier to inform Basville and his brother-in-law de Broglie, commander of the troops in the Languedoc, of the archpriest's murder. The military wheels began to turn.

Meanwhile the operation at Devèze further blackened the name of the Camisards, and not only in Catholic eyes. The Calvinists of Geneva and Rotterdam showed a growing disapproval of the insurgent violence as they learned of it piecemeal through messengers and from press articles.[36] The château was occupied by the widowed Louise d'Arnal, her two younger sons and a twenty-year-old daughter known for her beauty. Between five and six in the morning as the Camisards approached, the farm valet turned towards the château to give a warning to his employer and was killed by a sabre blow. The door was imprudently opened to their hammering by a servant, Anne, who was to be the only survivor of the massacre as the Camisards considered her to have been in forced employment. The younger son was in the hall and turned away without answering the demand for arms "in the name of God"; he was promptly shot in the back. The elder brother, carrying a loaded gun, stood behind the locked door to the upper rooms which was soon broken down. He had time to kill one of the insurgents, Jacques Couderc who was the first to enter, before falling under the attack of every man in the troop. The château was ransacked for arms and perhaps money, then set alight after the murder of the widow and young daughter who pleaded for her life but was killed in revenge for the hanging of the equally innocent Françoise Brès. An elderly uncle, ringing the tocsin which could be heard for a league around from one of the turrets, was either shot dead or left to die in the burning ruins.[37]

After burying their companion Couderc, the group of now thirty-four men withdrew and made their way to one of the historic sites of the Camisard War, the Plan de Fontmort, a plateau between valleys high in the mountain with few trees (though now reforested) and with a view over the untouched country of the Cévennes almost as far as the sea beyond the coastal plain. Here, the men rested and a fateful disagreement arose between Séguier and Mazel of a kind which Cavalier later used all his authority to avoid. Mazel received an inspiration that the party should at once leave Fontmort, while Séguier was commanded by the Spirit to remain, and it was he, as the senior prophet, who was obeyed. Since the Spirit commanded, human precautions were thought superfluous, no outlooks were posted and the encampment was unguarded.[38]

Due to the demands of the Spanish war for manpower, the comte de Broglie had no more than two hundred and forty soldiers under his command in the entire province. As soon as the assassination of the archpriest was reported he sent eighteen fusiliers to Le Pont-de-Montvert under the orders of the famous horseman captain Poul. Half an hour after reaching Barre following a night's march Poul was informed of the presence of insurgents at the château de la Devéze whose owners were valued figures in the small but powerful Catholic community of the Cévennes. Without pausing to rest, Poul and his eighteen men, followed by a group of twenty-five militiamen rapidly summoned, set off in the direction of Fontmort at five or six kilometres distance from Devèze where it was reported the Camisards had encamped. Poul was a professional soldier who had fought in Hungary and Germany and had been particularly ferocious in the crusade against the weak and impoverished Vaudois heretics in the Piedmont. He was described as "cunning and impetuous, giving no quarter and terrible in the assault ... tall and strong, his bellicose appearance and hoarse voice, his ardent and austere manner ... his audacity and taciturnity, the length and weight of his Armenian sabre ... all rendered him formidable."[39] Sighting the Camisards at rest in the shade of trees, Poul instantly charged them on his Spanish horse, almost flattened from the horse's ears to its tail in the curious position he adopted for a mortal attack. There was on this occasion no fight. Taken by surprise the Camisards ran for the woods, losing several men decapitated by Poul in his charge. The heads were later impaled on the bridge over the Gardon at Anduze.

In an age when torture was usual and execution by the most savage methods invariable, it was better to die in the field; but the unfortunate Pierre Nouvel was wounded and taken prisoner, the first of many. Séguier, in thrall to the Spirit, awaited new inspiration hidden in the gorse undergrowth where he was seen by the lieutenant of the fusiliers who at first thought him drunk. Mazel was critical of Séguier's actions: "Fear took hold of Pierre Esprit, he fled without fighting and so gave a very bad example to the others..." Poul, triumphant in spite of the escape of the majority of the Camisards, led Séguier and Nouvel in chains to Florac. "So, after your crimes, how do you expect to be treated?" he asked. "As I would treat you if I'd taken you," Séguier replied, although the slow death by breaking on the wheel could not be compared to any Camisard execution of a fellow countryman. Séguier and Nouvel were tried, with nineteen others, by a chamber of the court of Nîmes on assize at Florac. Eighteen of the men were sent to Montpellier for further interrogation and sixteen of them released for want of proof, evidence that at this stage some degree of judicial objectivity still obtained.

Séguier answered nothing under torture except that his "soul was a garden of shade and fountains". He was condemned as the first to strike down du Chayla to have his right hand cut off at the wrist and to be burned alive in the square at Le Pont-de-Montvert. It was reported that the sword blow to amputate his hand left it hanging by long shreds of skin which he tore away with his teeth while holding tied to the other a two-pound torch of burning wax. Led to the stake, he sang Psalm 69, *Sauve moi, ô éternel...* and continued to prophesy as the iron collar was fastened round his neck, entering into trance with such convulsions that he was strangled before the flames reached him. On 12 August Nouvel was broken on the wheel before the ruins of the château de la Devèze, and another captive, Moïse Bonnet, was hanged before those of the church at Saint-André-de-Lancize, both of them, like Séguier, undergoing before death the *question ordinaire* and *extraordinaire*, a civil service euphemism for the two degrees of torture applied to force abjuration and denunciation of fellow-conspirators. In all the accounts of the Camisard War there are very few instances of either of these aims being achieved. Many more such executions followed those of 12 August in different towns and villages, in all cases the expense of the preceding trials being born by the *communes* of origin of the accused whether innocent or guilty.

Capital punishment by smashing the limbs repeatedly with an iron bar as the wheel to which the victim was lashed revolved, was in wide use in medieval Europe though never, apparently, in England; the last such execution in France was of Jean Calas, a Protestant condemned in a questionable trial in 1762 which led to Voltaire's revolted attack on intolerance. Breaking on the wheel continued, though cases were rare, in Germany into the nineteenth century. It would be anachronistic to suppose that the repugnance felt today was inevitably shared by thoughtful people in the seventeenth century; the gentle and discriminating John Locke, one of the first leading figures of the Enlightenment paid three pounds on 18 February 1678 for hire of rooms in Paris from which he watched "the danceing master broke on the wheel", making no judgement and giving no details either of the crime or the punishment. And all accounts of the deaths of Huguenots and of Camisards in particular by these and other fearsome methods make it evident that those suffering them expected and sometimes seemed even to invite them as facts of their struggle for freedom of belief and as the gateway to paradise.

By the time of the judgements and executions Basville, attacked by gout, and Broglie his brother-in-law had departed to Montpellier after their hurried arrival to meet the crisis in the Cévennes. They and the authorities under their orders perhaps believed that the examples given of the treatment that rebels in the mountains could expect would be enough to bring a return of the unhappy peace that had reigned since 1685. But not all the clergy were so sanguine; J.-B. Louvreleul the parish priest of Saint-Germain-de-Calberte, who had preached the panegyric of the archpriest and became a historian of the uprising which he believed demoniacally inspired, wrote that "these prompt and terrible executions, very far from softening and dispersing the fanatical mob, served to augment their fury." Nevertheless, since the skirmish at Fontmort there had been no further disturbance of public order and by 13 August it seemed that the incident of "the disagreeable adventure" was closed. "The mob gatherings in the Cévennes have ceased," wrote Basville in an official report. But on that day the baron de Saint-Cosme, master of the château of Boissières, a former Protestant appointed to the lucrative post of inspector of the new converted with wide powers in the fertile saucer of the Vaunage between Nîmes and Sommières, was attacked on the road to Montpellier. Saint-Cosme was one of those new Catholics whose zeal in implementing the persecution outstripped that of the old. His wife refused to abjure her Huguenot faith and he took their two daughters from her to place them in a convent. He operated a system of venal insurance leaving those too poor to pay indemnity open to all the rigours of persecution from which those who could pay bought his protection. He directed the service of espionage in the region including Nîmes and Montpellier and being held "responsible for countless arrests, imprisonments, condemnations to the galleys or to death ... became the target for all the anger ... inevitably his days were numbered. He had no illusion about it."[40] The young men who followed his rapid poste chaise on foot and caught up with it when the baron halted to dismount and urinate, were typical of those who would become Camisards—sons of small farmers, of cattle-herds, of agricultural labourers—and acted on instructions from the Spirit uttered through the mouth of one of them, Pierre Bouzanquet. Though the baron's coachman and the huntsman accompanying him were both armed, one was knocked unconscious and the other fled. Saint-Cosme, returning to the post chaise and to his pistols from behind the tree where he had relieved himself, was attacked by the group and beaten to death with heavy sticks. Only Bouzanquet, who claimed innocence, was captured, tried and condemned to be tortured and broken on the wheel. The others took to the forest and were among the earliest recruits to the Camisard bands.

Official policy, offspring of administrators, had characteristically failed in the face of inspired opposition and the Camisard War had begun.

Notes

1   Patrick Cabanel, *Histoire des Cévennes*: 17
2   Nicolas Lamoignon de Basville, *Mémoires pour servir à l'histoire du Languedoc*: 76-9
3   Marcel Pin, *Jean Cavalier*: 136
4   Ibid: 39-40
5   Emmanuel Le Roy Ladurie, *The Peasants of Languedoc*: 175
6   Cabanel, *Histoire des protestants en France*: 99-100
7   Ladurie: 271
8   Philippe Joutard, *Journaux Camisards 1700-1715*: 8
9   Grégoire Vidal, *Lettres et rapports sur la guerre des Camisards*: 33

10 Cabanel, *Histoire des Cévennes:* 55
11 Henri Bosc, *La Guerre des Cévennes,* vol.1: 28-32
12 Geoffrey Treasure, *The Huguenots:* 362
13 Michelle Magdelaine, "Les Cévennes et le refuge huguenot", in *Les Cévennes et l'Europe:* vol. 4, 229-241
14 Cabanel, *Histoire des Protestants en France:* 202-3
15 Ladurie: 273
16 Cabanel: 679
17 Ibid: 686
18 Ladurie: 273-4
19 Cabanel: 661
20 Bosc, vol. 1: 183
21 Ibid: 159
22 Ibid: 183
23 Ibid: 164, 182
24 Patrick Cabanel, "La canonisation avortée de l'abbé du Chaila", in Cabanel and Joutard (eds.), *Les Camisards et leur mémoire:* 203
25 Bosc, vol. 1: 163
26 Ibid
27 Abraham Mazel, *Relation:* 5
28 Bosc, vol.1: 169
29 Marcel Pin, *Chez les Camisards:* 53
30 *Lettres et mémoire de Jean Rampon,* BPU de Genève, Papiers Court, vol. 17K folio 74-98
31 Pin: 58-60
32 Henry Mouysset, *Les premiers Camisards:* 68-9
33 J. Mingaud, *Journal:* 311
34 Ronald Knox, *Enthusiasm:* 363-4
35 Mazel: 12
36 Philippe Joutard, *La légende des Camisards:* 92-3
37 Mazel: 13; Rampon: 74-98
38 Pin, *Chez les Camisards:* 68-9
39 Bosc, 1:223
40 Ibid: 214

The 'Fanatick Rage'. Courtesy Le Musée du Désert, Mialet

Chapter Four
Camisard Logistics

Personnel

The men and women who fought against the army of the Crown were almost all very young, more than half of them under 24 years of age.[1] None, except an uncertain but small number of former soldiers, had ever fought before with arms and discipline; until now none could have imagined himself standing, with pike, firearm, sword or sometimes only sling and stone, against the authority of the king. Their preferred collective name for themselves was *les enfants de dieu* and the words "children of God" were often repeated in the written memoirs that have survived. These devout young people had never, for the most part, seen a pastor; they were instructed in the reformed religion at night by parents who for survival's sake observed the demands of Catholicism in the daytime, and growing into adulthood the new generation rejected the implied hypocrisy of those who accepted the form but detested the content of Catholic practice. The cries of "repent!" or "renounce idolatry!" mouthed by prophets and *inspirés* of both sexes were aimed at elders who, to protect children, property and lives, had knelt to swear this *abjuration de façade*. "The most pious of these young readers of the Old Testament were convinced that persecution was the expression of God's great anger at the impiety of their parents," wrote the historian Jean-Paul Chabrol. Emmanuel Le Roy Ladurie offered a Freudian interpretation for this scene of accusation against the fathers: "In the case of these young, sometimes adolescent youths ... a violent oedipal conflict found its justification in contemporary circumstances."[2]

However, the violent conflict that was the real daily experience of young Cévenols was between fealty to a king given to them by God, and endurance throughout their lives of fierce military and ecclesiastical oppression and cumulative impoverishment of their families by a system of punitive fines enforcing obedience in the forms of their belief which they held to be due to God alone. Jean Cavalier wrote that his father was among the first punished under an edict of 1688 "because his wife and children were absent from Mass ... and he was threatened with confiscation of his property and banishment." Obedience of the new converted, numbering in the intendant's calculation nearly two hundred thousand, to ritual Catholic practice was overseen by parish priests and any noncompliance denounced to the agents of Basville who openly admitted that "at the time of the general conversion there were very bad people filling most of the positions of parish priest in the Languedoc." The maréchal de Villars, most intelligent of the military commanders sent to bring the uprising to an end declared that "too much liberty was given to the priests and to some bishops, not for the exercise of zeal but to cover their avarice with an appearance of fervour ... and to put despair into hearts forced to sacrilege."[3] Even more convincing is the remark of the *Nîmois* judge Charles-Joseph de La Baume whose history of the Camisard revolt is among the principal contemporary sources: "It cannot be hidden that a number of ecclesiastics ... abused the kind of authority given them ... They, and above all Du Chayla, treated (the new converted) with so little charity and such rigour as to give them a pretext for revolt."

The uprising was not an insurrection of poverty nor of fiscal protest but of conscience. Its only demand was freedom of belief and worship, but contemporary writers could not conceive of a rural rebellion for other reasons than the popular hatred of the tax system, and this misunderstanding is repeated by Ladurie: "The Camisard uprising reveals itself ... as an explosive mixture of prophetic neurosis and anti-tax ferment." But Philippe Joutard denies the interpretation, arguing with evidence that not only had the uprising no social background but more surprising still, showed an entire absence of anti-fiscal motives. No correspondence or report of Basville or of any military commander mentioned such a motive and only one bishop (of Alès) alluded to it at all.[4]

Every account emphasises that the Huguenot young men—Cavalier being the best attested—both affirmed their loyalty to the king and humbly implored this distant solar sovereign to let them worship as their forebears had. The Camisards were not a rural proletariat of manual workers arrested in oedipal crisis, nor necessarily the poorest section of the rural population; the only established manifestation of social anger during the uprising was that of the Catholic militia who became known as the *cadets de la croix*, or *Camisards blancs*, who were moved by hatred and envy of the Huguenot bourgeoisie and were sharply condemned by La Baume.[5] Another singularity of the revolt was that unlike those of Rohan, it was not led by the nobility, which took very little part in it. Only twelve members of the noble caste have been identified in the Camisard ranks, and at the bourgeois level, two notaries, two surgeons, a procurator's clerk and a merchant.[6] This reticence of the nobility and bourgeoisie could be explained as political and financial expediency, as exhaustion from religious wars, or as revulsion of the better-educated Calvinists and the new converted from excesses of fanaticism and above all of inspiration with calls to repentance, and prophesying trances, seen as a proletarian manifestation. Monahan points out that the "pull of Catholicism was particularly strong for the Protestant nobility ... in the face of increasing pressure from their peers and the crown",[7] though this violent pressure and much more were resisted to the death by the lower orders among the Protestants of the Cévennes. Furthermore, both bourgeois and *gentilshommes* rightly believed themselves to be under close and individual surveillance. Basville drew up a list of those among them who were newly converted and kept himself informed of their attitudes, opinions, and regularity of attendance at mass; any thought to be potentially seditious were watched and the situation of their châteaux studied for possible strategic importance.[8] It is argued that most of the newly converted class of *notables*, many of whom worked in the administration or the law, were wilfully blind to the action and deaf to the prophetic words of the young Cévenols calling them back, with sermon and psalm, to the Church they had abandoned.[9] It would seem that centralization of power and wealth under Louis XIV and the growth in French society of a single social and religious culture at the expense of local variety, noted by Saint-Simon, caused a decline in initiative and independence in the ranks of the aristocracy which remained a feature of national life in the eighteenth and nineteenth centuries. The Camisards' readiness for martyrdom was not shared by those who had more than only their lives to lose.

Nevertheless, and paradoxically, the authorities and particularly Basville, unable to believe that the startling Camisard successes could be solely the work of young, uneducated, naturally gifted leaders, were convinced that the movement was clandestinely directed by Protestant noblemen with military experience; and so strong was the assumption that the movement must be led by noblemen, as movements had always been, that it appeared occasionally even among Camisards themselves. In September 1703 Pierre Laporte, the leader who became known as Rolland, wrote to inhabitants of cévenol villages signing himself "le comte Rolland," a title by which he was sometimes known to English supporters of the Huguenots. But among the only three veritable nobleman who came to be interrogated, tried and condemned, on circumstantial and fragile evidence, was the tragic figure of François Pelet, baron de Salgas, born to one of the leading families of the Languedoc, a landowner and possessor of several châteaux in the Cévennes. To preserve his estate Salgas abjured in 1685, but his wife did not and departed to Geneva in 1701 leaving her youngest child with its father. Despite his abjuration Salgas unwisely remained in contact with one of the Camisard prophets and leaders, Henri Castanet, who was responsible with the men under him for the violent massacre of thirty-nine Catholics in the village of Fraissinet-de-Fourques a few days after Salgas' last meeting with them. Salgas, wrote a diarist from Nîmes reporting popular Catholic attitudes, "was regarded as king of the Camisards". He was arrested in May 1703 and tried before Basville whose unchecked judicial powers supplemented and completed his power as governor making him, as some said, virtual king of the Languedoc. Interrogated many times by the sinister but routine methods of the *question ordinaire et extraordinaire*, he was condemned, despite declarations of his innocence by all witnesses except one, to the galleys for life. After the death of Louis XIV and the retirement of Basville, who remained always convinced of a secret aristocratic directorate behind the activities of the Camisards, a number of Huguenot *galériens pour la foi* were released at the request of Queen Anne, among others. Salgas, a remnant of human endurance after fourteen years as a galley slave under Basville's order that "he suffer all the rigour of his punishment and none of the complaisance that money or the Huguenot party might obtain for him", was at last freed on 4 November 1716 to rejoin his wife in Geneva where he died in August of the following year, without ever having renounced his faith during captivity.[10]

Of approximately ten thousand identified Camisards (there may have been as many as ten thousand if men and women who occasionally lent help and material support and shelter are counted), the age and occupations established with certainty are of those who were captured and interrogated. The professions of two hundred and seventy-seven of these are contained in the police records and show a large majority of textile workers, with the rest divided between labourers and shepherds. Textile work was paid and seasonal and most of the men practising it, generally very young, were unpaid for the work they did during the rest of the year on family farms under their fathers' authority. It is argued that many of the captives remained silent under questioning about their possible ownership or expectations of inheritance of land since if condemned, as most were, the property would be confiscated and their families punished.[11]

Another indication of a close link between Camisard manpower and the farming background was that large numbers, quietly dispersing and melting along forest tracks, returned to their villages during the harvest season. Cavalier recorded that his force ceased activity between May and September 1703 and went into hiding.[12] The vocabulary used to designate the insurgents changed as the authorities began to appreciate the seriousness of the movement and the monarchy realized that it was faced with a popular war, "the original modern guerrilla".[13] At first they were referred to as blackguards (*scélérats*), a contemptuous term which was dropped as their numbers and successes grew. Then they became *attroupés*, vagabond troops, or *osards*, a word thought to derive from the Hussar revolt in Hungary against the Habsburg monarchy.

Camisard, the name by which history knows them, made its first appearance in official correspondence on the 5 April 1703; but Mazel in his memoir stated that it was after the death of the bold and dangerous captain Poul in a pitched battle with Cavalier's force in January of that year that "we began to be called camisards. I don't know whether it was because we often made night attacks (*camisades*), or because we fought in shirts or *camisoles*." The question has never been decided but from that time they were considered, and war was made on them, as a guerrilla army rather than as a band of inspired criminals and this rise in evaluation of the Camisards' military prowess and effect resulted, in

1704, in the consideration given by the government to Cavalier as the most prominent leader, and offers of amnesty in place of extermination as a means of bringing the uprising to an end. Guerrilla techniques left the royal forces in the early stages at a disadvantage that later they were only able to overcome by force of numbers. After a particularly daring action by Cavalier's group at Sauve on 27 December 1702, the governor of Saint-Hippolyte, where one of the new garrisoned fortresses had been built to subdue the Cévennes, wrote to Basville: "I scoured the whole countryside without finding the *scélérats*, nor having any news of them as they had vanished in the forest, among the rocks, into the mountains..."

Official astonishment in the face of unknown tactics was reinforced by the discovery of the numbers of women in the Camisard ranks. This led, as night follows day, to outraged assumptions of sexual promiscuity evidencing a prurient and scandalized interest in *libertinage* from Catholics who often mocked Huguenot moral rigour as puritanical. It cannot be known how puritanical in sexual matters the young Camisards really were. If one of the early leaders, Henri Castanet, was tried in a summary court of his fellows for alleged "illicit commerce with a widow of Saumane", it was not the only charge made against him and he was acquitted. It is certain that discipline among the Camisards was strict and based on religious precept. Booty was shared and looters immediately eliminated; Sunday was a day not of fighting but of prayer. Some among the women were wives, either regular or "common law", that is, pronounced in the absence of pastors to be wives of men by the authority of the group they belonged to. Both Cavalier and Rolland had female companions, though their status and private relations are not fully known, and this might seem to show that the more powerful leaders made their own rules in the matter. At the moment of his death, intransigent to the last in the Camisard cause after Cavalier's accommodation with the government, Rolland was accompanied by one of two sisters of the Cornély family, Protestant gentry from near Lasalle in the Gard, the other sister being the companion of his lieutenant Malhier who was taken at the same time but survived to be broken on the wheel on the esplanade at Nîmes. The two sisters escaped, were later arrested and imprisoned but released, and departed to Geneva. Historians sympathetic to Basville have claimed this as an example of his relative clemency in dealing with women brought before him for judgement, seldom condemning them to anything worse than public whipping and imprisonment in convents or in the fearsome Tour de Constance at Aigues-Mortes where many Huguenot women spent all the years of their maturity in heat, cold and dark, hearing through slit windows only the lapping of water in the canal leading to the Mediterranean.

Catholics claimed that many of the women with the Camisard groups were prostitutes. Protestants, on the contrary, claimed them to be prophetesses who carefully preserved their virginity since that state made them eligible for visitations by the Spirit. But either way, the strong female presence adds to a sense of the uprising as rooted in the land where families were the ruling unit. The number of women Camisards is variously calculated at between a few dozen and a hundred and twenty, the figure arrived at by Pierre Rolland who identified them in the *Dictionnaire des Camisards*. Fifty-one were prophetesses and all were dispersed among small highly mobile groups and therefore hard to pinpoint. Others have estimated the figure far higher. The presence of these women in a fighting force, some of them active in the fighting and some known to have played a part in finishing off the enemy wounded since guerrillas on the move could take no prisoners, offended the prejudices of the bourgeois whether Catholic or Protestant, and was another forerunner of the conditions of partisan warfare. Cavalier wrote of a girl of eighteen at the battle of Nages that "she was the first that jump'd over the wall with a Hangar (sabre) she had taken from a Dragoon, who was wounded, crying Kill, Kill, and cutting in Pieces every one she met with undaunted Courage."

But the role of women was for the most part in the supply lines of armed groups and perhaps in nursing their own wounded; and just as young prophetesses had been the first to urge resistance to persecution, so now the inspiration of these female seers among the Camisards was often determinant in deciding the details of attack or retreat, although Cavalier, the most strategically successful of the leaders, relied on his own moments of inspiration, authentic or assumed, to order the action of his force as his men implicitly did also. This put the twenty-one-year old Cavalier in a position of almost limitless authority and independence. La Baume accused him of keeping two of his followers as mistresses. One of them, known as la grande Marie, born in Lussan, was captured in January 1704 and imprisoned at Uzès. Cavalier kidnapped the sister of a leading Catholic of the town and threatened to treat her as la grande Marie was treated; the two women were exchanged. Cavalier valued Marie as the most gifted of the prophetesses and told Voltaire that if she was disobeyed she would go into inspiration and denounce the offender who was at once executed. This extreme example, and the numbers of prophetesses marching side by side with the men through the hazards and terrors of the uprising, demonstrate the active part played by women in Huguenot religious life in the Languedoc after the disappearance or destruction of pastors and preachers. Marie was aged thirty in 1704, was said to be without charm or beauty and is less likely to have been Cavalier's mistress than was the other woman named by la Baume, Isabeau Chanurel, a childhood neighbour. Daniel Guy, one of Cavalier's lieutenants, declared in 1708 that his leader had been always accompanied by a young peasant girl who ate and slept with him.[14] Cavalier's humanity, his private weaknesses and strengths, are among the aspects of personality for which he has not generally been credited by stern Calvinist historians such as the pastor Antoine Court rescuing the Huguenot reputation from the uncertain personal morality of Camisard fighters.

Organization

The first need of the small but growing and sometimes coalescing groups of men was for arms. In the Camargue where peasants depended for food on wildfowl shot in the waters of the Rhône delta, firearms had been confiscated and forbidden from March 1702, leaving families hungry; but as in the Cévennes, it is believed that from the date of the Revocation of the Edict of Nantes small arsenals of guns had been laid up in secret. Until the preachers were eliminated, most of them had a pistol. But as the number of groups and of the men in them grew these reserves ran out and many recruits were armed with no more than a sword, a pike, a halberd, a scythe, a metal-tipped stave, a sling or a club; throughout the uprising these weapons were often the only armament they used. Some sources describe encounters in which the insurgents fought with bare hands or with stones. For the acquisition of guns and pistols the

Camisards relied from the beginning on pillage of châteaux belonging to Catholics or new converted, or of presbyteries where priests were known to keep weapons for defence. The other chief source of supply was from soldiers killed in ambush. Bullets were manufactured from lead taken off church roofs or presbytery windows; other metals such as pewter could be molten in homemade furnaces and cast into shot, and Cavalier gave detailed accounts, which there is no reason to doubt, of these methods and of the technique developed for making gun powder which he rationed out to his men in a pewter spoon. In April 1703 the maréchal de Montrevel reported to Basville that several of his men had been shot with silver bullets. Cavalier also recorded that for money a number of soldiers in the royal army supplied Camisard agents with both powder and shot, a statement corroborated in a letter from a senior serving officer to the Minister for War.[15]

Cavalier's *Mémoires* were the earliest and remain the most detailed account of the war by a closely involved participant and leader; also of the organization of his force and of the negotiation to amnesty which was rejected by most of his companions, particularly Rolland and the other leaders. His account has been criticized for omission of detail or events on which for one reason or another he chose to be silent—a ground of criticism where as a rule no memoirist is spared. An exception to the rule was Élie Marion, one of Cavalier's most virulent critics who was both selective and sometimes evasive in what he chose to mention in his own account in the *Théatre sacré des Cévennes*, without it being held against him. But denigration of Cavalier's work by Protestant historians would appear to have another origin than only that of historiographic discipline, and probably stems from Antoine Court's acceptance and repetition of the judgement on the English text by the anonymous author of *Histoire des Camisards*, whose many errors Court himself found and corrected, that it was "the refuse of bookshops, without date, reasoning, or sense".

Cavalier's memoir appeared for the first time in a fully annotated French translation by Frank Puaux in 1919 citing corroborative contemporary documents for the greater part of the account. Marcel Pin, generally sympathetic with a lawyer's caution to the subject of his biography, claimed that careful study showed Cavalier to have invented nothing and to have told the story almost always exactly as it was; "the great merit of Cavalier was to pile up reserves and organise warehouses ... in caves and caverns; these contained clothes, arms and ammunition, wheat and flour, salted beef, wine etc ... the largest cavern, between Euzet and Fontcouverte was arranged as a hospital where two surgeons received the sick and wounded." Nevertheless, on the following pages he ranges himself with the majority conclusion by adding that in his preface and notes Puaux "too easily accepted all of Cavalier's affirmations", and that by the time the uninstructed Cavalier wrote, he had "completely changed in mentality".[16] This ambivalence where reliability is positively or negatively weighted by "mentality" suggests a bias with sources to be traced.

Cavalier's Camisards formed by far the largest group, reaching on occasion a thousand men though more usually between six and seven hundred with fifty or sixty horsemen, compared with that of Rolland which never exceeded three to four hundred and was without cavalry. The movement of so many summarily armed men accompanied by horsemen along narrow river valleys or villages on mountain roads could be observed and reported by informers existing even in close Huguenot communities, or by those frightened by the sudden appearance out of the forest night of a force the size of a brigade whose reputation for inspired ferocity went ahead of them. Cavalier sub-divided his group into smaller detachments more easily hidden, directed by signals or messengers and able, in classic guerrilla form, to regroup rapidly for joint action. This technique baffled the commanders of the royal army, incredulous of tactical and organizational skill in untrained leaders, for many months, as did the wild energy of these fighting men emerging from the forests after days and nights of lightning march on mountain tracks. Cavalier was often accused of boastfulness in the *Mémoires*, and the apparently artless style of his narrative may seem to lay stress without false modesty on the exploits he or any other of the Camisard leaders could fairly claim. But he made no secret of his defeats. In May 1703 his troop of four hundred men was severely depleted in a wood near Uzès, due largely, he claimed, to poor discipline:

> In that unlucky encounter, I lost fourscore Men ... We were obliged to abscond from the latter End of May, to that of September ... And yet during that Time we were not idle, for we were carrying

on, and finishing several Works already begun; such as our Arsenals, Magazines and Hospitals, to fill up this great interval of Time, I shall give an account of the Methods we used to get Bread, Arms, Powder, Bullets, Money, and other Necessaries towards the Maintenance of an Army...

At the time that he composed or perhaps dictated his memoir, in a relatively incorrect French later translated with some flair by an unidentified hand to eighteenth-century English in the reporting style of Defoe, Cavalier had become a professional soldier in the English army with the rank of colonel but with no men under him. It is unsurprising that the book, dedicated to Lord Carteret, Lieutenant-General Governor of Ireland, should be presented in terms of routine military ordinance and in a style which can seem to swagger in itemizing actions taken and hardships overcome. Moreover, part of the undeclared purpose of the book was undoubtedly to present the author as a highly employable man of gallant exploits and with strategic and organizational talent out of the ordinary; both these claims being true and well-attested, they led to his eventual promotion to major-general. Voltaire, who met Cavalier in Holland and London in April 1727 and heard his and other accounts of the Camisards, later wrote that "the most creditable of their leaders and the only one worth mentioning was called Cavalier ... he was a small fair man of pleasing appearance."

Long before Bonaparte and the democratization of the class of officers in the French army, Cavalier the "little baker's boy", as denigrators called him, had thus risen through the military ranks to within a grade of the summit. True, he had achieved this in another country yet it seems anomalous that the main body of criticism of Cavalier should come from the Protestant and not the Catholic party. Basville's great-nephew de Malesherbes, chief censor of the book trade and minister to Louis XVI wrote, "I confess that this fighter who had never served before ... this simple peasant ... this Camisard who by gift of nature proved himself a great general ... seems to me one of the rarest characters that History has brought down to us." But Protestant historians seem never to have forgiven Cavalier for escaping martyrdom in the cause nor, possibly, for his expatriation and worst of all his engagement in the English army with which he fought against the French in Spain in 1707. The negotiator and renegade was doubly condemned. But the most repetitious criticism, still more contradictory on the part of Huguenot historians such as Antoine Court who rejected the inspirations and prophesying of the Camisards and their female companions, was that Cavalier denied his own past as a prophet at war and in his *Mémoires* passed over the phenomenon of prophecy and its uses during the *guerre des Cévennes*, arousing suspicion that this silence was by deference to his English superiors or patrons at a time when English opinion was turned towards a naturalistic apprehension of history and of the world.

That Cavalier's often vivid and always detailed account of his part in the fighting and the organization of his own group, which can be taken as true enough of many others that have left no portrayal of their own, has been discredited by historians is partly due to the personal attacks made on him by the popular journalist Madame du Noyer, Protestant by origin, exiled in The Hague and editor of the fashionable periodical *La Quintessence des Nouvelles*. In a series of venomous assaults on his birth, his record in the war, his truthfulness and his ambitions, she deployed every device, false or merely plausible, of a woman apparently scorned. She had some grounds for this. Cavalier owed her money, he had promised to marry her daughter, he is thought to have been her occasional lover, and he reneged on all these counts. Yet before she became his enemy Madame du Noyer wrote enthusiastically of him as prospective son-in-law: "A man who with a handful of people had held his own against several Marshals of France and obliged his King to yield, this defender of religion—all this was most agreeable for someone who had given up everything for that same religion." But unfortunately for Cavalier's reputation it has usually been the vitriolic attacks of the angry and perhaps humiliated woman that many historians have repeated in outlining the later career of the peasant's son who became Governor of Jersey.[17] Nevertheless his *Mémoires*, wrote Frank Puaux their editor, "must be considered the most important document we possess, from the Camisard side, on the events in the Cévennes". His conclusion on the polemic surrounding Cavalier's role and record was that "it was the great honour of the young Cévenol peasant to have personified the noblest of causes, in defending the liberty of conscience in the reign of the most absolute of kings."

The royal troops in the Languedoc available to attempt the repression of the uprising, and which very soon had to be heavily reinforced as the Camisards not only eluded but repeatedly trapped them, consisted at the outset of not more than eight companies of thirty fusiliers.[18] In August 1702 the king authorized the raising of ten companies of dragoons at his expense and two at the expense of the province. To these were soon added three hundred ferocious *miquelets* from the Pyrenees, regiments of Swiss and Irish mercenaries, grenadiers from northern France, all more given to pillage than to the exhausting pursuit of fast-moving guerrilla groups hidden in impenetrable forests and waiting to ambush the military in narrow valley defiles and river crossings. By December 1702 the comte de Broglie, commander-in-chief of the army in Languedoc, disposed of approximately four thousand men, largely ill-disciplined, often ill-equipped, of mediocre quality as soldiers and difficult if not impossible to deploy effectively in the cévenol mountains and ravines. A Huguenot partisan in London published in 1703 an account of the problems faced by the army and the opportunities to be exploited by the Camisards:

> If those in command in the Cévennes understand the profession of war, they will draw the king's troops into narrows where a hundred will defeat a thousand or ten thousand: and even though roads have been built both along the rivers and to the summits of the mountains so that a carriage or waggon can climb them and wheel about, these roads are so narrow that a battalion cannot be put into battle order there. And cavalry is absolutely useless in that country and would do more harm than good.[19]

In the silence of the forest the march of troops along hard-surfaced roads would announce their movement directly and by echo to watchers and their scouts from far off, and these difficulties for the army were aggravated by the attitude of some of the population toward the uprising. If the bourgeoisie in the towns and the *notables* generally, having so much to lose, were generally hostile to the uprising, although in towns such as Nîmes and Alès there were hidden supporters, in the country and particularly in the mountains there was almost universal backing to the Camisards from families connected to them, by providing food, shelter, hiding places and intelligence gathered by shepherds. Cavalier said that his group was authorized to take sheep but only did so in case of extreme necessity. On occasion men from the farms would join the ranks of the rebels for an operation or encounter, and then return home. General de Julien, a notably successful enemy who had been born Protestant but converted wholeheartedly to Catholicism, wrote that the inhabitants were "in constant correspondence with them, supplying them with all they lack ... walking ten leagues to warn them of the least movement of the king's armies ... and more camisard than the rebels themselves. There," he said, "is the true situation in the communities." All this ended in a scorched earth policy, the destruction by fire and pickaxe of hundreds of villages, hamlets and outlying farms in the autumn of 1703 with expulsion of inhabitants who were driven without means of support into the plain or foothills. A combination of military failure, Camisard violence and the hatred of Catholics against Huguenots led to the deployment of the *milices bourgeoises*, a civilian army without training or discipline and motivated by vengeance; this was to prove the worst conceivable means of attempting to control the uprising, by this time of a whole displaced and persecuted people, since it entrenched and perpetuated a religious, geographical and social split among the Languedoc population which has remained, notably in the Cévennes with its largely unchanging demography, as an enduring scar, and which in 1702-4 drove the Camisards to reprisal by atrocity rather than to submission.

Fifty-two regiments of Catholic *milices* were formed under Basville's rule in the Languedoc, and urged into action by the papal bull of May 1703 declaring a religious war and crusade against the "heretics of the Cévennes". This force served originally to track down and disperse illegal assemblies and to protect the Catholic population where it was in the minority and exposed to risk of violence. The men were unpaid and were, like the Camisards, mainly peasants or artisans, led and exercised by retired army officers where possible and otherwise by members of the gentry or the leading bourgeois. Their use for policing purposes directed at their fellow-subjects of different religious faith, and their part in the pillage and destruction of four hundred and sixty villages and hamlets of the Hautes-Cévennes in September 1703 naturally brought back to life the hatreds and inherited memories of the wars of religion. No one pretended that the *milices* formed a disciplined body of militiamen able to hold their own in the field against Camisards descending on them with the wild energy so often remarked on with wonder. They were nervous and quickly routed by groups such as that led by Cavalier, but worse still, those of the *milices* known as the *cadets de la croix* had the reputation of being thieves rather than soldiers. The maréchal de Montrevel wrote to the minister for war that "all this rabble is good for nothing but to excite the uncommitted to join in a general revolt". The total of army forces including the *milices* reached twenty-five thousand men at the height of the war against two thousand permanent opponents aided by the population, proof that the authorities believed they could only overcome the Camisards by massive numerical superiority. The *milices* were at last ingloriously dissolved in 1717 but by their share in the expulsion from demolished homes and burned out lands of the Huguenot population of the Cévennes they bequeathed to following generations a legacy of sectarian hatred and contempt which is still active, though diluted in the growing current of religious neutrality. However, when the pendulum of oppression swung with the Revolution, the National Guard was recruited above all from Protestants employed to track down and bring to execution the "Catholic royal brigands".[20]

Protagonists

Nicolas de Lamoignon de Basville, appointed Intendant of Justice, Police and Finances in the Languedoc at the moment of the Revocation and remaining in office until 1718, came from an eminent family of lawyers and was an advocate who had risen rapidly through the legal ranks; and perhaps more important, he was a friend of Madame de Maintenon before her marriage to the king, which according to Henri Bosc made him a redoubtable figure at court. Marcel Pin pointed out that the calligraphy of Basville's letters, mostly in his own hand, was always excellent, reflecting calm, impersonal clarity and the love of order which he associated with commitment to the institution of the absolute monarchy. Basville's personality, with some sign of depressive tendency, would seem to have been of the obsessional type as defined by Freud who considered himself potentially obsessional, "orderly, parsimonious and obstinate". Other psychologists have suggested that the obsessional personality may be driven either toward submission, or toward tyranny leading to annihilation of the other and hence to isolation.

Basville's defenders have pointed out that the cruelty of the tortures and deaths carried out under his authority and often in his presence, and their frequency, were a routine part of the exemplary imposition of law and obedience in the seventeenth century; but this, if true, ignores the influence on the uses of power by tendencies in the personality such as those observed in Basville by Saint-Simon who described him as crafty and implacable, and added that his "domination broke all resistance". The historian and marseillais professor André Ducasse, on the other hand, claimed that the intendant's lack of imagination and his hardness prepared the way for the *convulsion extrême*, and Monahan states that "Basville's harsh policies certainly played a role in igniting the Camisard Rebellion"[21]

Basville's remark in a letter to his friend Bishop Fléchier that "it is a sad life that one should have to deal with such matters" is not easy to accept at face value in light of his treatment, for example, of Salgas which was marked by unnecessary vindictiveness without mercy and continued until his retirement from the Languedoc. Yet the fair-minded Marcel Pin claimed that in spite of the legendary Protestant hatred accumulated against Basville, "it must be recognised that he discharged his functions scrupulously and with honesty", which was certainly Basville's own opinion and matches the description by psychologists of the behaviour of obsessional personalities. Henri Bosc reinforced this interpretation of Basville's character: "He was totally alien to the notion of ... an interior cult not manifested in civil life ... and a magistrate's essential duty was to force those refractory to Catholic dogma and discipline out of that state."[22] One historian of the Camisard rebellion remarked that the most curious thing in the life of Basville was that he died in his bed; but it is true, the historian added, that he almost always dealt with chivalrous enemies.[23]

The first of the military commanders answerable to Basville as well as to the court was his brother-in-law the comte de Broglie, "the most disagreeable of men" according to Basville. Pin called him merely unlucky and added that it was truly comical to see him, in all his letters to the minister for war, complaining of the spite of the rebels who dispersed without waiting for him; when, on 12 January 1703 they did wait, he was imprudent enough to charge them with sixty dragoons, was soundly defeated and dismissed from the command shortly afterwards.

His successor was the maréchal de Montrevel, a personal friend of the king and raised in the court, of whom the king's son the duc du Maine said that he could never tell his left from his right and that he covered his universal ignorance with audacity protected by the royal favour. In his time in the Languedoc he devoted himself to his pleasures and, said Pin, never personally confronted the Camisard rebels; it took several months for Basville to relieve the province of this "burdensome nonentity" who was dismissed from his command after a defeat by Cavalier on 14 March 1703 though he defeated Cavalier in his turn, with heavy losses to the Camisards, on 16 April. Cavalier generously described him as an amiable gentleman "inclin'd more to amorous Speeches than his own Profession ... however to save his Honour, he came now and then after us with a strong Body of Forces, and not finding us, suddenly return'd to his Mistress." But he was not invariably amiable. One of the worst atrocities of the war, the massacre of the Moulin de l'Agau never forgotten and repeatedly avenged, was carried out on his orders on Palm Sunday the 1 April 1703 (see p.167).

By this date, and after repeated urgings from Basville, the king and Chamillart his war minister had grasped the seriousness of the uprising and of the humiliations inflicted on the royal forces under incompetent or distracted commanders-in-chief. Both king and minister are credited by Pin with refusing the use of even more violent methods of repression recommended by local authorities, particularly ecclesiastic, and the king with sometimes remembering that the rebels among the new converted were his human subjects. The decision was taken in April 1703 to send to the Languedoc the most famous of French marshals, Louis Hector de Villars, described by Pin as "courageous, intelligent, active, very liberal, not at all devout", a man with diplomatic experience and determined to bring the insurrection to an end with the good humour that would carry all before it. Villars' memoirs claimed that he told the king before setting out that he would "try to finish with gentleness the misfortunes that severity has produced", and whether or not this was the working of retrospective vanity, the flattering and sometimes duplicitous methods he employed in inducing Cavalier to accept amnesty in May 1704 were largely successful in leading to an end that in Pin's words "excused the means."

On his arrival he brought together the leading figures of the chief towns of what is now the Gard department, the region with most Camisard activity, and explained to them that although the king would never allow public religious assemblies, they were free to pray as they wished; "Adore God according to your opinions, and if you believe you must, adore him in your hearts. The good and just God asks no more." This, says Cabanel, restored life to Article 12 of the Edict of Fontainebleau, or seemed to do so. It certainly went much further than the king's known intentions and its diplomatic message bound no one, smoothed the path to negotiation and amnesty, and left the detail of the religious cohabitation it hinted at to be settled (or refused) by others later on. Villars withdrew from the province in March 1705 and was in due course rewarded with a dukedom which until he acquired an estate appropriate to it remained a title without a territorial name.

Under Broglie and Montrevel, action on the ground was ordered and executed principally by another ambiguous figure of the Camisard story, the subordinate general Jacques de Julien, chosen by the king and charged by Chamillart with the duty of confiding his opinion on and reporting the performance of the commanders-in-chief in weekly letters to the minister. In the Cévennes after his appointment, being eager to prove the sincerity of his conversion and have his Protestant origins forgotten, he showed a pitiless zeal found excessive even by Chamillart who recommended greater moderation. Julien was one of the first to grasp that the Camisard revolt was a war of an entire people and that it was necessary to destroy the insurgents' resources by wiping out the population supporting them, through destruction and massive deportation. Named by Cavalier "Julien the Apostate of our Times", he was the instigator and executant of the burning of the villages, farmhouses and lands of the High Cévennes. Allegedly a hypochondriac complaining frequently of the state of his chest and stomach, he died in Orange in 1707 at the age of forty-seven.

If Jean Cavalier's military talent and successes, his later career, and the mental change or development that removed him from the influences of prophecy and inspiration combine to make him the most interesting, as a man, of the Camisard leaders, he has never been the most admired by Huguenots whose veneration for their faith's martyrs can seem like a vicarious taste for immolation and its eternal reward. The hero for the devotees of this deep religious and tribal cult was Pierre Laporte, known as Rolland, who refused to join in Cavalier's negotiations for peace, rejected their outcome and continued the fight until he was killed in August 1704. He was believed to have served some time as a dragoon and had a basic military training in the handling of arms which he put at the disposal of the men of his group. He was tall, robust and handsome; other words often used to describe him are uncompromising and unsubdued, implicitly contrasting him with Cavalier the flexible negotiator.

Bosc shows his preference for Laporte by describing him as the most famous of the Camisard leaders, but whereas the personality of Cavalier often appears through his written memoir, Rolland left nothing similar and although his leadership and skill are apparent enough in the records of his actions, the image of the man himself remains indistinct. Cavalier is a memory contested or disputed; Rolland is a legend that like a magnet has drawn to itself the iron in the Huguenot soul. In a letter composed the day before his death he presented himself, in the words of Jean-Paul Chabrol, as "the champion of sacrificial resistance and upholder of the faith of the ancestors", and it is in this saint-like role that the Protestants have cast him; and in that mood that thousands of them attend annually at the mas Soubeyran in the Gard, the home of his family forebears, for the three-day celebration of the *Assemblée du Désert* when the identity and cohesion of the international Huguenot peoples are reasserted in psalm, hymn and sermon.

It is the want of any other full account by a protagonist in the war that has led to many attacks on the good faith and reliability of Cavalier, by partisans of different versions of the story unsupported from convincing written evidence but depending on oral and often contradictory recollections. There can be no doubt that the brutality of the war, its privations, losses and horrors, affected the psychic stability and memories even of rebel fighters used to the cruelty of the seventeenth-century penal system. For these reasons, some parts of Rolland's experience and actions during the two years of the uprising remain a grey area of the unknown. Criticism was sometimes heard, even among his followers, of his quiescence and inactivity during the height of the burning of the Cévennes and the crisis of despair that accompanied it, while Cavalier created diversions in the plain with a succession of lightning attacks. Julien, returning in December 1703 to the plain after completing his work of destruction wrote to the minister for war expressing astonishment that none of the mountain groups had attacked him: "I can say to you that the rebels ... are true cowards to have watched while their country was burned by a handful of men without daring to oppose it." The tactical speciality of Rolland who was, in the words of Cavalier, "a Gentleman of a good Family in Miallet in the Cevennes ... well educated", seems to have been in laying highly effective ambushes in his home mountain territory. He was less at ease in operations in the open plain where he seldom ventured. On one occasion when he did, in the absence of Cavalier who was ill with smallpox, he was seriously defeated and Cavalier's troop suffered heavy losses for which Cavalier blamed him. During the negotiations of 1704 Rolland did not inform Cavalier that he was in touch with an emissary of the Dutch and English governments, Tobie Rocayrol, who fortified him in his intransigence with the delusory hope of foreign intervention in the Cévennes. Rolland's final refusal, despite his mother's pleas, of the truce agreed by Cavalier, was believed to be partly the result of pressure on him from the ferocious Laurent Ravanel who by that time had turned away from his leader Cavalier with violence, accusing him of treason and of being a "vile slave" to Villars, and who shouted at Rolland's assembled men that God had warned him Rolland, too, was about to betray them.

The relations between the two principal leaders were therefore troubled on both sides. Unlike Cavalier, Rolland never turned his back on the *prophétisme* that both had made use of in the war. And there was a not unexpected personal rivalry, specially felt by Rolland due, possibly, to superior social origins and education, resentment that Cavalier's forces were much larger, more organized and could mobilize more cavalry than his own, and because Cavalier with his brilliant successes in the field at times seemed to assume the more authoritative position. It is recorded that during their heated argument over the terms of the proposed truce to end the war Rolland claimed seniority in the Camisard ranks and complained that the *maréchal* did not treat him on an equal footing with Cavalier. In the end Rolland, after a period of doubt and contradictory signs, declared that he "offered his body in sacrifice to God" and that his fight must continue. This was the turning point after which he was taken by historians and pastors such as Antoine Court, though they disapproved of the war, as the uncompromising hero of the *enfants de dieu* who went to his death for the cause that in their eyes transcended all.

No other group reached the size in manpower of Rolland's which was far less than that of Cavalier, and accordingly no other leader had the influence of either of them. But there was a degree of equality among the Camisards which was only superseded by inspiration; both Rolland and Cavalier were frequently inspired and led their men into action as the Spirit ordained. Élie Marion affirmed that inspirations were the law, the guide and the military discipline of the insurgents. The most frequently and perhaps most influentially inspired of all was Abraham Mazel whose dream of black bullocks had lit the fuse of war and who was the last Camisard to die in action, in October 1710, years after the rest had fallen silent. Mazel more than any other epitomizes the simple and unpretentious rank and file of the Camisard army, courageous, sometimes bloody in action, vengeful and totally committed to the faith of his fathers and, what was never forgotten by the cévenol Huguenots, of his mother. He led a group of men based in the hills between the Massif du Bougès and the Mont Lozère but operating wherever they could join forces with the larger groups and particularly with Cavalier who was first introduced into the company of those Camisards already enrolled as fighters for conscience by Mazel who had come down into the lowland plain to meet the baker's assistant, almost a boy but already notorious as a preacher at assemblies. Mazel seems never to have entirely rejected Cavalier after the negotiated truce and amnesty so violently repudiated by Rolland and other leaders. On 17 November 1705 he was one of a group of fifty former Camisard exiles at Lausanne arrested as they attempted to cross Lac Léman by night to join Cavalier, their former commander and now a professional army officer in Savoy.

After the burning at the stake of Esprit Séguier there was a pause in guerrilla activity as if in shock from the assassination of du Chayla and the attacks following it and, said Mazel, out of fear of what had been done. This phase, mistakenly thought by Basville to mark the close of the disturbance, was brought to an end by Mazel's renewed inspirations: "The order was given me to take up arms against the persecutors, and that those in whose hearts God put the desire to fight for his cause should assemble ... this assembly was of about four hundred people, men, women and children," and showed that the fear inspired by Séguier's execution had been overtaken by his example of defiance. Abraham Mazel's most spectacular and famous exploit, for which he gave the entire credit to the Spirit, was his escape in July 1705 from the Tour de Constance in Aigues-Mortes, prison of living death for the Protestants enclosed in the massive stone walls and surrounded by the salt marshes of the little Camargue.

Among other leaders of smaller groups or in subsidiary roles the most notable were Catinat, Ravanel and Castanet. The first, whose given name was Abdias Maurel, commanded Cavalier's cavalry and was active chiefly in the plain to the south of Nîmes, in his native Camargue and in the Vaunage to the west. He was one of the many Camisards who, after an exile in Switzerland, returned to France to fight again and was burned at the stake in April 1705.

Laurent Ravanel, Cavalier's lieutenant, led a group of three hundred after Cavalier's amnesty, never surrendered, and was burned at the same time as Catinat. The Catholic historian Louvreleuil described him as "small, dark-haired, with a face like a monkey, uneducated, brutal and cruel", and several accounts refer to his subsistence on alcohol and chewing tobacco. Castanet, a forester in the Mont Aigoual, had some education, was considered a great preacher and was described by another historian, Brueys, as "having the size and appearance of a small bear with all its ferocity". His troop was of several hundred men and took a principal part in the massacre of the Catholic population of Fraissinet-de-Fourques which led to the arrest of the baron de Salgas. Castanet's morals were thought dubious by some of the stricter Huguenots; he was reproved, but redeemed himself by an informal marriage to Marie Planque, a Camisarde later imprisoned in the Tour de Constance, and their marriage was regularized after they both reached exile in Geneva. But Castanet was another who returned to the Languedoc from

Switzerland, was caught and executed in March 1705. He was the subject of a biography in part-fictional form and of great emotional empathy and truth to historical detail by André Chamson, *Castanet le Camisard de l'Aigoual* which ends with the agonizing scene of Castanet broken on the wheel on the Esplanade at Montpellier from where he can see, as the wheel turns, "the line of his mountain crests, undulating like a melody in the chanting of a psalm".

Violence and the Scriptures

The bilateral atrocities of the Camisard War show the debasing influence religion can have on the human faculty of compassion, an effect now most often seen outside the fading boundary lines of Christian belief. If the persecution of the Huguenots under Louis XIV and the barbaric cruelty of punishment for dissidence had at least as much political as religious motive, on the Camisard side the motivation of atrocities committed by one or other of their independent troops was entirely apolitical, vengeful and above all religious. These victims of oppression believed themselves to be acting as the agents of God's anger, a divine attribute familiar to such readers as they were of the Hebraic Old Testament. Retaliation and revenge operated on both sides, since the burning of the Protestant assembly by the army under Montrevel at the Moulin de l'Agau in April 1703 followed the Camisard massacre of the population of the village of Fraissinet-de-Fourques in February. In historical writings, the painful empathy of Protestant sympathizers contemplating the horrors of persecution is set off by the assumption, not always unspoken, of Catholic authors that persecution was an act of state and that resistance to it was sedition to be put down by any means. Even in the twentieth century this assumption can be seen at work in Ronald Knox's *Enthusiasm*:

> ... the year 1704 alone saw the murder of eighty priests and some four thousand lay Catholics ... It is not to be denied that cruel reprisals were sometimes taken ... nor were the official methods of repression less odious than such methods commonly are ... Unfortunately such records can be matched from the history of many nations which have had to deal with internal rebellion ... of many armies engaged in the thankless task of stamping out

guerrilla warfare, with its secret and silent movements, its hidden bases among lonely hills, its dependence on the tacit support of a friendly country-side ... But what lends an added touch of horror to the Camisard murders is that they were done not merely in the name of religion but under the direct influence of a religious inspiration.[24]

Knox cites only the work of another priest, the abbé de Brueys who like himself had started life as a Protestant, as his authority for details, and exaggeration can be suspected since the figure of four thousand Catholics massacred in 1704 is not supported by Bosc. But the lapidary account of the Camisard means of sustaining the uprising is prophetic of that chosen to abolish it, demolition of every farm and village in the high country, destruction of livestock and burning of land and forest. And Knox's impugning of religious inspiration for extremes of violence is justified by the accounts of the Camisards themselves through the statements of survivors, particularly Abraham Mazel and Élie Marion. Cavalier in his own interest as an English army officer was too circumspect about his past to admit involvement in a mode of waging war that relied on a resource as suspect, to English eighteenth-century eyes, as religious "enthusiasm"; simple rebellion against the oppressor would be enough for those who followed Locke's view that government should be justified.

The methods of the twenty years of oppression before the uprising are itemized by Jean-Paul Chabrol: "deportations to America, prison, galleys, torture, the wheel, the gibbet, summary executions, rapes, floggings, *dragonnades*, individual and collective fines, children taken from families, young girls and women put into convents, houses razed to the ground, goods confiscated..." To argue that sensibility to suffering in the seventeenth and eighteenth centuries was relatively blunted by custom and that perception of it today is anachronistic ignores the logic that fear of suffering was relied on by the monarchy to enforce a terrified obedience. However, a catalogue of misery that might justify any rebellion leaves out the all-important theological element for Huguenots. The violence towards civilians and the frenzied attacks by Camisards streaming out of forest obscurity to fall on village as on château inhabitants, on presbyteries and churches, must be explained by some psychic factor beyond the need to retaliate and by accumulated hatred, humiliation and loss of identity; but to name an unconscious psychological origin for a problem of uncontrolled fury is to explain it away while leaving it in place. No explanation has ever been found necessary for the violence of the state towards its citizens, of the king against his subjects, the *raison d'état* being taken as its own sufficient cause. In contrast, the violent reaction of subject against monarch appears by definition to need some ulterior aetiological ground. And in the case of the Camisards it was the Bible.

Large-scale destruction of enemies is approved and even ordained in some parts of the Old Testament; the massacre of the Canaanites or of the priests of Baal, the killing of a thousand men by Samson with the jawbone of an ass are examples out of many episodes of divinely sanctioned violence in the book that was for Huguenots the guide to all life, its purpose and meaning. Their biblical reading predisposed the Huguenots of the Cévennes to believe that extermination of the enemies of God, including idolaters, was a rightful aim and they held the teaching and practice of the Catholic Church to be idolatrous and superstitious. The systematic burning of Catholic churches by the Camisards was not only a revenge for Catholic destruction of their *temples* but a purification of the sites of idolatry, and the assassination of priests was God's punishment of its celebrants. But the self-justifying argument does not cover post-mortem mutilations of the bodies of murdered priests which could only be the work of individual frenzy, and the same must be true of the massacres of entire village populations including women and children.

Protestant apologists including those hostile to the Camisard War have always been trapped into relative silence on this seemingly indefensible record which only a psychological origin—beyond the truism that state atrocity breeds atrocity in revolt and that reciprocal killings on a sufficient scale create a "vertigo of massacre"[25]—could fairly explain. The possible origin generally chosen has been the millenarian belief that the children of God carrying out God's work would be rewarded with eternal life. Man's hallucinatory dream of immortality was operative on both sides and could dehumanize Protestant as well as Catholic. Many of the Camisards, including the comparatively open-minded Cavalier, fell on weaker enemies and their dependents without mercy; but the long Catholic record of violence disqualifies the rhetoric of histories such as that of Jean-Baptiste Louvreleul, another priest like Brueys writing as a contemporary, in his *Rise and Downfall of the Camisars: giving an Account of ... their brutish Carnality, their many bloody and inhuman Murders and Massacres of Persons of all Ages, Sexes and Conditions, and their horrid devastations of Towns and Villages by Fire*. More charitable and more hopeful were the words of a mountain *curé* addressing his new converted parishioners about to be driven from their homes by fire and the sword in October 1703: "... you should set to work at once to remove and carry away everything you have and uncover your houses so only the walls remain, removing even the beams ... If one day the King allows you to return to your property, you will rebuild your houses more easily by having all these materials and the frames of doors and windows in a place where the all-consuming fire will not reach them ... I deplore your suffering with all my heart, my very dear children..."[26]

Notes

1 W. Gregory Monahan, *Let God Arise*: 89
2 Emmanuel Le Roy Ladurie, *The Peasants of Languedoc*: 281
3 Archives Historiques du Ministère de la Guerre, vol. 1796: 76
4 Philippe Joutard, *La légende des Camisards*: 37; *Les Camisards*: 153-4
5 Joutard's *Présentation in Charles-Joseph de La Baume, Relation historique de la révolte des camisards*: 20; *Relation historique*: 218
6 Pierre Rolland; *Dictionnaire des Camisards*: 34-5
7 W. Gregory Monahan, "Between Two Thieves", in *French Historical Studies*, vol. 30, no. 4: 538-9
8 Marcel Pin, *Jean Cavalier*: 94
9 Didier Poton, *Les notables nouveaux convertis devant la révolte in Les Camisards et leur mémoire*: 67-8
10 Gaston Tournier, *Le Baron de Salgas*: passim
11 Pierre Rolland, *Dictionnaire des Camisards*: 34-5
12 Jean Cavalier, *Mémoires sur la guerre des Camisards*: 87
13 Philippe Joutard, *Les Camisards*: 176
14 Pin: 154-5
15 Archives Historiques du Ministère de la Guerre, vol. 1707: 270
16 Ibid: 35
17 See Jean-Paul Chabrol's *Jean Cavalier, une mémoire lacérée*: 101-15
18 Henri Bosc, *La Guerre des Cévennes*, vol. 1: 262
19 Anon: *État et description des Sevennes par rapport à ce qui s'y passe aujourd'hui*: 4
20 Robert Sauzet, *Les milices bourgeoises cévenols pendant la guerre des camisards in Les Camisards et leur mémoire*: 103-110

21 W. Gregory Monahan, "Tyrant of Languedoc?" in *Proceedings of the Western Society for French History,* vol. 37, 2009: 3
22 Bosc, vol. 1: 15
23 André Ducasse, *La Guerre des Camisards*: 42
24 R. A. Knox, *Enthusiasm*: 363
25 Patrick Cabanel, *Histoire des protestants en France*: 699
26 Joutard, *Les Camisards*: 128

JEAN CAVALIER.

Jean Cavalier: 'one of the rarest characters that History has brought down to us' (de Malesherbes). Courtesy Le Musée du Désert, Mialet

Chapter Five
Soldiers of Liberty

1702

Gibbon's *Decline and Fall of the Roman Empire* portrayed Christianity, with its divisions, consecrations and anathemas, as unfit to bring peace on earth. Theological debate, continuous for at least seventeen centuries, was generally closed by outbreaks of lethal violence, the "final argument of kings", and thereafter resumed. And as intolerance grows from infallibility, so religious war might follow on some similar failures of intelligence. It is not difficult to trace this in the reaction to the Camisard uprising, in its human responses and consequent horrors.

An example running through the period of persecution and especially during the uprising was the systematic disempowerment of the provincial gentry, still generally held in popular respect, in favour of a centralized civil service manned by officials promoted into the ranks of the oligarchy, ornamented with new titles and drawn from the levels below. The king's jealousy of power was more soothed by created servants in the corridors of the palace than by any rustic nobleman great or small, in distant hereditary *château* or *manoir*, useful only for the tax on his coat-of-arms. In the Languedoc many of these were known to Basville the intendant as *gentilshommes laboureurs*, squires who worked their own fields and could not afford, in the growing rural poverty, a journey to Versailles in quest of gratuities through obedience. These were the men, Catholic or Protestant, who during the uprising were strictly deprived of any initiative in their own region. When the hamlets and farms of the Cévennes were being put to the torch, the comte de Peyre-Montbreton, nominal lord-lieutenant (*lieutenant-général*) of the Languedoc, was ordered to return to his château de la Baume and leave the work of destruction to the professional army, and he received the same order on his appearance with fellow gentlemen leading a disciplined troop of militia at Le Pont-de-Montvert within hours of the assassination of du Chayla. One result was the uncontrolled formation of leaderless, lawless *milices* responsible for the worst of the pillaging, the rapes and atrocities of the later months of the uprising:

> If the command had been left to the lords-lieutenant ... the revolt would most certainly have evolved quite differently ... They had cordial relations with their tenantry; their own interest would have advised them to act with moderation. Besides, the peasants still usually respected and esteemed the local country lords.[1]

The last claim can be confirmed by the peasant leader Pierre Laporte's adoption of the address "Chevalier Rolland", and later of *comte* and *généralissime* to accredit himself with the military powers and increase his authority among his men by assuming a feudal title, imaginary but time-honoured.

The civil administration of the Languedoc was in the hands of Basville and the military responsibility in those of Michel Chamillart, minister for war and controller of finances. Chamillart was the grandson of a merchant of Sens and was the type of civil servant of the later reign of Louis XIV, not spoiled for office by aristocratic connection; he became a supporter of Madame de Maintenon and financial administrator of her École de Saint-Cyr, and formed a more or less servile friendship with the king at the billiard table. Historians of the eighteenth century criticized him for weakness and lack of character but later studies have suggested that his chief lack was of confidence and this naturally kept him close to a sovereign to whom he could offer no kind of rivalry. A stream of express despatches from Basville and from the three successive commanders of the royal forces in the Cévennes—Broglie, Montrevel and Villars—and held in the archive of the Dépôt de la Guerre with a parallel series of letters to and from officers junior to the marshals but encouraged to make their own reports to the minister, kept him in close control of the state's responses to an uprising whose progress and early successes astonished the army, the court and unfriendly foreign powers taking an interest in it. Chamillart, says Bosc, controlled all military appointments and was ignorant of almost no detail of the military operations or of the functioning of the chain of command in the region, including written orders given to subordinate officers by the marshals or their staff. Every paper concerning the province and the war passed across his desk and was noted by him. He either read the reports or a summary of their content to the king; many original papers bear phrases and sometimes the text of replies in the king's hand. This raises the often discussed question of how far the king's knowledge of the horrors committed in his name went, and how aware he was of the pitiable condition of life of a number of his faithful subjects. The Huguenots of the far-off Cévennes believed him innocent:

> This distant king cloistered in his palace of Versailles, separated from them ... by the insurmountable barrier of a powerful Court, was he truly informed of their physical and moral suffering? This sovereign whom they still loved and respected in his royal majesty must certainly be ignorant of all that...[2]

However, the question of the king's awareness can be answered with certainty and in the opposite sense. Chamillart and La Vrillière, the secretary of state for affairs of the "so-called Reformed Religion", vied with each other in the completeness and speed of their reports to the king on the progress of the war, Chamillart complaining that La Vrillière's assertion of a right to receive directly or to see copies of reports from the marshals or the intendant was officious, went beyond the limits of his departmental role and encroached on that of the minister for war, a tension between bureaucrats that the king may have found it convenient to leave unresolved. But undoubtedly it was Chamillart who worked closest with him in a relationship of which the minister wrote that "in the eight years I have had the honour to fill the high position confided to me by his Majesty, I have lived so entirely free of constraint with regard to him that I have reserved nothing to myself until he has either seen it or had it read to him."[3] Chamillart wrote still more specifically in answer to maréchal de Villars' hesitation in bringing disagreeable details to the king's attention, that he had never hidden anything, however disagreeable, from him, and that only a bad courtier would avoid speaking of matters that concerned the king's service.[4] All the highways of centralization led finally to the writing table in the *cabinet du Roi*. Louis XIV personally authorized the burning of the Cévennes and the condemnation of the baron de Salgas; it must follow that he knew well enough of the *dragonnade* outrages, the inventive barbarity of the executions, the routine use of torture during questioning and the misery of his cévenol subjects about which it is inconceivable that he, ruler of every Frenchman and woman, did not inform himself, to carry the ultimate responsibility for them all. In the dawn of the eighteenth century, wrote Marcel Pin, "the war of the Camisards can be considered as the first advance sign of the decline of the power and prestige of the absolute monarchy",[5] and so considered, could account for the brutality deployed in the effort to defeat it and the apparent callousness of an omnipotent and beloved sovereign seen by his people as God's representative on earth.

The Camisard groups had no intention at the outset to attack royal troops, nor ever questioned the authority of the king and his intendant. The uprising was not a rebellion but a protest in extremity against persecution and the leading part in it of some of the Catholic clergy, of Catholic laymen such as Saint-Côme, and of informers who denounced Huguenots quietly continuing the practice in the *désert* of their own form of Christianity, or less quietly, the hearing of prophets. The clash with the forces of the Crown that followed on early assassinations and burnings was inevitable but not sought. An appetite for guerrilla warfare against the army came later with the flourishing of tactical and strategic gifts particularly under the leadership of Jean Cavalier, but at first there was a period of mounting reciprocal terror without planned action. The army units present in the Cévennes were too slight to control so large and wild a region and one of the first reactions of the intendant, while awaiting the reinforcements he had demanded, was to order *communes* to arm their Catholic populations and to join forces *en masse* with the regular troops to spy on, interrogate and punish their fellow-subjects suspected of sympathizing with or helping the *troupe de vagabons*. A contemporary gave an account of the process:

> These *milices bourgeoises*, old Catholics ... pass over the countryside pillaging, beating, sacking, with a horrible cruelty; they chain and imprison and rigorously punish whoever they catch, innocent or guilty ... in a word, a single old Catholic enemy is absolute master of the most "purified" new converted who is entirely exposed to his hatred.

This letter, says Bosc, "reveals the prodigious tension existing between old Catholics and new converted, reflecting the deep antagonisms that later events would transform into civil war." Equally prodigious and fateful would be the failure of intelligence on the part of Basville, a man whose clear head was often praised by historians on both sides, in mobilizing and arming one part of the population against another in the context precisely of the issue that divided them, violent religious prejudice.

The peasant groups, not yet organized and meeting secretly "in the hollows of the mountain and the solitude of the *désert* ... spoke with moving gravity, before taking up arms, of their hope that the king would let them live in peace with their families and their faith ... they never abandoned this aspiration and would fight and die for it."[6] Critics of the account given by Cavalier who with his first eighteen followers had marched into the foothills near Euzet to join the assassins of du Chayla, have nevertheless always relied on it for the accuracy of details to be found nowhere else. At this decisive hour it was recognized that the men assembled must have a single leader: "It was necessary to choose a Commander; for it would not be prudent to put it off to the last, by reason we were under an apprehension we might be every Moment attacked, and were in danger of being defeated at the first Onset, if we had not One to head us."[7]

Soon after this meeting on 1 September Gédéon Laporte was unanimously chosen as general following his threat to withdraw and "let them shift for themselves". Companies were formed from this first Camisard group of about a hundred men present, and officers nominated including Cavalier as lieutenant. Laporte at forty was older by far than the rest; he had served in the royal army, had been a travelling merchant, bankrupted, and had journeyed in Protestant countries where he may have been encouraged by Huguenot exiles to take the leadership in the Cévennes when the expected uprising began. The savage executions of his friends Séguier, Bonnet and Nouvel, and lately of Bouzanquet, determined him, says Bosc, to raise the standard of revolt. Laporte was not one of the "inspired"; he made no claim to be so or to cultivate prophetic powers but kept beside him Mazel and Salomon Couderc, both veterans of the du Chayla assassination, to supply the prophecies that were for all the Camisards the fount of action. Cavalier, aged twenty-one but noted already for his preaching gift, must have observed in the company of these three men the interaction between military command and prophecy, with communications from the Spirit guaranteeing obedience. By the end of September he was recognized by the early Camisards of the mountains as one of the chief prophets and there is evidence, though he said nothing of it in his memoirs, that throughout his ascendancy and his often startling military successes he made use of a capacity for prophetic trance giving him complete control of his men until the day when realism and intelligence led him to the negotiating table.[8]

Prophecy was recognized as an arm of war, and few fanatical fighting men would follow a leader who abandoned this arm in favour of compromise and peace. The implication is that Cavalier, and perhaps others, used their supposed prophetic powers like a weapon that can be laid down once the time of its usefulness is over. Many historians have repeated the criticism of Cavalier that he reneged on his prophetic past, as if this was an apostasy and not an implied admission by a gifted preacher that he had taken advantage, in a world stripped bare of public joy and starved of theatre, of his innate histrionic ability—the thundering perorations of Bishop Bossuet are the period's leading example—to defend his faith; and had ceased to exercise it only when interest in life overtook taste for martyrdom.

The organizing of a band of fervent but irregular insurgents into companies, with officers elected, entitled and appointed, would fortify them against attack as Cavalier said, but also stir them to fight in the basic unit for joint aggressive action. Once formed, the nucleus of the rough, unpaid, untutored army embarked on an aggressive rampage which, while sometimes provoking battle with the royal armies, would remain always essentially an attack on the religious adversary. The Camisards began their assault on 7 September at Saint-Paul-la-Coste, where they burned the church and presbytery, then pillaged a farm where a depot of arms was known to be found.

From the first, the seizing of arms was the priority of men most of whom carried only a pick, an axe, a scythe. On the 8th they reached Le Collet-de-Dèze in the high Cévennes; after luring the garrison out of the town by reporting the presence of an insurgent group in another direction, they entered the former *temple*, a unique building as the only survivor of the Huguenot churches built with a single-span longitudinal arch along its centre line from end to end and as the one Languedoc *temple* left standing in the destructive wake of the Revocation. Having destroyed the tabernacle and other insignia of "papism" they held a service of their own before burning the house of the *curé*, seizing whatever arms they could find and requisitioning a quantity of shoes, indispensable for troops covering distances on forest tracks by night and day.

The mainly Protestant population of Le Collet received the Camisards in a welcoming silence and many of their men enrolled before the departure of the group at two in the morning in the direction of Champ-Domergue, a small cultivated plain surrounded by dry-stone walls. On the 9th the news of their movement reached Saint-Germain-de-Calberte as the formidable Captain Poul arrived with a detachment of a dozen fusiliers; he chose a dozen more men to add to the number, and was shortly joined by the garrison of Le Collet. With this troop of eighty, Poul marched through the chestnut forest into the mountain in search of the Camisards, found them encamped on rising ground above the plain, and launched his attack which was the first set encounter of the Camisard uprising and the first occasion for Cavalier to show his courage in battle. "Poul marched towards us with so grave and daring a Countenance, that it might have frighted better Soldiers than we were," Cavalier admitted. But by a majority vote quickly taken the Camisards stood their ground, though Cavalier later agreed that they would have been wiser to avoid a fight against superior numbers which they were certain to lose. Cavalier, by his own account, was in command since the newly elected general Laporte was lame and feared he would be unable to leave the field and continue to serve the cause. The Camisards raised and flourished their hats at the enemy as a challenge, chanted a psalm and fired first. The trained men facing them returned the fire with greater effect, then charged. Cavalier found himself aiming at an approaching officer but his powder failed to light; seeing the men behind him in retreat he joined them unharmed. But an uncertain number of men were killed or wounded, and several were captured to be broken on the wheel the next day in Alais. Cavalier recorded that the Camisards were so discouraged at first by this defeat that for some time they did no more than "bolt from forest to forest like foxes tracked by a pack of hounds" as the forces of the Crown chased after them.

In the following days the Camisards melted away into the familiar forest and many returned to their farms before absence could be proved and punishment brought down on their families; the remainder reformed, assimilating newly recruited men drawn from the apparently limitless resource of the like-minded population, while Poul, joined in the chase by general de Broglie and companies of cavalry and infantry, was forced to admit to the intendant that he had failed to track them down. "The comte de Broglie has been in the mountains of the Cévennes for the past week and has not managed to find these villains ... They are so well hidden that we could not discover them," wrote Basville. Despite Poul's victory at Champ-Domergue, the continuing trail of burning churches across the countryside and the flow of Catholic priests into the safety of garrisoned towns, together with the silence of the inhabitants of farms and villages taught Broglie and Basville that defeat of the insurgency would need heavy reinforcements at a moment when the king's European dominance and his pride were challenged in the war of the Spanish Succession.

Basville, however, understood from the quantity of guns taken from buildings in raids by the insurgents in the aftermath of the battle that a true revolt had broken out and that Camisard numbers were growing. His consequent policy of lodging violent troops in the homes and at the expense of inhabitants who were accused of no more than tacit sympathies was another fault of intelligence, since its immediate result was to increase the anger of the population and further swell the Camisard ranks. Soon, many houses in the Cévennes would hold only women, children and old men, while the young took their strength and knowledge of the mountain forests to join the expanding war against priests, and against officials who, however badly wounded their prisoners, put them to the rack, the pyre or the wheel, tortures which they bore, like their families at home suffering the *dragonnades*, mostly in silence. Maréchal de Villars, generous as well as intelligent, wrote of the Camisards' astonishing contempt for death and added that "the cruellest tortures of hell (*géhennes*) had never made any of them reveal the least of their secrets".

If the discourse of prophets must be, as Marcel Pin remarked, an unconscious manifestation of their desires and hopes,[9] it would seem that Cavalier was able when necessary to work without it. At the beginning of October he made a decision, apparently unguided by the Spirit, which was characteristic of his career both as a Camisard and later in life. For reasons combining the strategic and the personal he separated himself from the mountain group commanded by Laporte, and made his way to Anduze and down toward the plain with fifteen companions, armed with three muskets between them. As for arms, Cavalier knew as well as anyone how to find them and better than anyone, as was soon shown, how to manufacture the powder and shot without which a musket would be less use than a scythe.

The strategic reason, which was to have a great effect on the development of the war and on Cavalier's standing and reputation, was to operate a diversion in the open lower country in order to disengage the Camisards (the "malcontents") of the high Cévennes from encirclement by royal troops by drawing some of these down into the plain to meet the new threat on a second front. "Knowing the Weakness of the Malecontents, I concluded it was absolutely necessary to make some Diversion in Order to prevent their Ruin and mine." In this, Cavalier was spectacularly successful. The personal reason, he gave in his *memoirs*:

> After I had been for some Time in the high Cevennes I grew Melancholy, and the Reason of it was, I knew not well that Country, and perceiv'd there was not among the Chief Officers of our Troop, that Unanimity and Concord with which they us'd to be closely joined, on which Account I left them and return'd home.

This apology suggests a half-conscious desire to lead and take first place which comes from innate knowledge of superiority in action; and it was not to be the last time that he would show it. From this time forward, the focal point of the war was Cavalier, the intelligence of his leadership, his reaction to success or failure. Other leaders had exploits and defeats, but the narrative of the Camisard uprising grew about the figure of the Anduze baker's assistant—stocky, thick-set, with a large head sunk into his shoulders, neither handsome nor imposing but blue-eyed, fair-haired, gentle-looking[10]—with his understanding, and sometimes his miscalculation, of the historical drama in which he would become the principal player. "Considering his appearance," wrote Basville, "a small, not good-looking man, son of a peasant, one cannot comprehend how he imposed himself and made himself absolute master of such a great number of villains." But "no other Camisard chief was able to make himself so loved and feared. It seemed as if done by enchantment," explained Sister Demérez, a nun whose contemporary letters described, vividly if erratically, the course of the action as learned from the talk of Nîmes.

On 4 October a band of young men with blackened faces gained entry to the presbytery of a church near Durfort, on the border of the plain, demanding arms. The *curé*, a man of friendly character described by Cavalier as a "joyful companion", not wishing to be martyred, handed over twenty guns or pistols confiscated from the new converted population, and many pounds of ammunition, and though made to kneel and prepare himself for death was spared as a non-persecuting priest, one of those criticized by Basville as "bad *curés*", lazy, indulgent, less zealous than the adherents of du Chayla and sometimes even charitable to their new converted parishioners. At the nearby château de Vibrac and in other Catholic houses the group seized as much weaponry again, then returned into the forest while the garrisons of Saint-Hippolyte and Anduze searched for them. Well-armed, they had, like the troop of Gédéon Laporte in the mountains, retributions to pay off as preliminary to wider action.

On 18 October Laporte and his men took care of du Chayla's secretary, Gardès, the informer to Basville of the assassination who was rewarded with a lucrative post of collector of punitive fines. "Commend your soul to God as best you can," Laporte instructed him before giving the order to fire; and sixty gold *louis* were taken from his pockets to go into the Camisard reserves. The revenge to be carried out by Cavalier's men was at Bagard, some twenty kilometres across country, uphill and down steep valley sides and over river crossings, from Durfort. The army could march along roads, the Camisards in the mountains moved through forests of high trees, but those in the plain and foothills could advance only on goat tracks among dense and spiked scrubby kermès oaks. The rapidity of movement of Cavalier's group across this terrain baffled the army commanders obliged to learn, seldom successfully, to anticipate it. On the night of 5 October they left the forest to knock on the door of Étienne Jourdan, captain of militia and murderer ten years before of the deeply revered preacher François Vivent. By the time they entered the house Jourdan was hiding under his bed. He was found, pulled out with difficulty and shot three times: "You are wrong if you think you killed Vivent. He lives through us." As Jourdan still seemed to move, he was shot again through the mouth before the insurgents moved on to the church which they set alight to the singing of psalms and the ringing of the church bells as if, said Bosc, "in mockery of the militia reinforcements that this nocturnal peal of bells would call out from Anduze". They then burned the church at Saint-Christol where was to be placed a garrison that Cavalier judged "would have greatly inconvenienced us."

In the Cévennes at the same time Gédéon Laporte's troop carried out similar burnings and arms raids; at Saint-Martin-de Boubaux in the forest north of Alais (now Alès) they killed a priest who had given them hospitality by shooting him in the back as he returned to his presbytery, one of the first of many discreditable or shameful actions by Camisard groups for which there was always the explanation that far worse had been done against them in the years since 1685. This, however, did not exonerate them in the view of Genevan pastors who preached that though it was normal to rise up in protection of one's faith, it was against God's law to murder priests, an illustration of the gulf separating these exiled clergymen from their former flock left under persecution.

Another leader, Pierre Laporte, uncertainly related to Gédéon, made his first recorded appearance on the night of 9 October when he preached a recruiting sermon at an assembly in the forest, presenting himself as a "man of war and of revelation". Anxious to form his own troop under his sole command he assured his "brothers of the mountains" that they would find caves to shelter in, springs for water and chestnuts, at this season ready to fall, to eat; that he was not a novice at military expeditions (Laporte is thought to have served in the army) and that he would know how to profit from the mountain and forest terrain to attack, to rally and to retire in good order. He was a man of unquestioned commitment and physical courage and whereas Cavalier, a few years younger, had the aspect of a sweet-tempered child, Laporte was tall, disfigured only slightly by marks of smallpox and irregular teeth, and with an impressive presence that made him a noted recruiter of men of the high Cévennes who might be reluctant to follow a village youth and offer their lives in the plain.

Christianity romanticizes martyrdom so that the personality of the martyr remains an enigma, immaterial and disconnected. Cavalier is familiar in his virtues and faults, not only thanks to his memoir but also because no attempt to idealize him has ever been made. Pierre Laporte, better known as Rolland, is still, to many Huguenots emotionally engaged with Camisard history, a romanticized martyr figure without substance, the ideal *récalcitrant* and beyond judgement. Enough of his actions and words in speech and letters is nonetheless recorded to allow a more objective account of a man one of whose chief characteristics seems to have been an understandable narcissism, different in kind from Cavalier's youthful vanity feeding on success. It is not surprising that the relations of the two men, though sometimes close, were often strained by a rivalry felt more, it seems, by Rolland than by Cavalier whom he could never regard as an equal.

Throughout 1702 Basville and his brother-in-law the comte de Broglie, commanding in the Languedoc, were urging that more troops be sent to prevent forest assemblies which they rightly believed to be the site of Camisard recruiting; and also relief from the rule that garrisons could only be taken out of their fortresses by order of the king—though before the end of the year Broglie, who distrusted the militias, had several times brought garrisons out on his own responsibility. In August the king authorized the raising of four companies of fusiliers and two of dragoons at the expense of the province, avoiding the withdrawal of troops from the armies at war. This minor but irritating disturbance of peasantry in the Cévennes was not yet seen from Versailles to be as serious as it would become without a massive reinforcement of men, and impatient criticism was directed by the minister at Broglie, of whom Cavalier wrote that he was "naturally haughty, cruel, brutal but greatly incapable of commanding an army".

Meanwhile, church burnings, murders or executions of Catholics and pillage of their homes continued in the hills above Anduze. On 13 October a detachment of fifty or sixty militiamen and soldiers was challenged by a group of three men led by Cavalier who narrowly escaped while one of his companions was killed and another taken prisoner. Attempts to rescue the prisoner failed due to heavy rain which soaked both guns and powder, and he was left to be broken on the wheel on 10 November. Marcel Pin asked what would have become of the insurrection had Cavalier who was to be its chief guide been killed at the outset, and concluded that the revolt would have been stifled within a few weeks.

Broglie, writing to Chamillart, complained of the conditions that made his work so ill-rewarded:

> No one denounces this rabble ... and in every *commune* they find other villains to follow them ... If this country was like others one would quickly put an end to an affair like this ... but where everywhere is mountain and precipice running with torrents too strong at this season to cross, it is no good searching, one finds nothing.

The rebels "disperse like starlings" in peaks and ravines where "only bears could turn round" was another complaint, showing that officers arrived in the Cévennes ignorant of what to expect and that the Camisards profited by it. On 22 October Laporte and eighty men, leaving behind them a trail of burning churches and presbyteries, found themselves blocked at Thémélac in a narrow forest valley near Barre-des-Cévennes by a force of five hundred men, some before them and some behind, commanded by Poul. In heavy rain, the insurgents had no more than thirty muskets in firing order; Mazel was inspired to advise retreat up the steep hillside but Gédéon Laporte determined to stand and fight. At the first discharge by the fusiliers he was killed beside Mazel who led the remains of the Camisard troop, still under attack, in retreat to Le Pompidou, outdistancing the military by their foresters' agility on mountain paths. Poul ordered the decapitation of the thirteen men killed and left the bodies to rot at the entry to Barre; the heads, including that of Laporte, were taken on pikes by mounted dragoons in triumph through Saint-Jean, to Montpellier and finally to Anduze on market day, where they were nailed to planks at the entry to the bridge over the Gardon and seen by both Cavalier and Pierre Laporte and their companions. Antoine Court claimed that this sight far from discouraging the rebels drove them on, and encouraged many of the Huguenot population to join or support them. But the lesson was not learned by the civil servants, with Basville at their head, and brutal methods of reprisal, punishment, warning and example continued to be the automatic response to the humiliation inflicted on intendant, minister and king by supple adversaries.

During October, Cavalier's troop continued to grow; Pierre Laporte had recruited some twenty-eight men near Nîmes but felt not sure enough of himself, says Bosc, to lead this troop alone; in consequence he and Cavalier joined forces on the 20th near Tornac and until the end of the month moved together in the vicinity of Anduze, pillaging arms and burning barns with Catholic owners, vainly pursued by Broglie, and attacking the châteaux of Tornac, Saint-Félix, Ribaute and d'Arènes which were all well defended. Between the 26th and 29th thirteen infantry companies arrived at Anduze, of which four remained while the rest marched into the Cévennes; of these reinforcements Vidal, the prior of Mialet who had taken refuge in Anduze wrote that "most of them are only children, naked and without arms, one can judge by that whether they are in a state to do the least thing for the king's service."[11] In reward for his success at Thémélac where Gédéon Laporte was killed, on 6 November the king promoted Captain Poul to the rank of colonel.

Atrocities committed by Camisards are first reported in November 1702, and many, though not all, are uncontested. None is defensible other than by appeal to the *lex talionis*, a code of retaliation used to justify an endless sequence of revenges in unenlightened societies. The royal government's reaction to instances of inhumane Camisard violence exemplified this repeatedly during the years of the uprising, while the foregoing seventeen years of persecution gave the pretext. On 1 November a group of rebels, apparently not commanded by either Cavalier or Rolland, murdered a Catholic farmer, his wife and two small children near Saint-Étienne-de-l'Olm. They continued to Deaux, entered a Catholic household where they announced themselves by name, drank three barrels of wine and savagely attacked the woman of the house who remained crippled for life. The group pursued their course of random and often unmotivated massacre across country until 4 November.

On 17 November a troop including Cavalier and Rolland captured an officer whose refusal to renounce his Catholicism enraged them; according to Bosc, who accepted the story although Court had rejected it, they stripped the officer, filled his mouth, ears and nostrils with gunpowder and lit it. Cavalier took his red breeches and coat and Rolland his gold-braided jerkin. At Courbessac near Nîmes on the same night a pregnant woman was disembowelled. It is claimed that Cavalier on one occasion piled into a burning church women and wounded men, and André Ducasse in his account of the war credits the accusation; he sets against these atrocities the well-established fact that in 1704 general La Lande massacred six hundred new converted of all ages and sexes without their having fired a single shot on the soldiers. "This execution," wrote La Lande, "gave great joy to the Catholics." The conclusion must be that only total religious conviction could have provoked such reciprocal savagery in the early years of eighteenth-century enlightenment, a movement seemingly more advanced in the land of Locke than, as yet, in that of Voltaire; and that in the Camisard ranks as in those of the royal army there were men of criminal or sadistic mentality, some of them escaped from the arbitrary violence of law enforcement that gave no mercy to the weak.

But often the Camisard expeditions, particularly those of Cavalier and his troop, were more temperate. On the night of 9 to 10 November he made use of a stratagem which was often successful. Approaching Saint-Chaptes, between Nîmes and Uzès, he sent in a messenger to the consuls of this important village to say that the comte de Broglie wished to see them. As they came out of the village they were arrested. The Camisards took provisions of food and wine, burned the presbytery and confiscated any arms they could find. Only one of the prisoners was assassinated before they retired. At the château de Fontcouverte Cavalier's men confiscated two of the three guns found there, leaving the third for the master of the house who was a sportsman, and later took the gun of a *gentilhomme* they met shooting in the woods but left him unharmed. In every case it was the supposed religious position of those they arrested or whose house they invaded that decided what would be done with them. Wherever the Camisards took action, violent or not, the local inhabitants were afterwards penalized by fines or imprisonments, sometimes of the entire population, on Basville's assumption that the unhindered passage of the insurgents through their locality was proof enough of complicity.

On 13 November and in the days following, Cavalier with a boldness never shown by any other of the leaders led his troop to the threshold of Nîmes, the fertile basin of the Vaunage where the population, spread among a dozen prosperous villages, was solidly Huguenot but not yet participant in the uprising. The rebels marched into Aigues-Vives, the largest of the villages, in ordered ranks and to the sound of drums as the crowds gathered in front of the church. An audience of two thousand joined the assembly to hear Cavalier "unleash their enthusiasm with his arousing eloquence".[12] In his account of this assembly Antoine Court gave an unflattering picture of the leader whom he came to think of as apostate to the cause:

> The most zealous among the lower order practically regarded him as another Gideon sent by God to deliver his people ... he was small ... with large expressive eyes ... a wide, reddish face, insignificant-looking ... people attributed quick wits to him and he must have had some..."

Another assembly was begun two days later but Broglie was informed of it, arrested all those present, hanged several, had a boy-prophet whipped round the town and sent a dozen men to the galleys for life. The meeting of bishops of the province proposed that all the seditious elements of the population be deported to Canada or the Caribbean islands, and Basville endorsed their recommendation though the king for the time being disapproved it. The anger aroused by these punishments without proof was thought to have brought about the dismissal of Broglie some months later, but resulted from the grant by the Council of State to Basville of an absolute jurisdiction overriding the powers of courts in the Languedoc. In six weeks of October and November 1702 he had more than fifteen accused men broken on the wheel and in October alone sixty-two prisoners of both sexes were arbitrarily and rapidly judged by a court in Alais presided by a judge appointed for the occasion and answerable to him. In parallel to this, prophets and prophetesses among the Camisard troops decided the fate of captured Catholics; in the first months at least those whose religion was their only offence were generally released; and from respect for the privileged classes "the god of the Camisards often ordered the liberation of gentlemen and Catholic bourgeois, while showing himself pitiless to the more humble."[13]

Cavalier and Pierre Laporte brought their troops together again on 16 or 17 November; during this period even Bosc admits that exact movements of men and their leaders are impossible to verify. An attack on the château de Mandajors in the hinterland of Alais was made on the 18th with losses on both sides, followed by a Camisard withdrawal into their redoubt of the woods where they carried out training exercises such as the five drill movements of ordered musket fire to the beat of drums, like regular troops in a walled fortress. The spirit of discipline and the appearance of men marching in ranks to drum beat made a strong impact on a fearful population and won recruits from among the new converted to take their place alongside deserters from the recently formed Languedoc regiments, or refugees from the prisons of Montpellier. During the last weeks of November the combined troop moved rapidly around Anduze, burning and pillaging Catholic houses; at Mialet and Générargues, villages nearest to the mas Soubeyran, Laporte's family farm, their murderous activities were intended to ensure that there would be no Catholic left in the vicinity. At the end of the month Cavalier and Laporte decided to separate, fearing their number (then about five hundred but fewer than Cavalier's group would soon become) made them vulnerable. There is no evidence of discord but these pretexts for dividing their numbers, which ceased to apply when Cavalier's force swelled to over a thousand in the coming months, may suggest a disagreement between the leaders that would later be fatal to the opposing hopes of both. Before their separation Cavalier and Rolland attacked the château of Sérignac, hidden in the wooded country between Nîmes and the cévenol foothills, and after setting fire to it threw the guides who had led them there, tied to one another, into the flames of the furniture of the presbytery and of the altar and ornaments of the church.

The ferocity of the Camisards was generally to be explained if not excused, said Bosc, by their disgust for renegades to the faith who as informers had joined the persecutors. In a meeting on 11 December the assembled leaders agreed the division of their forces because it was found impossible to nominate a single general accepted by the others to take the place of Gédéon Laporte; fragmentation allowed ambitious individual leaders to command their own unit in relative independence. Rolland's troop assigned to itself the area around Anduze, Mialet and Lasalle, with a "resting-place" at Saint-Félix-de-Pallières where the woods are dense and the approach from all sides is from lower ground. Salomon Couderc and Jouani occupied the high Cévennes, and Castanet the Aigoual massif. Cavalier's troop was the largest and most mobile, almost permanently in movement between Nîmes, the Vaunage, the lower valley of the Gardon, the direction of Beaucaire and the Camargue with its cavalry, and even as far as the outskirts of Montpellier. Thanks to the daring of its leader it was the only group actively seeking direct combat with the royal troops.

Cavalier chose the densely wooded and rocky foothill of more than a thousand hectares of the Mont Bouquet between Alais and Uzès and near to Euzet, where caves in the limestone offered a great choice of shelter and hiding places for men and stores: "A vast labyrinth and safe refuge allowing Cavalier to get out under cover either towards Alais, or to Uzès, toward the river Cèze, or, crossing the Gardon and the bois de Lens, to the outskirts of Nîmes."[14] The caves of Euzet became Cavalier's headquarters and refuge after setbacks, his ammunition and arms store, the underground hospital where two surgeons worked in the light of braziers at caring for the wounded, and the workshop in which he set up an installation for the manufacture of powder and shot. They were the rallying point of his troop after any dispersal and where recruits came to join him and to receive the training and discipline which made his force the most effective of the Camisard groups.

On or about 20 December Laporte and Mazel with a hundred men, and Cavalier followed by his two hundred, met in a wood in the foothills between Durfort and Saint-Hippolyte. Arms were scarce and shortage of powder acute. A bold ambition was formed to seize the town of Sauve with its stock of materials, their first attempt on such a scale, and the three chiefs agreed to study the plan over the next days. But Cavalier was perhaps too impatient to delay action while slower men turned the project round in their heads. Moving with his usual speed between Durfort and Euzet, on 21 December he launched an attack by stratagem on the château de Servas where he knew a garrison would shortly be posted. Servas was in a commanding position in the region of Euzet, Lussan and the Mont Bouquet which he considered as the base and theatre of his future operations; he dressed most of his men in uniforms taken from the army dead and wounded in previous actions and he wore an officer's coat. Ordering his two hundred men into columns of four with three of them roped together as if taken prisoner, Cavalier on horseback led the group toward the château. Calling himself the "captain Saint-André" and flourishing a written order of de Broglie found in the coat pocket, he required shelter, food and a safe place for his prisoners. A hundredweight of bread and a barrel of wine were produced and while his men were quartered in the village Cavalier and three of his officers were led inside. Later in the evening they murdered all those living in the château except a boy who pleaded for his life and was allowed to run away, rifled the contents which included six guns and a quantity of powder, and set fire to the remaining furniture and woodwork. As the troop, chanting their ritual psalms, retired into the Bouquet woods a huge explosion from a powder store undiscovered in the cellars came from the buildings within and around the château which were left in wreckage, though the thick exterior walls survived. "They knew the strength of our château," wrote its owner, the sieur de Servas, to the war minister sadly complaining of his ruin. He was partially indemnified in the sum of nine thousand three hundred *livres*, four years later.

On 21 and 22 December a succession of church burnings, with the usual complement of executions, was carried out in the Cévennes, and on the 24th Broglie left Alais with a part of his forces heading for the mountains. The same day, on learning of these movements, Cavalier and his group burned the church at Saint-Privat-des-Vieux, then encamped in the open in a field below the mas de Cauvi, a farm three miles from Alais, where he called on a large assembly to celebrate Christmas. It is remarkable that while the mountain groups led by Rolland, Jouani, Castanet and Couderc moved mostly at night under cover of the forest, appearing and vanishing as fast as they came, sometimes setting an ambush in a narrow valley before again disappearing, Cavalier in the plain on Christmas Eve beside the high road to Montpellier from Alais openly challenged the royal armies to come out to meet him. With his force of eighty men and a few horsemen his action was more that of the commander of an opposing army than the twenty-one-year-old leader of a group of peasants described by Mazel as "poor, wretched, clumsy and inexperienced with arms".

The battle of the mas de Cauvi that followed this act of temerity was to be the first set battle of the Camisard War. The governor of Alais was quickly informed of the assembly and emerged from the city walls with four hundred men stiffened, it was hoped, by the presence of the local gentry and to be followed by two hundred men more. Cavalier ordered the assembly to take shelter half a kilometre away from the mas de Cauvi and to observe the battle at a distance. Of the eighty Camisards some favoured retreat but Cavalier, having an inspiration of victory, placed them in an entrenchment beside the road where the military would pass, giving some cover from fire and concealing their small number, approximately one against seven of the approaching force. A group of the best riflemen was placed in front and opened fire as the advancing cavalry came within range, killing two of the leading officers. The return fire of the cavalry made little impression and while the horsemen reloaded, the Camisards rose from their entrenchment, chanting their psalm, and charged, firing as they went. A number of cavalrymen and horses fell, the rest including the gentry and bourgeoisie specially called up for the occasion hesitated and then turned tail, riding through and over the infantry behind them.

The retreat became a stampede, pursued by Camisards with bayonets, in which an uncertain number of the royal force was killed. Cavalier claimed a hundred, Broglie, minimizing as usual the losses in his report to the minister, admitted to twenty. Some of the fleeing men took refuge in the château de Montmoirac which was the nearest safe building, while others were chased as far as the walls of Alais: "We pursued them for half an hour like hounds," wrote Cavalier. On the deserted field the Camisards recovered arms and ammunition and uniforms, and found the coils of rope that the governor of Alais had brought with him to tie up prisoners. Terror took hold in Alais at the thought that Camisard marauders might enter the town; the governor's efforts to calm the population were slow to have effect since a month later the brigadier Julien wrote to the minister: "I have never seen a town more alarmed ... it surpasses the imagination, particularly the canons of the cathedral who dug themselves hideouts in the church..." Since the defeat of Champ-Domergue the Camisards had learned to fight and hold their own against a force far larger than theirs. "Cavalier," wrote the commandant Louis Blachère, military historian of the uprising, in 1970 "had shown himself to be a leader naturally possessing military qualities of organization and of tactics. He was to be the best leader of the revolt and his troop would only succumb through betrayal and in face of a crushingly superior adversary."[15]

On Christmas Day a great assembly was called in a wood near to Vézénobres, five kilometres from Alais, and lasted from early morning to afternoon. After religious observances, uninterrupted by authorities too intimidated by the defeat of the previous day to show themselves, had been completed the assembly turned to the fateful question of electing a leader for all those of the plain and the low Cévennes, the *mécontents* willing to fight or to support the fighting groups of the area which now amounted to several hundred. The need for a lucid and firm structure of command was felt by all.[16] At the first vote Antoine Rastelet, who had served in the army and was to become Cavalier's principal lieutenant, received a large minority of votes. At the second, Cavalier was elected unanimously. His success of the day before, his intrepidity and the quality that must have been evident to the sagacious Cévenols, his exceptional intelligence, made him the inevitable choice: but it must be remembered, according to Bosc, that the assembled men and women were above all influenced by his reputation as an *inspiré* to whom the Spirit sent messages of coming victory. When Rastelet came to be interrogated by Basville under the usual torture, to the question "Who was it gave such credit to Cavalier among the insurgents?" he answered, "It was by enchantment." Whatever the motive of the voters, Cavalier made it clear that "if they wished to choose me as their chief I intended to be obeyed as such. Unanimously they invested me with the power of life and death without being obliged to call a court martial, which I never did without the advice of my six principal officers."

The most feared of his threats was to abandon the "brothers", on which they would beg him to stay and return to absolute obedience. Marcel Pin with an understanding of his fellow Cévenols remarked that "It was the Spirit of God that the Cévenols, individualistic, rebellious, insubordinate and retaliatory, always obeyed. The day that inspiration leaves the little shepherd, his soldiers will abandon him and follow those of the prophets who are still favoured by 'the gift of the Lord'." The unanswerable question is how well Cavalier himself made the same forecast, how far he gambled on successfully defying it, and to what extent were his commands from the Spirit simply the expression of wishes and designs of his own? An inspired leader may provisionally but sincerely convince himself that his inspiration has some transcendental source, especially if his followers already believe it, justifying him in his conviction as he in turn follows them.

The planned attack by Laporte, Cavalier and Mazel on the medieval town of Sauve took place on 27 December following an inspiration of Mazel. The same ruse as led to the occupation of Servas was applied, and with the same success. Two officers and forty Camisards in captured army uniforms gained entry to the walled town and were received with hospitality by the officers in the château and the men in the town. On an agreed signal the town guards were arrested and the gates opened to the flood of Camisards waiting outside who entered chanting the Psalm 137, "Put to sack, to sack, let it be set ablaze and razed to the foundations." The customary pillage of houses followed, with confiscation of arms and clothing, and the burning of the church and buildings belonging to prominent Catholics.

The Camisards withdrew at two in the afternoon on being warned of the approach of a strong detachment from Saint-Hippolyte, alerted in turn by smoke filling the sky, and retreated with their booty most of which they abandoned in the woods as they escaped from a much larger force. Five priests who had taken refuge in Sauve were said to have been killed along with a number of inhabitants who made the mistake of resisting the invasion. Marcel Pin observes that in the beginning of the insurrection the Camisards generally respected ecclesiastics not known to have actively persecuted Protestants but that once reprisals and indiscriminate punishments had inflamed their fanaticism "they killed all wearers of the *soutane* who came within reach". In the last days of the year Laporte and Cavalier separated, Cavalier returning to the area of Uzès within reach of his base at Euzet, but both groups continued day and night attacks and burning of churches in the dioceses of Alais and Uzès, destroying at least a dozen including the monastery of Tornac whose ruins, incorporated into farm buildings of the later eighteenth century, are half-hidden in a valley between the plain and the wooded hills. If the authorities had thought to see the end of the insurrection with the end of the year they were proved to be mistaken.

The minister's dissatisfaction, and the king's, with progress in the repression of this inconvenient uprising while the royal armies were engaged in a war far more important, elicited in reply a string of complaints from Broglie and Basville regarding manpower. Both agreed that more troops and better were required, and both felt distrustful of the undisciplined and predatory Catholic militia. From the regular companies recently raised in the Languedoc a significant number of men had deserted, were on the run and presumed to have joined the Camisards. Army officers trained for fighting set battles in open country found the woods, precipices, ravines and rivers of the Cévennes beyond their competence and the Camisard guerrilla methods with the support of the mountain population outside their tactical experience. Broglie insistently demanded the sending of a *maréchal de camp* (brigadier) to lighten his duties and this request was met by the posting to the Languedoc of Julien, a former Protestant and scourge of his ex-fellow religionists. Basville, admitting his impotence in face of opponents who regularly outwitted him, remarked to the minister that even if the reinforcements promised (the Irish regiment of Lord Gallmoy proved like the rest a ghost) were one day to arrive, they would still be too weak for "so great an ill".

> It is no longer a matter of assemblies in what they call the "camp of the Eternal". One knew where they were and one finished them off in a single action ... It is now the whole country in revolt without appearing openly to be so ... there are more than forty thousand new converted able to bear arms ... most of them look on these events with pleasure ... and it is certain that the rebels have all the money they need...

At the same time, the alliance of Protestant countries with the Emperor Leopold of Austria hardened against France and was joined by Savoy and Portugal in the New Year. The war, sometimes called the first war of nations in Europe, made the removal of well-trained troops from the frontiers to an internal region which few Frenchmen could identify on a map a necessary evil for a minister harassed by events beyond control. The general scapegoat for the misfortune would be the hard-working but eventually ineffectual de Broglie, an easy sacrifice whose brother-in-law Basville wrote of him that "it requires patience to endure his moods".

1703

Early in the New Year the inhabitants of Anduze found a letter on their doorsteps stating the motives of the revolt, especially that it was not against the king but those priests "who have left no means forgotten to massacre us". The letter was signed by "La Pierre Rollante" (rolling stone), *nom de guerre* of Pierre Laporte, and "La Rivière du Gardon", that of Cavalier who soon dropped its use. The poetic image of the rolling stone seems an expression of Laporte's more romantic disposition and not a reference to his action in the war which was in fact much more static than Cavalier's; this first *nom de guerre* was later changed to "le Chevalier Rolland", a conscious borrowing of the name of Charlemagne's heroic nephew Roland whose legend was so well known in the Cévennes that the church of Moissac was built to commemorate him. Laporte's later title for himself as "Comte et Seigneur, Généralissime des Protestants de France" suggests a romantic temperament loosened by war from the ties of reality.

There was no lessening of the attacks on churches and Catholic families and their homes. On 2 January Castanet's troop attempted to take Saint-Germain-de-Calberte and was repelled; the setback was repeated two days later at Sainte-Etienne-Vallée-Française but they and others carried out dozens of burnings and executions both in the low Cévennes and in the diocese of Uzès, where Cavalier made a series of assaults on the Catholic village of Belvezet whose population was almost wiped out. The growing frequency and occasional atrocity of these murders was logically accounted for by Marcel Pin:

The murders committed by the rebels in 1702 were isolated and individually motivated executions; the victims were traitors, persecutors, or personal enemies. In 1703 the cruelty of the insurgents continued to grow in parallel with the severity of the sanctions against them ... The fanatics ushered in the new year by applying to the community as a whole the ancient law—an eye for an eye.

The royal troops acted often like gangs of brigands, said Bosc, their recruits for the most part more or less criminal. And the progression of inflicted horror was accelerated by the arrival on the bloodstained scene of the brigadier Jacques de Julien on 14 January 1703.

Of all the military commanders in the war Julien most polarized the opposite judgements of Catholic and Protestant historians. Marcel Pin gave a synthesis: "The king made a good choice in appointing this officer. Julien had the qualities of a pitiless partisan leader ... crossing the Rhône, he announced that he would have 'the heart of a tiger,' and he went on to prove it." Julien, grandson of a pastor of Orange, had been in the service of William III who made him lieutenant-colonel and gave him a regiment; in 1690 he thought himself overlooked for promotion, quarrelled with his superiors, returned to France and abjured his Protestant faith, preferring his interest to his religion and taking care to amass a fortune as he went, claimed Antoine Court. Louis XIV was said to be gratified by this abjuration and rewarded it with an infantry regiment. Julien remained solidly in favour at court and cultivated a special relationship with the minister of war to whom he sent regular reports, including his opinion of the work of the three commanders he served under in the Cévennes.

Julien was the man for the situation, said the fair-minded Bosc, and his arrival strengthened the badly compromised authority of the army and government; but Bosc also went on to quote Pin: "Julien, like all ambitious apostates anxious to have their heretic past forgotten, exaggerated the outward signs of Catholicism and the cruelty he showed towards his former co-religionists." Some of the success Julien was credited with was due also to the simultaneous arrival in the province of the long-awaited reinforcement of men; five infantry battalions, a regiment of dragoons and five hundred *miquelets*, the formidable mountain troops from the Pyrenees, reached the Cévennes by the end of January.

Success, however, was neither immediate nor invariable. Cavalier and his troop, by now much the largest and most enterprising, were making themselves "masters of the country" in the Vaunage[17] where they held numerous assemblies attended by Huguenots from Nîmes and the surrounding country. These gatherings under Cavalier's protection, and where he among others regularly preached, contributed as much as his victories in the field to the extraordinary popularity that surrounded him among the inhabitants of Nîmes by the time of the amnesty negotiations of 1704. On 12 January Cavalier was in Nîmes buying gunpowder and a stock of the indispensable shoes; his troop, commanded in his absence by Ravanel and Catinat, was near Caissargues, a village five kilometres from Nîmes where they had spent the night and were preparing an assembly at the moment they were discovered. The royal troops, with Captain Poul in command, were brought forward hurriedly while a messenger was sent to Broglie who, on his arrival, had to decide whether to retire before a force possibly superior to his own, or attack. Broglie and Poul disagreed but Poul fell in with the *maréchal*'s decision to attack. Part of the Camisard force had meanwhile occupied a shallow hollow in the land with banks on either side known as the Val de Bane behind which they took cover, using Cavalier's well-tried method.

The battle was short and sharp. Broglie, believing that sixty well-mounted dragoons would make quick work of eighty ill-armed peasants, sent in his cavalry, awaited by the Camisards singing the psalm of battles "If God only shows himself, and one will see in a moment..." The charge of the dragoons was met by intense and accurate fire which drove them back, turning on their tracks, into the ranks behind them. Poul was unseated from his horse and killed by several peasants using axes, forks and sticks. At the moment when Broglie attempted to rally his men he saw the approach of a larger Camisard force and retreated precipitately with his escort in the direction of Bernis where he spent the night before making an apologetic report of his defeat to the minister, minimizing his losses and claiming heavier losses on the Camisard side than any other account has borne out. The triumphant Camisards stripped Poul of his uniform, released the famous sabre from his fist and decapitated him with it in revenge for the decapitation of Gédéon Laporte. It was after the death of Poul, claimed Mazel, "that people began to call us 'Camisards'".

On the same day, Rolland in the high Cévennes ambushed a consignment of provisions for the château de Mandajors, hanged one of the mule drivers, shot the other and savagely mutilated a third person with them. On the 14th, Cavalier drove the garrison of Moussac, which was following him and waiting to attack, into the Gardon in flood where most of them were drowned while the rest fell into the hands of his men who took no prisoners. Julien announced on his arrival at Montpellier, at the end of his first journey across the Languedoc, that he could not understand how a mob of about nine hundred villains could terrorize every class of the population in such a beautiful and flourishing province.

In the country between Uzès and Alais, where Julien installed his headquarters, the Camisards showed themselves particularly vengeful and violent in the days after their success at Val de Bane. "They intensified their massacres," wrote Bosc, "and were guilty of many crimes ... with cruelty that makes one shudder." Some smaller groups, notably that of Jacques Couderc known as "La Fleur" were also active in the high Cévennes, where with extreme mobility they "hurt the enemy more than any other in proportion", according to Mazel. At the abbey of Cendras near Alais Rolland's group burned the buildings and massacred twenty-two unarmed occupants on 21 January; at Malataverne, possibly inflamed by wine, they cut the throats of twenty-three others including women and children, causing panic at Alais and in the surrounding villages. On the 24th Julien, who was to prove himself expert in brutality, wrote to the minister, "my hair stands on end to hear of such cruelties."

Until now, Camisard operations had been limited to the Lozère, the foothills and the Languedoc plain, but the neighbouring region of the Vivarais had a predominantly Huguenot population which had so far remained quiet. It became Cavalier's ambition to raise the Vivarais in revolt alongside their Camisard "brothers". To make this attempt it was necessary to cross two fast-moving rivers, the Cèze and the still faster and deeper Ardèche, in the depth of winter, and in the country between the two the Camisard troop left a trail of burning churches and Catholic corpses as they passed. At the beginning of February Cavalier with his troop of seven hundred approached the Ardèche in flood and crossable only by bridges; from the outset of the movement into the Vivarais, Cavalier showed signs of uncharacteristic hesitation, while Julien with eight hundred men advanced from the direction of Alais. However, before Julien reached the river the commander of royal forces and militia on the other bank had crossed it in hope of finding and crushing the Camisard troops.

On 10 February at dawn Cavalier saw the enemy advancing; dividing his troop in two he placed one in battle order facing the advance, and the other half-hidden behind trees along the roadside. Both groups opened fire together on his signal, killing all the chief officers in the royal detachment. The soldiers behind them broke and fled, abandoning their arms as the Camisards pursued them with bayonets. The battle was followed by numerous atrocities committed in the village of Vagnas on wounded survivors and those of the inhabitants judged insufficiently cooperative. After this quick unexpected victory the bridge over the river was now open to Cavalier but, for reasons which have never been clarified, he did not take it though he had learned that five hundred Vivarais men were ready to join him on the other side. His lieutenant and great friend Espérandieu, the only one of his companions to have known military service, was killed on the field, and Cavalier gave as another reason in his memoir that he was unfamiliar with the country and felt exposed. The vital qualities of decision in military leadership may be anticipation and strong nerve; these are possibly not different from the inspiration relied on by the Camisard chiefs and in this case absence of *inspiration* might translate as sudden loss of assurance understandable in a leader twenty-one years of age.

The outcome at the second battle of Vagnas was disastrous, and it is characteristic of Cavalier's treatment by historians who give martyrs kinder treatment that he has been criticized equally for this, and for the disaster that followed in 1704, at an even more decisive moment for the uprising and for his followers, when his self-assurance and nerve held firm. On 10 February the troops of Camisards, making their way back toward their familiar Cévennes, met an army force sent to meet them near the wood of Barjac. As soon as engaged, the royal troops were reinforced by the arrival of Julien with another eight hundred men; the

Camisards were heavily outnumbered, and trapped by the positioning of the enemy force which was similar to that used by Cavalier himself on several occasions—the combination of a frontal array and one or more lateral, concealed detachments attacking from the flank and blocking retreat. At the second combat of Vagnas it was only the failure of the royal troops to occupy the wood that allowed Cavalier himself and a remnant of his men to escape the battlefield in which more than two hundred of his men were killed. The wounded were first tortured for information in Julien's presence and then massacred. "I spared the king the expense of justice and of the executioner," he wrote to Chamillart. Cavalier, exhausted, spent twenty-four hours in the snow, crossing the Cèze in darkness with water up to his neck and walking barefoot since the loss of a shoe in the river, before reaching the other survivors at Euzet.

If Cavalier's prestige was affected by this avoidable defeat, it was not so for long. Until the end of his active participation in the uprising he was everywhere regarded as its prime leader with a troop of variable numbers; at harvest time he had no more than a hundred men but at others and for important expeditions he could count on thirteen hundred or more, divided into brigades of twenty to fifty. Daniel Guy, a gardener from Nîmes, was his friend and confidant in charge of provisioning for the troop, assisted by the mason Pierre Claris who became one of the last Camisards to be eliminated; Laurent Ravanel, violent and fanatical, was lieutenant-colonel and commanded in Cavalier's absence with Rastelet as major; Abdias Maurel, known as Catinat and also noted for violence and brutality, commanded the growing cavalry detachment; and Pierre Cavalier, the leader's younger brother, was aide de camp, agile, brave and mounted on a Camargue horse. Among the brigade leaders were Samuelet from Générac and Francezet from Beauvoisin, both at the limit of the Camargue, who for three months with a dozen horsemen blocked the route of communication between Montpellier and Nîmes and terrorized the villages from Vauvert to Nages where the last decisive battle of the war before negotiation would later be fought.

But in 1703 negotiation did not enter into government thinking, as the comte du Roure, baron de Barjac, was to learn. When Cavalier and his troop passed near to Barjac, Roure, believing himself useful as an intermediary able to open a dialogue with the Camisard leadership, delivered into Cavalier's hands a letter in which he asked his reasons for taking up arms and his conditions for peace. Cavalier answered that he and his followers were ready to put themselves at the service of the king in exchange for liberty of conscience and for the liberation of galley slaves and prisoners for the faith. Roure replied that he had no order from the court to negotiate and that he had made the attempt on his own account. When the minister for war learned of this exchange he rebuked the count, a provincial gentleman to be kept subservient and inactive, on behalf of the king: "Make sure that this move which seems innocent at first sight is not repeated." He pointed out that it was "not suitable for subjects in revolt who could be crushed by force, to put propositions to their masters",[18] an example of politicians rejecting an initiative towards compromise that they would later be forced to adopt.

On 14 February Broglie, criticized on all sides, was replaced as commander in the Languedoc on the arrival of maréchal de la Baume de Montrevel, a personal friend of the king who respected the marshal's reputation as a lover of women probably more than as a soldier. "He was short and stocky and his kind of self-complacency, though extreme" said Saint-Simon, "was ready-made to fit the king." For Marcel Pin, Broglie was more unlucky than incompetent, Protestant historians blaming him for excessive severity at the start of the revolt while the Catholics accused him of incapacity in repressing it. The marshal's arrival with a numerous staff of officers and aides comforted the clergy, the Catholic population and the bishops. Basville, whatever his opinion of Montrevel, received him with magnificence matching the marshal's magnificent apparel, and with solemnity knowing how sensitive he was to honours. Montrevel's first action after these ceremonies was to use his influence at court to support Basville's demands for more troops, which were not long in coming. Six battalions of mature and trusted soldiers arrived in the Languedoc about 19 March. It seemed that at last the government had understood the seriousness of the situation in the Cévennes and that a new phase in the repression was opening. In fact the period of the greatest activity by the Camisards, and of their most striking successes, was about to begin.

Notes

1 Marcel Pin, *Jean Cavalier*: 274
2 Henri Bosc, *la Guerre des Cévennes*, vol. 1: 234-5
3 Archive du Dépôt de la Guerre: vol. 2042, folio 38
4 Bosc, vol. 4: 454
5 Pin, *Cavalier*: 8
6 Bosc, vol. 1: 234
7 Jean Cavalier, *Memoirs of the wars of the Cevennes ... in defence of the Protestants persecuted in that country*: 43
8 Pin, *Cavalier*: 106
9 Ibid: 98-99
10 André Ducasse, *La Guerre des Camisards*: 82
11 Grégoire Vidal, *Lettres et Rapports sur la Guerre des Camisards*: 69
12 Bosc, vol. 1: 293
13 Pin, *Cavalier*: 153
14 Ibid: 130
15 Commandant Louis Blachère, *La Guerre des Cévennes*: 29-30
16 Bosc, vol. 1: 325
17 Ibid: 372
18 Ibid: 808

de Montrevel, 'inclin'd more to amorous speeches than his own Profession': Gillot Saint-Evre, 1835 (Wikimedia Commons)

Chapter Six
Maréchal de Montrevel

Scorched Earth

After the Camisard defeat at Vagnas with the loss of four hundred men (the figure, probably inflated, reported to Basville) he and the government at Versailles hoped to see the uprising rapidly extinguished, with the presence under the marshal's command of six companies of *miquelets*, several regiments of bourgeois militia, twenty battalions of regular troops and three regiments of dragoons. In spite of these overwhelming military numbers, however, the government's illusion was brief. Montrevel wrote to the minister on the day after his arrival in the province that the war could turn into a general revolt beyond control: "The Camisard band beaten by Julien on the 10th February has quickly reformed in several very aggressive groups, again burning farms and châteaux with as much vigour as before ... Faced again by Julien's troops near Barjac, the Camisards cried out, 'Here are more of those same scum, let's wipe them out.'"

The violence of the Camisards aroused Catholic village populations to equal violence, massacres matched by massacres, victim numbers depending on which side was in the minority. The village of Fraissinet-de-Fourques had a population of fervent Catholics active in the persecution of Huguenots in neighbouring farms and hamlets and considered responsible for the murder of the mother and sister of Castanet. On Ash Wednesday 21 February 1703 Rolland and Castanet attacked the village which was armed and defended itself with gunfire, killing twenty of the Camisards. This exacerbated the rage of the attackers and a massacre of forty inhabitants, men, women and children, followed, often with extremes of brutality, and the houses destroyed. This slaughter in an isolated village became emblematic in later history for all Huguenot atrocities and by its savagery allowed both contemporaries and those who followed to overlook the long chain of oppressive violence that led to it. In 1840 Napoléon Peyrat wrote simply that "A century has not effaced the mark of Camisard bullets on the walls..."

In spite of the quick recovery of his troop from the decimation of Vagnas, Cavalier recorded that his men, soon numbering thirteen hundred, included many young soldiers without training and that he was at a loss how to arm them, adding that after meeting Rolland at Colognac in the mid-Cévennes he found that "Rolland's Troops were very ill-provided with Powder, Shoes and other Necessaries, and had no money to purchase any." Cavalier and Rolland remained together for three days and "came to the following Resolution, that we would immediately attack Sumène and Vigan, in order to get Arms, Powder, and what other Necessaries we stood in need of, and also to endeavour to increase our Forces to the number of two thousand men." Unfortunately, Cavalier added, he now fell ill with smallpox and was obliged to leave the command of his troop to Rolland, "which troubled me very much, and occasioned a great Consternation among my Men..." when he parted from them at Tornac on 2 March. It can easily be supposed that the nervous equilibrium of irregular partisan troops, living in permanent great danger and reliant on leaders whose inspiration came from an invisible authority, could be precarious and that this fragility would be increased in the febrile atmosphere of prophesying, trance and visionary belief that accompanied their heroic march across plain and mountain, and always preceded their engagement in battle. Cavalier withdrew to Cardet, possibly to the house of his companion Isabeau Chanurel, to get through his illness while Rolland was left to carry out the actions decided between them and intended as the start of the year's campaign.

Montrevel, while making acquaintance with local society in Montpellier, Nîmes, and Alais and, according to Cavalier among others, measuring the amorous possibilities offered by these towns and deciding, after researches and despite Basville's canvassing for Montpellier, in favour of Nîmes (though later Alais found greater favour) continually bombarded the minister with demands for troops, artillery, staff officers, guides and postilions. In particular he was determined to use artillery against the Camisards, and this provoked the minister's exasperation and the king's disapproval, although the appointment of a marshal of France to deal with a peasant uprising was likely to lead to insistence on equipment, manpower and supply befitting the rank of the commander. Chamillart expressed his irritation to the intendant: "It seems he needs a considerable army to destroy the fanatics. He is asking for teams of artillery, quantities of general officers and artillery commanders ... at a time when his Majesty has all Europe against him." The minister went on to advise the avoidance of anything that looked like a war by the king on his own subjects, and also to minimize the revolt in the Cévennes and not show its true gravity either within or outside the kingdom. The marshal had to be mainly content with the arrival in the province of the Irish Brigade known for its extreme aversion to Protestants, and of the ferocious Pyrenean *miquelets* more fit for mountain work than were the soldiers, often mercenaries, from the flat plains of northern France.

From the time of Cavalier and Rolland's meeting at Colognac, and because of it with the growing disparity between the principal leaders, the Camisard uprising became increasingly two separate wars—one of guerrilla attrition, burnings, murders, ambushes, revenge, capricious executions or pardons—another that was the simulacrum of a war of states, of the servants of God; less petty, equally brutal, but with a horizon beyond that of the blue interlocking hills of *la Cévenne* under its vast sky, which were far from the earthy realities of the plain in general avoided by the mountain leaders. The exception to this, which in its outcome confirmed the separation of types of action in the field, was Rolland's first and last venture in command of troops into open country beyond the foothills, and may have been the period he alleged in 1704 as the time when Cavalier carried a musket under his command.

On 4 March his own troop and that of the absent Cavalier entered Sumène, took what provisions they could find but were vigorously repelled by the militia of the town. They continued their march toward Ganges, were joined by Ravanel and his group bringing their total to eleven hundred men, and massacred twenty-five young naval recruits unlucky enough to meet them on their way to the coast. The population of Ganges, former Protestants, received the Camisards hospitably and while several hundred men of the troop were sent to burn churches and Catholic houses in the vicinity the rest spent the day acquiring arms and supplies. A fast-moving detachment spread terror in villages of the diocese of Montpellier and alarm in the city and its suburbs which until now had seen none of the action. The presence among Rolland's assembled force of several leaders—Ravanel, Catinat and others—with their own men evidently resulted in a loss of centralized discipline that Cavalier would have used his authority and prophetic powers to prevent.

On 6 March, leaving behind them a trail of destruction and execution, Rolland and the reassembled troops reached Pompignan, forced an entry against the courageous resistance of the mostly Catholic inhabitants and began the burning of the town. Montrevel, however, was not far off; by the use of a ruse which convinced Rolland that the marshal and his force were continuing on their way, he encircled the Camisard troops in Pompignan and drove them out street by street. Rolland, said Pin, showed himself incapable of organizing the defence. Cavalier in the worst of difficulties would hold firm and protect his rear guard; even completely surrounded he would counterattack and escape with minimal losses. Rolland attempted to retire into a nearby wood; the *miquelets* were posted there to trap him and drive him back into the plain where the dragoons were waiting; retreat then turned into rout. Four hundred rebels were killed, according to Montrevel's report, but Rolland escaped.

Historians of every camp have condemned his generalship on this occasion which greatly weakened the Camisard groups, particularly that of Cavalier who wrote, "That Day was very fatal to us, for we lost half of our Men, and that thro' Roland's forwardness: For had he stay'd in the Mountains as I advised him, the Mareschal's whole Forces could not have attack'd him." For once, no one coming afterwards and making retrospective judgement coloured by knowledge of his later career has argued with Cavalier. According to Bosc, Rolland was "very clever at setting ambushes in the mountains but incapable of waging a battle in open ground and of standing up to an officer of some military experience like Montrevel." Pin was incisive: "Rolland, sick with exhaustion and pique, returned to his mountains; for the reputation of this peasant, obstinate, cunning, brave, but presumptuous and incapable of directing an important action, it would have been better never to have left them." And the military historian Louis Blachère stated that Rolland, knowing the strength of Montrevel's force, should have distanced himself rapidly. "When they separated Cavalier advised him to do that but he ignored the advice. Why? Presumption, pride, incompetence? Whichever it was, the Camisards paid a heavy price for this unforgivable mistake." The cautious and painstaking Antoine Court, however, supported Mazel's claim that there were as many royal soldiers killed as Camisards.

On 20 February Ravanel, with Cavalier's reduced troop, rashly approached the walls of Nîmes with the intention of finding necessities in the town. Montrevel in person rode out at the head of a troop of a hundred and sixty dragoons and four hundred foot soldiers to encircle them. Ravanel was forced to retreat along a narrow ditch, abandoning horses and mules, and losing a hundred and seventeen more men. Montrevel, who like Basville was convinced of an invisible directive behind the Camisard front, affirmed in his report to the minister that among the rebels were people as clever as career soldiers and that he believed the instructors who had taught them to fight must be deserters from the royal army. He became alarmed at the possibility of the uprising, which grew from day to day, spreading beyond the Cévennes and even into neighbouring provinces. A royal ordinance of 22 February and one issued by Montrevel on the 24th established a systematic repression even more draconian that that existing, the instant execution of captives without trial, judgement by the intendant or his delegates without appeal of those suspected of complicity with the rebels, with confiscation of their goods and destruction of their houses, and the application of collective guilt and responsibility of inhabitants in whose villages or farms Camisard activity took place. The countryside was soon crawling with the painful movement of a displaced and penniless population, many of whom would never return to the ruins of their homes.

Court pointed out that these extremes of repression had the immediate effect of turning the stream of recruits to the Camisard ranks into a flood. On 26 February Montrevel assembled for the first time the new converted gentry of the region and delivered them a stern lecture on their feudal duties and their neglect of them. He pointed out that an attitude of haughty unconcern was unfitting for the nobility of the kingdom and that they must make themselves useful to the king's service. Since everything possible had been done for many years to reduce their influence, and it was well known that to restore authority to the provincial nobility was contrary to the policy of the court, this lecture may have been sceptically received; Basville in any case had a deep mistrust of the formerly Protestant nobility whom he suspected of watching the rebellion with secret pleasure from their town houses in the region's safe cities. "We will see what is their conduct in the future," he wrote to Chamillart. On 12 March there was a second assembly of the local gentlemen at which Montrevel set out both threats and offers. He would punish with the utmost severity those who continued not performing their loyal duties; "It is not a question of religion, I would like everyone to be Catholic but I will force no one to carry out Catholic functions. I only ask that they be faithful to the king." Bosc says that the new converted gentry appreciated the apparent tolerance of the marshal's words, but were unconvinced. They applauded, but remained secretly in agreement with those fighting for the religion of their heart. Above all, while preserving the forms of politeness, they tried as they could to protect their own lives and property.

Montrevel set out at the end of February to make a tour in the Cévennes, a region entirely unknown to him, in order, supposedly, to grasp better the nature of the country where his authority ran. It fell to Basville to oversee the comforts of the marshal on his tour; the cortège of the commander-in-chief was followed along hilly roads by a train of mules loaded with linen, silver, decorations and nourishment of every kind including wines chosen by Madame Basville herself. The tour was not a long one; between 22 February and 12 March the caravan of horses and mules and splendidly dressed officials visited Anduze, Alais, Quissac, Ganges, Saint-Hippolyte and Anduze a second time on the return journey. No penetration into the valleys and forests of the Cévennes was attempted. In Nîmes, the marshal, had found several women to impress. "Pray don't despise our town of Nîmes, since a number of beautiful women have chosen to stay in it," he wrote to Basville who in the end tired of hearing about Montrevel's intrigues which he suspected of depriving the marshal of his attention to duty. But it was only in Alais, according to Cavalier, that the marshal fell in love: "He gave himself up to this Lady, so that he could leave her but seldom; however to save his Honour, he came now and then after us with a strong Body of Forces, and not finding us, suddenly return'd to his Mistress ... a very Sweet and agreeable War for him after his Fatigues..."

On 11 March Montrevel divided the region of the revolt and delegated that of the high Cévennes to Julien, with drastic later consequences for the inhabitants. Julien made his headquarters at Saint-Jean-du-Gard while Rolland, whom Cavalier "comforted ... leaving him in his County" (apparently a reference to Rolland's use of the title of comte) "that is to say, to stay in the Mountains", burned and pillaged in the surrounding villages. Cavalier meanwhile, recovered from his illness, took his troop in charge and proceeded to make a number of attacks in the plain between Uzès and Pont-Saint-Esprit on the Rhône in quest of arms and money, and on 14 March carried off one of his more notable victories at Martignargues near Alais. On 16 March Cavalier's troop ambushed a supply train from which they took two hundred pairs of shoes and a quantity of wine and salt. On the 17th Rolland's troop arrested two young men making their way home from the assembly of the nobility, let one go free and shot the other in the back after ordering him to march towards a bridge on the road over the Gardon.

Rolland's seemingly capricious judgements, generally adverse, on the fate of prisoners can be compared with those, equally capricious since both of them were governed by "inspirations", of Cavalier which tended, though not invariably, the other way. During March a manifesto printed in Holland and intended to be studied by sympathizers to the Huguenot cause in Protestant countries and to create hopes of foreign intervention in aid of the Camisards, began to circulate in the Cévennes. For the same reason, the authorities in France, and in particular the intendant Basville, were strengthened in their belief that foreign advisers and money were concealed behind the rebellion. In fact, although sympathy was stirred up in England and Holland, those countries' planned or attempted interventions in the affairs of the Languedoc were throughout minimal, came too late, turned out unlucky and were finally useless. From first to last the Camisards were on their own and, with the growing influx of trained army units, left to face a crushingly superior enemy ready to use the most ruthless methods to bring the insurgency to an end. The foremost advocate of these extreme measures was the apostate Julien, in his command in the high Cévennes, whose purpose was to "exterminate the rebels, because the evil is in their blood". Any village in which the Camisards acted should be destroyed and all the inhabitants including children massacred.

On 5 April these proposals were put to the king, who refused them as they would make it appear that he was waging a war on his own people. The preferred method was that of scorched earth, or systematic pillage of any suspect village or locality. Chamillart noted on a letter from Julien, "let him do it." The threat of destruction and ruin for the entire Cévennes and the brutality of reprisals encouraged some of the inhabitants to press the Camisards to seek an amnesty, but drove others to join them. On 27 March the *commune* of Mialet, close to Rolland's home at Soubeyran, was invaded by Julien with four hundred and fifty soldiers. The next day the entire population of six hundred was deported and their homes destroyed, while an attempt by Camisard groups to rescue them was repelled with loss of sixty lives; the prisoners, men, women and children, were marched to Anduze and later to the prisons of Perpignan where most of them died. These aggressive means were applied in twenty-six parishes of the plain as well as in the hills, with the marshal's encouragement, though Basville was more hesitant since it was not until 5 April that he received the king's approval.

The more striking the Camisards' action, the more brutal and widespread were the reprisals. In the last week of March Cavalier carried out burnings of farm buildings close to Nîmes and held an assembly of two thousand near to Saint-Gilles. Many of those present were arrested and taken to Nîmes for interrogation. Court wrote that "scarcely a day passed in Alais, Nîmes or Montpellier without bloody executions ... by fire or the wheel of innocent people on pure suspicion, without trial, that they favoured the insurgents." In a pastoral letter of September, Bishop Fléchier reproved those of the clergy who took pleasure as spectators of the torture and execution: "The Church, so circumspect and charitable, cannot approve such sad and indecent curiosity." Nevertheless, the Bishops of Montpellier and Lodève are reported to have visited the galley on which Salgas was chained like any criminal to the bench and asked to watch the sixty-year-old baron working at the oar. The spectacular executions, not only in the main towns of the region but in villages and farms and suffered with great courage by many of the victims, hardened the rebels and their recruits rather than discouraged them. A contemporary witness wrote that "the new converted regarded the condemned men as martyrs and their courage in death confirmed the public in their religion ... producing the opposite effect to the one expected." This courage beyond normal understanding was taken by witnesses of both parties as a sign of physical and moral resistance in the Camisard revolt that would be hard to break.

The second great emblematic massacre of the uprising was an immediate result of this. On the morning of 1 April, Palm Sunday, a group of friends and related families gathered, despite the threats hanging over them, outside the walls of Nîmes for prayer and meditation, assembling in an oil mill at the foot of the walls known as the Moulin de l'Agau, a hundred metres from the Roman Porte d'Auguste, which was the principal entry from the road to Rome and is still standing. Bosc describes this move as aggressive and extremely dangerous since Montrevel was in the town. The sound of psalm singing and the raised voices of the inspired were heard for several hours and the news that they were audible in the cathedral during vespers was carried to Montrevel who reacted to the interruption of his dinner with fury. He ordered the massacre of the congregation and destruction of the mill, and rode out with his personal guard and a troop of dragoons to see to it. Those attempting to escape were shot or attacked with bayonets, the survivors forced back into the building which was then set alight, watched by an enormous crowd of horrified Nîmois who heard the cries of women and children in the flames.

Montrevel was henceforth known to the Nîmois both Catholic and Protestant as the slaughterer of the Agau, and his presence in the town was felt to be unbearable. The numbers of the dead have been exaggerated by both sides but twenty-five identifiable bodies were buried the following day, leaving the remains of others in the building which was then razed to the ground. Montrevel, once his rage had subsided, was apprehensive of the court's disapproval but his account of the day's work won the minister's praise and that of Fléchier, Bishop of Nîmes: "This example was necessary to stop these people's pride. But the heart of a bishop ... is touched and his entrails moved..." The moral balance, in weighing these atrocities on both sides, tips inevitably in favour of the persecuted minority, though not to the point of acquitting crimes so revolting to the Huguenots in exile that their historic spokesman Antoine Court felt it necessary to atone by his work for these excesses, many of the most repellent of which, he claimed, were in fact the work of uncontrolled Catholic groups looking for vengeance or for gain and were wrongly attributed by other historians to the Camisards. It has been established that the Catholic militia, and particularly the *cadets de la croix*, worked with ecclesiastical support and occasional participation, and relied on the tolerance of their activities by royal officials whose duty was rather to quell the risk of civil war than silently favour it; but from 1 May the Catholics were authorized by Montrevel to form armed groups to work beside the army.

During April the arrests and deportations continued; two thousand people are thought to have been sent to the prisons at Perpignan in April and many of them, referred to as "vermin" by the marshal, shipped to the Caribbean or to Canada, a penalty more dreaded by the Cévenols than the executions. The forced depopulation, in punishment of guilt by passive and often accidental association, continued in the following months at the same rate. Camisard reprisals followed the emptying of each village; on 2 April Cavalier, at the head of six hundred men, attacked a Catholic village some kilometres from Nîmes and massacred the inhabitants. Rolland and Cavalier together destroyed the Catholic-owned mills at Anduze, and assembled at Lussan a gathering of more than four thousand people as part of the holy week celebrations that brought together Huguenots from every part of the Cévennes into the *désert*, under the protection of the Camisards but in the end at the expense of the *communes* where they met which were punished, without mercy or pretence of legal process, by the army under Julien.

Increasingly, as the months of destruction and of family tragedy went by, some inhabitants of hill and valley villages pleaded with the Camisards for what they had left of security in their homes and farms; but as their sons themselves formed the Camisard troops the pleading went generally unheard and the burnings and murders of suspected Catholics continued. In April, Cavalier decided to join forces in the high Cévennes with the groups of Salomon Couderc, planning to capture the strategically placed town of Le Pont-de-Montvert on the Tarn. Along his route through the hills Cavalier deliberately sought out and successfully attacked the groups of *cadets*, his inferiors in guerrilla tactics and intelligence, leaving a trail of the executed as he progressed toward the Mont Lozère. Julien, however, was informed of this gathering of Camisard troops and moved in force from Saint-Jean-du-Gard to prevent it, with the result that the three diverse groups dispersed, Cavalier returning to the plain. Marcel Pin alleged that Cavalier carried away a disagreeable impression of the cold highland from this adventure: "In the Vaunage ... every farm could offer white bread, abundant wine ... the mountain wine was scarce, the bread made of barley or chestnuts unappetising. Cavalier and his men, used to a softer climate, gentler gradients, other food, were soon disillusioned by their visit to the mountains." Several witnesses also described Cavalier's way of life, the dressed table, the silver, the comfortable bed, the domestic aides, and all this may have been out of place in the forests of the Bougès and the Lozère, and was evidence, perhaps, of the vanity which critics alleged as one of the causes of his eventual downfall.

Between Alais and Anduze on 29 April a great assembly of two thousand people was held in the woods, with preaching and prophesying. In the evening Cavalier led his men, exhausted after a march of forty kilometres from the high Cévennes, into a disused formerly fortified small tower near Ribaute, known to him since childhood. His defeat at the Tour de Billot was the result not of hubris but of imprudence and betrayal. Two brothers Guignon in his troop were sons of a carpenter in a nearby village and Cavalier thought it unnecessary to hide from him where they were going. The carpenter carried the confidence to the military command at Anduze and claimed the reward offered to informers. Sentries posted at the tower fell asleep and Cavalier himself relaxed his vigilance. At midnight a force totalling eight hundred and fifty men attacked the tower simultaneously, the sentries' throats cut before they woke, Cavalier led his men out of the building and rallied them behind trees but forty were caught in the stampede within the tower on the arrival of the soldiers. Cavalier made two attempts at rescue but was forced back by the arrival of yet more troops, the building was set alight by grenades and the last Camisards killed as they fought to get out. "It seemed," Cavalier wrote, "that the earth and sky were on fire and the shadows of the night redoubled the horror of the sight."

Cavalier retired with the wounded to his caves at Euzet calculating his losses at two hundred men though other witnesses put the figure at four hundred, confirmed by Bosc. The carpenter's sons formally condemned their father to death; he was later found and killed with the reward still in his pocket, but once again the authorities believed they had struck a blow that would quickly bring the uprising to an end, a belief that perhaps accounted for Montrevel's generous judgement in victory: "The resistance of the Camisards was what could be expected of the best troops." However, the authorities learned that recruits continued to join Cavalier at Euzet, "regrouping like starlings" so that they were "stronger after a few days than they had been before they were beaten",[1] and very soon returned to the attack wherever their unpredictable and generally undetected movements took them.

These repeated resurrections, and the proven military gifts, despite defeats, of the peasant leaders confirmed the beliefs of the intendant and marshal in the existence of an occult consistory, advised by officers from Protestant countries, "carefully organized, inspiring the manoeuvres of the Camisards and communicating to them the inner flame of resistance".[2] In fact, the exiled religious consistories fiercely disapproved of the Camisard violence, credited the stories they heard of licentious and obscene practices with the women accompanying the groups as prophetesses, and most of all rejected the practice of prophecy itself. They sent in May a pastoral letter to be distributed among the cévenol population urging submission and an end to all violent action. But, asked Bosc, "at the degree of exaltation and anger they had reached, how could they halt their terrible élan?"

In June there was constant movement of royal troops in search of Camisards who remained invisible. It was becoming evident to Basville at least that Rolland and the other mountain leaders could indefinitely repeat their sudden attacks, followed by disappearances into the forests where no amount of military manoeuvring could bring about a face to face battle. But the plain was different, as later events would prove. On 11 June, after a series of murders in the region between the Gardon and the River Vidourle, including in the immediate vicinity of Nîmes, the largest royal force so far assembled, almost five thousand men led by the marshal himself, was marched to the Vaunage to look for Cavalier, still at this time far too circumspect to let his group of a few hundred men be encircled by an army. "Cavalier ... runs about with impunity wherever he likes in spite of all the troops engaged in the region," wrote Julien to the minister. After fruitlessly scouring the woods and vineyards for three days and nights the marshal retired in frustration to Alais.

For some time, Basville had reviewed the possibility of bringing the uprising to an end by an offer of amnesty to those giving up their arms. Montrevel, a single-minded proponent of the severest methods, was constitutionally opposed to this, but in April nevertheless let it be known that an amnesty might be considered; at that time none of the rebel leaders, and notably Cavalier, would hear of it, and accordingly the Spirit gave no encouragement to those among the Camisards who, by the month of June and the approaching harvest, became affected by "a kind of collective and contagious psychosis inducing them to lay down their arms".[3] The king, in any case, considered that an amnesty would be seen as a weakening of the royal authority. The amnesty that would bring the insurrection to an end the following year was impossible in 1703 since the figures whose mutually recognized intelligence would bring it about, Cavalier and the maréchal de Villars, had yet to meet. For the moment the Camisards were showing themselves, in the view of foreign diplomatic agents following developments in the kingdom's underbelly, more combative and daring than ever. They were conscious of their strength with the support of a sympathetic population and encouraged in their illusions of the sailing to their rescue of English warships by the appearance in May in London of a pamphlet, *The Necessity of giving prompt and powerful Help to the Protestants of the Cévennes*, which argued the advantage to the Allies to be drawn from the revolt and particularly the potential territorial profit for England from the ease of disembarkation near the sandy shores of Aigues-Mortes. The Camisards, said Pin, "awaited the summer, the English fleet, and an army." On 4 July a detachment of Cavalier's troop carried out a premeditated massacre at Valsauve, a property of the Ursuline convent at Bagnols-sur-Cèze where a large number of harvesters were at work; fifteen were tied together and executed where they knelt, nine or ten others, less badly wounded, escaped as night fell, while the women were spared and locked into farm buildings. Neither the harvest nor the buildings were destroyed but booty was carried off on the backs of mules in the direction of Lussan.

The massacre at Valsauve created fears throughout the province wherever harvesting was in progress and men in the fields owned by Catholics were relatively undefended. Montrevel took hostages in Lussan and other villages nearby, while Cavalier announced that the operation was in reprisal for the numerous executions recently carried out at Nîmes and Montpellier; it was also well known that close to Valsauve were grouped the most aggressive bands of armed Catholic peasants.[4] Cavalier in a memorandum headed "Cavalier, established by the grace of God to guide the flock and defend the cause of our Law..." assured the minister to whom it was addressed that "God forbid we should act against the king who would have no more faithful servants than us and if he gives us the liberty of our conscience we ask nothing more in the world." But the letter sets out the Huguenots' complaints against the Catholic clergy and their abuses and accuses the priests, especially those in inferior positions, of responsibility by their "intolerance, intransigence, tenacious obstinacy ... their violence and harassment ... for this war that ravages one of the most beautiful provinces of France and sets French Christians one against the other."[5] In the Cévennes on 18 July Rolland, having learned that the prior of Monoblet had sold eleven barrels of wine to mule drivers from mountain villages, broke into the priory cellars, drew off the wine and carried it away on the mules to the woods of Tornac where he and his group remained for the rest of the day and night following; there are many records of the Camisards' hauls of wine or eau-de-vie, seeming to support allegations against them that pillage, arson and murders were sometimes carried out under the influence not only of communications from the Spirit, but of rough alcohol and hallucinatory substances in other forms, as was suspected later of the London Prophets

As summer passed, the certainty of the authorities grew that despite punishments and deportations, the people of many villages and farms of the Cévennes, if not in the plain, secretly received the Camisards, often their own menfolk absent on sacred duty, on occasion hid them, and kept them provided with the stores to support their epic rapid marches through forest and mountain. Julien wrote to the minister that "all the peasants are Camisards today at their work, and tomorrow with a gun". From this time onward all events in the Languedoc tended toward the drastic solution, for long rejected by the court, which came to be known to military and civil service alike as the "great work" (le grand ouvrage). But for a time Basville held back from authorizing those most draconian measures, urged by Montrevel, that would lead to the ruination of the highland and, as a result, a serious fall in the tax revenues on whose successful collection his own regard at court partly depended. The unwillingness of civil servants to displease the king was not due to fear for their heads as in the past, but for their income, their titles, their mansions and their rank. Basville gave the better part of his life to the defence of these assets and was left until the age of 71, deaf and gout-ridden after 33 years as intendant, to labour at it in the Languedoc, far distant from the gilded theatre where they could be enjoyed and displayed. The baron de Salgas, released from the galleys in 1716, could have drawn some grim satisfaction from the thought of his enemy still chained to duty in the provinces many years after the Camisard uprising had become a memory.

In the meantime, awaiting the authorization for the grand ouvrage, the authorities depended on the violence of the troops and the efforts of spies who were often priests, "the most active and redoubtable agents of the intendant and the commander-in-chief," said Pin who believed that had the curés remained in their parishes their service of information on their parishioners could have paralyzed the movements of the rebels and stopped their activity. As it was, the pitiless vengeance of the Camisards against them was the "just wage of their spying and informing", an activity energetically pursued on both sides in an epoch when the shifting movements of war made frontiers and boundaries permeable and difficult to control.

On 31 July, Cavalier and Rolland met in the hills near Anduze to receive the visit of an emissary from the marquis de Miremont, a bitter enemy to his cousin Louis XIV and now established in England as a major general in the English army. Miremont had emigrated at the Revocation of the Edict of Nantes, was an active proponent of an Allied intervention in France in aid of the Camisards and had distributed a pamphlet entitled *Europe enslaved if the Cévennes are not supported.* He dreamed, said Marcel Pin, of returning to an independent and Protestant Languedoc that might become his principality. His emissary, who was to reappear several times in the Camisard history, was David Flotard, a native of the Cévennes in exile who also held an officer's commission in the English army and acted as Miremont's man of confidence and secretary. The object of his mission was to encourage the Camisards in the belief that Allied help would come, to agree with their leaders a system of secret correspondence and to announce, without detail, the expected arrival of an Anglo-Dutch fleet in the Golfe du Lion. "It is easy to imagine," wrote Cavalier in his memoir, "our joy at this good news, though we only knew the marquis by reputation." Flotard advised the appointment of a chief and let it be understood that Miremont would accept the position to which his rank would give valuable authority. Both the foreign governments and the upper class of the exiled Huguenots would look on the Camisard movement more sympathetically with a Bourbon at its head.

The spy network of the French authorities was extremely well-developed, both at home and abroad; Montrevel was soon informed of the arrival of this emissary though he could not identify him. "He is a man of about fifty held in great respect by the rebels, very cold and communicating hardly at all." Flotard assured the leaders that Queen Anne took a personal interest in their fate and was determined to help them. However, as would be often repeated, the promised help was slow in coming or came not at all though it left the Camisards "attached henceforth to the marquis de Miremont who was never seen: the phantom prince ... the Protestant Bourbon who was to restore the destroyed *temples*."[6] Cavalier, the most realistic, wrote that the promise of help "did us great harm because at the moment when we were beginning to win against our enemies we waited, and gave them time to take measures to stop us..." But, as later events showed, Rolland was more credulous and more attached to the same chimerical belief in foreign help as that which always convinced and troubled Basville. Perhaps both—the smallholder from Mialet and the son of the *premier president* of the Paris *parlement*—were overly impressed by the titles and antecedents of Miremont who was, however, to prove incapable of translating these advantages into action.

On 6 August, on the banks of the Gardon, a priest rashly visiting his parishioners was captured by a Camisard band and murdered: "They began," alleged the cloistered Soeur de Mérez whose accounts were necessarily second-hand, "by tearing out his teeth and then his tongue." Bosc pointed out the great disparity between the written accounts, official or hearsay, of the Camisard atrocities, and the much scarcer and more lenient records of those they and their families suffered. He recalled again that the violence of the Camisards answered an anterior and continuing violence against them. Soeur de Mérez, who reported the construction of a new scaffold on the Place du Marché at the foot of the cathedral in Nîmes on which several victims at a time could be broken on wheels, and the addition of multiple gibbets for a faster turnover in hangings, was a source for this too: "Some speak before dying; they are all tortured but most say nothing ... those who abjure do so to ease their suffering but all the ease they are given is to tighten the knot that strangles them." Non-abjurers could be taken off the wheel, broken but still alive, and left shackled beside it while others took their place, and all wait until nightfall for the executioner, his day's work done, to finish them off.

The only result, other than the horror gradually spreading through Europe from reports of the savagery at civilization's centre, was the redoubling of reprisals in Catholic farms, churches and villages of the Cévennes and in the plain. By 30 August an estimate of the destructions by Camisards put the number of houses at six hundred (a fraction of those soon to be destroyed on the king's order), and two hundred and fifty of churches. "For murders, the number is so great that an exact account could not be taken ... but they have massacred entire villages regardless of age, sex or condition, and as for soldiers, they have killed almost as many as have been killed of their own."[7] Soeur de Mérez understood well that the Camisards at this time were masters of the countryside and with two or three thousand men could dominate the military whose numbers would soon reach twenty five thousand soldiers. Cavalier was known to issue orders to local owners including Madame de Lussan to plough, harrow or sow on land neglected due to fear of the insurgency. The sole solution urged on the court by bishops, officials and officers was to suppress the population, presumably by execution or deportation, or ruin the countryside to starve the Camisards out.[8]

On 5 September Cavalier returned to Ribaute with an escort, murdered in passing three Catholic masons against whom he had a grievance, and went to the family home where his mother was dying. Immediately after her death Montrevel arrested Cavalier's father and brother, who had never supported the Camisard cause but quietly continued cultivating their land. Cavalier wrote to the marshal ordering him to release his father and brother or if not he would come with ten thousand men and burn Alais to the ground, though he was "not sorry to see them arrested since they had never wished to follow the inspiration of the Spirit". Montrevel, outraged by the insolence of this letter, at once had the Cavalier house at Ribaute razed (it was later rebuilt, but Cavalier's father and brother went into exile in Switzerland).

The month of September 1703 saw a drastic development of the conflict leading to destruction of part of the kingdom of France on the king's own order. By this time the number of troops in the Languedoc had risen to twenty five thousand, well-armed, commanded by a marshal of France with a staff of experienced officers but unable to crush an army of exasperated peasants advancing from one offensive to another and spreading terror as they went, their makeshift armaments contrasted with the equipment of the soldiers. On 7 September near Alais Cavalier with some of his men discovered in an isolated building used for the production of vitriol a number of lead cauldrons each weighing three hundred pounds. Too heavy to carry away, they were cut into strips and taken the same night to the caves at Euzet to be made into shot: "they were a lead-mine for us and for Rolland for a long time," Cavalier wrote, showing that Rolland relied on him for his ingenuity.

But the chief weapon of the Camisards was the unfailing supply of recruits, driven by despair and crossing the forests to join their fellows attacking the common enemy. The most vociferous advocates of extreme measures against these vengeance seekers were, naturally, the bishops and their clergy. "The rebels are masters of the countryside," wrote Bishop Fléchier, "the court has been too slow in making up its mind to ... punishments more extreme than those which have been rejected as too cruel." Julien expressed the general sense of adamant authority succinctly: "Not a single one of these vermin should be left alive if we wish to cut the evil at the root ... I would send them all to the Indies, males to one island, females to another..." Basville had for some time urged extreme measures against the population of the highland although for many months Cavalier's troops had been far more active in the plain than were those in the mountain, and had inflicted far more damage. The intendant's well evidenced belief was that it was from the mountains that the rebels in the plain obtained their sustenance; therefore his plan, at first rejected by the king, was for the devastation of the Cévennes, with demolition of four hundred and sixty-six villages or hamlets and the deporting of a population of thirteen thousand from three hundred and thirty-one parishes, a "*Saint-Barthélemy des maisons*" in Michelet's phrase, to transform this region into a desert where the Camisards would die of cold or hunger. Chamillart wrote that "although I am not cruel by nature, it seems to me that on occasion one must strip oneself of all humanity..."[9] Authorization for this *grand ouvrage* reached Basville by express on 16 September, with the king's single approving word, *bon*, in pencil on the margin of the page. The work was assigned to Julien, its most forceful military advocate filled with unforgiving resentment against his former co-religionists. He set to work on 29 September with a thousand militiamen and two hundred *miquelets* as bodyguards. Very soon the militiamen tired of the exhausting work of demolition of stone houses and vaulted roofs with picks and axes, and began to desert as the weather turned cold.

Julien demanded, and on 12 October obtained permission to use the more quickly effective means of fire. "Soon," wrote the Catholic historian Jean-Baptiste Louvreleul, "groups of houses, remote farms, barns, cottages, every building fell to the fire set by Catholic troops like wild flowers, weeds, and wild roots fall under the blade." The immediate consequences were not those envisaged by the intendant: "Every night the progress of the burning could be followed from the plain; in village after village from the Mont Lozère to the valleys the thatch flamed, the barns, the sheds, the sheepfolds. Beams fell ... but the walls remained up and the vaults intact ... the peasants, far from joining the convoys arranged by Basville, hid themselves in woods, rocks and caves ... and all the young people, left to the devil, went to join the Camisards." Patrick Cabanel in his monumental *Histoire des protestants en France* pointed to the futility of the cévenol burning since the theatre of war had almost entirely removed to the plain; and emphasized the modernity of this large-scale destruction designed to punish the region where the hostilities began. "It witnesses the cruelty of the state against part of its own population."

Reprisal

Eight days before the king's authorization was received the bishops made the details of Basville's project known; and during the last three weeks of September Cavalier, with the intention of keeping as many of the royal troops as possible in the plain, led a campaign of preventive reprisals, often of extreme violence, in the Vaunage and the vicinity of Nîmes itself in spite of Basville's repeated threats to punish the inhabitants of the nearest villages without trial. Cavalier, according to his memoir, sent a warning to Montrevel that for every village burned by the soldiers he would burn two, and the massacres that followed the carrying out of this threat spread panic in the plain where the army was either inactive, impotent or absent. "These execrable monsters," wrote Montrevel to the minister on 22 September after a massacre at Saturargues between Montpellier and Nîmes, "only stay half an hour to carry out their horrible executions and then retire so promptly that it is impossible to find them". The following day, one of the suspected men was arrested with his thirteen-year-old son; the father was burnt alive and the boy hanged three weeks later. In the Vaunage bloody attacks were made on the villages of Aigues-Vives, Bernis, Gallargues,

Aubord, Boisseron, and in the vicinity of Alais. A Catholic witness reported that Cavalier was venerated by his men and that he had recognized him by his costume of iron grey overcoat, black jacket and a large black band in his hat worn as mourning for his mother who died on 5 or 6 September. Catinat, meanwhile, made an excursion into the Camargue, came away with between sixty and eighty horses and left a trail of violence behind him including the murder of the Grand Prior of the Order of Malta, possessor of a domain near to Saint-Gilles set alight by the Catinat troop. Between Nîmes and Uzès in the last days of the month the pace of the incendiary work accelerated so that at night from the walls of either town the populations watched the sky reddened with flames. Soeur de Mérez described the growing fury of Catholics against Huguenots making themselves masters of the burning landscape: "They could destroy one another ... One can hardly believe this in the reign of Louis the Great."

Montrevel, impotent to prevent the ravages, continued destroying suspect villages and farms for each of which there were the promised reprisals, until it was feared that Nîmes itself was directly threatened and Fléchier asked that the garrison be redoubled. At night, the streets were patrolled every quarter of an hour by groups of officials and citizen guards. But in the mountains, the activity, or lack of it, of Rolland at this time puzzled the military authorities and has never been elucidated by historians. On 22 September he and his group broke into a château in the Cévennes, drank all the wine they could find, smashed the furniture and disappeared into the forest they had come from. Julien expected an attack from day to day but nothing happened. "They are ... only capable of fires and massacres where there is no resistance and are very careful not to approach me," he wrote to Chamillart, and this assertion was to be repeated from both sides a month later with reproaches aimed at the mountain Camisards by village representatives and ruined families whose houses, with their contents, food stores, animals, fields and implements had been destroyed village by village, farm by farm, while the Camisard groups of Rolland and other mountain leaders seemed to stand passively by.

In a history charged with so many elements of dramatic tragedy, not the least was the sighting, early in September, of an Anglo-Dutch fleet of fifty to sixty vessels, mostly warships of sixty to seventy guns, entering the Mediterranean. The fleet transported, according to the information received by the French authorities, two and a half thousand soldiers of whom the Dutch were better disciplined than the English. Two ships, the *Pembroke* and the *Tartar*, were detached from the main fleet to reconnoitre the French coast at Agde and Sète. The men on board suffered an epidemic which in three weeks caused the burial at sea of twenty-three of them. On the 28th the two ships were visible from Montpellier in the offing from Sète, and it was rightly supposed that they brought men, money and equipment to the aid of the Camisards. Advancing cautiously through the water, and at one moment pursued by galleys, they took depth soundings as they approached the coastline, then hove to in sight of Maguelone and the line of hills beyond Montpellier where it was expected that the Camisard troops would be awaiting their signal. At midnight the captain of the *Pembroke* had a bright fire lit on the bridge of the ship; there was no answering signal from Maguelone or the Pic Saint-Loup at the south-eastern extremity of the cévenol heights. Four launches were put to sea to row to the coast and repeat the signal, but with the same result: "no fire, no kind of sign answered them," said Bosc. In the night the Mistral wind got up, blowing strongly from the north, and the fleet was driven out to sea where it remained until a landfall on the sheltered Italian coast became possible at Livorno (Leghorn) on 5 October.

In examining this missed opportunity the question usually asked is not, where was Rolland, but where was Cavalier? The assumption of historians and chroniclers was that a response to the ships' signals could only come from the effective leader. Cavalier, in fact, was leading his men in lightning attacks on churches across the villages of the plain and had sent Catinat with his cavalry toward the sea where he might have joined the disembarked Allied infantry. The conclusion drawn by Bosc was that the Camisard leaders were not aware in time of the proposed landing, and that Marion, who was the best informed thanks to his interception of a letter addressed to the marshal, failed for unknown reasons to pass on the knowledge of a rescue operation whose results could have changed the course of the revolt. "His apparently passive attitude," said Bosc, "makes his conduct strange, not to say inexplicable ... was he blamed for it later?"

And it could also be asked whether this blame, if it was laid, could account for Marion's bitter antipathy toward Cavalier in their London encounters. Marion's account of the episode was brief and could seem disingenuous: "Towards the end of August Rolland told me ... that Flotard had said that the English and Dutch fleet would sail into the golfe du Lion and make such and such signals, that if we were able to come down to the coast we should be given arms, ammunition etc. But the enemy had already taken measures to prevent us. About three months later only two ships came ... and made signals as Flotard had said." It is evident that Rolland would never venture so far from his native hills where he knew every path and gully; Flotard had relied on the wrong man and Marion seems to have been responsible for Cavalier's not being informed in time to meet the men from the sea.

Although the history of the Camisards has since been carried around the world by the Huguenot diaspora, at the time of the uprising and for differing reasons it never succeeded in passing the local boundaries of its origin. The Allies, though interested in the possibility of striking at France from within, and occasionally capable of some more or less bungled initiative, at no moment formed a concerted plan to engage. Even the funds they sent from time to time came in amounts too frugal and too arbitrarily distributed to make any impact. The Camisard groups themselves generally limited their action to the terrain where their separate leaders felt most at home; only Cavalier's aborted move into the Vivarais, which he never repeated, was an attempt to break out.

A second chance presented itself, in another direction, in mid-September. In the Rouergue to the west of the Cévennes there was a strong new converted presence and it was thought possible that some of these former Protestants might join the Camisard troops. Cavalier, after some hesitation, sent Catinat with four others into the diocese of Castres on reconnaissance, and to make contact with a nobleman of the region, the abbé La Bourlie, marquis de Guiscard, known for inflammatory political views fed by a personal hatred of Louis XIV and thought to be preparing an insurrection, political rather than religious since La Bourlie was Catholic, which could make common cause with the Camisards. On both sides there was naivety and lack of the strategic caution which Cavalier's presence would have supplied. Catinat, intemperate and indiscreet, was not the best choice for the mission. He succeeded in enrolling a number of recruits but far from reconnoitring, he set about burning churches, attacking Catholics and advancing on the city of Castres where panic took hold, houses were barricaded and the bishop believed excited reports of a plan to kidnap him. The militia were called out in great numbers from nearby towns, the forests were scoured and some of the band captured so that Catinat with the rest was forced to retreat into the Cévennes.

The attempt to raise the Rouergue was quickly over, and as the captured men, under torture, might give his name, La Bourlie prudently reached the Swiss frontier and crossed it, continuing his political activities on the other side. Bosc judged that the political ideas of this erratic nobleman ecclesiastic were forerunners of those that inspired the Revolution eighty-five years later. "His misfortune," wrote Michelet with a familiar tendency to export blame, "was to be too far ahead of his time and badly supported by Holland and England."

In October the duke of Savoy, Victor-Amédée II, changed sides in the war and joined the Allies against France. The territory of Savoy adjoined the Dauphiné and it was hoped, not least by Miremont, that this would make a penetration into France and the Languedoc more feasible, and also bring support to the insurrectionists. A good number of Huguenot refugees in Holland joined the Savoyard army in a regiment composed solely of Frenchmen. At the same time the Camisards of Cavalier increased their activity in the country round Nîmes as their numbers and experience grew. "We expected that during your expedition in the mountains the rebels would fall on us," Fléchier wrote to the marshal, "but we didn't imagine they would come here and burn churches and domains and villages under our very eyes." On 2 October Cavalier attacked the important town of Sommières and held the outskirts for several days though fired on by cannon from the tower at the top of the town. On the 8th, Cavalier and his troop approached Saint-Ambroix, some eighty-three kilometres away, where they also attacked the outskirts, churches and presbyteries.

Montrevel remained in Alais with a strong bodyguard of gentlemen and Irish officers known as the "noble brigade", and left the Camisards free to come and go at will, pillaging and burning with impunity. Paradoxically, and as though to demonstrate their failure to understand the strategic realities of the uprising, it was at this moment that the Allies began to reduce the modest financial help they sent, and by the end of the year there was left only a superficial effort in favour of the Camisards and their cause.[10] On 26 October at Lussan in the region of Uzès Cavalier provoked an encounter with a force the most aggressive of whom were Irishmen. He claimed in his memoir that this battle, not one of the more significant of the uprising, ended in victory for the Camisards and humiliation for the army; the Catholic version was the opposite. Bosc concluded that there were neither winners nor losers except those, uncertain in number, who died on the field. The Irish attacked a defended bridge leading to the village while the inhabitants joined in the fight from the safety of the walls by firing on the Camisards; for two days afterwards bodies of the dead and wounded were still found in the woods and approaching roads and though there is no agreement about casualties it is not contested that the cavalry of Catinat lost most of their horses.

The battle of Lussan was perhaps representative of a great number of such combats in the plain, with its violence, loss of life, bravado and inconclusiveness. Even Cavalier's major successes, which astonished Basville and the army, could in any case lead to no conclusion; guerrilla warfare can only result in the political or ideological changes the partisans seek when help comes from outside and the balance of force changes. Michelet was right in thinking that the English and Dutch failed the Huguenots, despite all expressions of sympathy for co-religionists and the oppressed, by their inaction and lack of will in face of the immensely complex and dangerous enterprise of invading a province of France.

From 25 to 29 October there were continual massacres in the vicinity of Nîmes and the Vaunage, but such operations needed no special supply of powder and were carried out by small bands of men. Cavalier after the losses of Lussan lay low in the woods of the Mont Bouquet while reconstituting his supply of both; recruits came easily but powder had to be either captured or created. One of Cavalier's exploits was its manufacture in the darkness of caves which he described in terms that easily could, and did, irritate the envious:

> When I was searching into the Cavernes of the Mountains, I discovered at the bottom of one of them a kind of a Natural Stone, which being a little cut and filed, was able to bear up a Kettle, and leave under it room enough to make a Fire sufficient to boil the Salt-peter. I made a trial of the Thing, which succeeded so well, that I used it as a Pattern for making of more in two other Cavernes ... There were by good Luck, at that Time two Gun-powder Makers amongst us ... and they, together with some Soldiers went into all the old Vaults, Cellers and other Subterranean Places round about us, gathered all the Salt Peter they met with, and boyled it in kettles ... We got Mortars, wherein the Soldiers by turns, beat the Powder with Pestles ... the Gun-powder being well beaten, was ... spread over Floors and Areas made for that purpose, upon the Top of Rocky and high Mountains, and soon dried up, the Sun shining perpendicularly upon it...

Roland was also running short of powder and shot and sent a messenger down into the woods of Bouquet urging Cavalier to join him in the highlands where the cévenol inhabitants were in despair as Julien's work of destruction continued unchecked night and day at a growing pace. Cavalier reached Saint-Bonnet where Rolland was encamped in the first days of November. It had been reported to Julien that almost the entire population of the Lozère driven from their homes were still in hiding in the mountains. The assembled leaders, including Couderc, Jouani and Castanet, attended a gathering of three thousand in the Vallée Française at which they were bitterly reproached for their passivity in face of the campaign of burning, some of the inhabitants even threatening to join the army and act as guides if within four days the Camisards failed to attack the forces of destruction. Cavalier who on his way into the mountains had demolished the château de Mandajors wrote later that on his arrival he found Rolland demoralized and in "great consternation" because the burnings by Julien deprived his troop of provisions. Cavalier favoured an immediate attack as demanded by the assembly but Rolland hesitated, believing, said Bosc, that any attempt was bound to fail, though he reluctantly gave way on Cavalier's insistence.[11]

For several days the combined force searched the region of the Vallée Française in bad weather hoping to lure Julien into confrontation until

Cavalier, who received messages of increasing assaults by well-armed Catholic militias, taking advantage of his absence, on the new converted in the plain decided to return. The passivity now and later of Rolland is among the great enigmas of the uprising, its corollary being the largely unexplained posthumous devotion to him of the Huguenot historians and their followers to the present day. After Cavalier's departure, Rolland kept his distance from the scenes of burning and made no intervention, preferring "according to his usual practice", said Bosc, to attack convoys, set ambushes and capture Catholics rather than go into battle with an enemy he was wary of. "Should he be accused of cowardice," asked Bosc, "for not coming to the aid of his fellows and attempting to stop the fires that were destroying their native land ... did the anguished supplication of a ruined people not touch him?" The answer he gives to these questions comes, like a number of vindications, from Marion and goes to the centre of the Camisard mystique without elucidating it:

> We were about six hundred men very resolute to attack the enemy ... the flames of our houses, and of our brothers', augmented the ardour of the impatience we felt to fall on the wretched incendiaries, but I was much surprised to hear from my own mouth an opposite warning ... that it was in vain that we try to prevent the fires ... since God had so decreed it.

"Inspiration" was considered decisive and beyond discussion and Rolland was, said Bosc, perhaps more sensitive than the other leaders to prophetic warnings. Between 9 and 15 November he and his force of six to nine hundred had three times avoided confronting Julien due to contrary inspirations, and then disappeared out of reach into the forests. On the first of these occasions they limited their action to the capture and driving off of a herd of seventy cattle belonging to the dispossessed peasants of the hills. On 24 November Julien completed the burnings around Sainte-Croix-Vallée-Française, his troops working in two parallel converging valleys while the Camisards watched from the heights above. When he reached Sainte-Croix Julien noted that in their recent passage they had wholeheartedly (*à coeur joie*) absorbed a large quantity of wine, there being a good stock of it in the town. The ambiguity of Rolland's record is emphasized by the ideas of grandeur that rumour attributed to him, exaggerating the importance of his role. Bosc adjusts the balance: "Despite the high-flown titles he liked to adorn himself with—'commander of the Cévenol troops in the Languedoc, general of the Protestant forces in France'—his authority never extended to other troops of Camisards than his own," and he points out that decisions taken by the Camisard council of war were signed by all the leaders equally. It would appear that Rolland to some extent toyed with fantasies of priority that he never attempted to assert until much later when he resisted Cavalier's moves toward peace.

Down in the plain the activities of the militia alarmed even the marshal who had encouraged and aided their formation, in some cases into uncontrolled bands of fifteen hundred men inflamed with hatred and avarice. "I am frightened to death," the marshal wrote to Chamillart on 12 November, "that in the end the old Catholics and the new converted will be equally in revolt." "It is already civil war," added Soeur de Mérez. Montrevel further claimed that the priests and their powerful bishops were at the bottom of the violence by exciting the *Camisards blancs* and silently approving the results. In the Cévennes it was the *curé* of one of the highland parishes who organized and led a band of seven hundred that devastated villages and farms so far untouched by the military burnings, and murdered any inhabitant believed to belong to the new converted. Rape, as in most fields of war, was routine and went unpunished.

The flamboyant but ineffectual Montrevel felt himself submerged by the movement he had at first encouraged. "So now, there we see two different kinds of Camisards, equally deplorable," he lamented to Chamillart from the comfort of Alais. But Chamillart, like Basville in Montpellier and several senior officers in the Cévennes, was wearying of the marshal's explanations of failure, as the sight of his magnificent regalia now wearied the provincial society whose lands, and revenues, were sacked by civil war. On 11 November Cavalier called an assembly near to Nages and its "sacred hill" which was attended by a thousand people come to hear him preach. The governor of Nîmes rashly sent out his garrison of a hundred and thirty, later reinforced by dragoons, to make arrests. Cavalier placed the assembled women and children behind his troop and stationed a detachment of men in the village below to lure in the soldiers who would then be encircled. Before the battle, Cavalier, returning alone from a reconnaissance along a hidden track, found himself face to face with an officer and two dragoons. Though for a moment he thought himself lost, he killed all three.

In the ensuing battle the royal troops were driven off despite the arrival of reinforcements from Sommières, and the Camisards withdrew from an exposed position, taking the women, the children, and the aged with them into the great bois de Lens which stretches from the Vaunage to near the foothills. Each side, as usual, exaggerated the number of their adversaries and minimized that of their losses. Bosc stated that once again there was neither vanquished nor victor, but Soeur de Mérez admitted, "we could win no advantage over the Camisards". And accounts agree that many of the protected women showed themselves as fierce as the men or more so at their first battle experience, leaping on the wounded with cries of "long live the sword of Gideon" so that, according to Cavalier, their enemies claimed "there were Men amongst us disguised in Women's Apparel, which fought like Devils".

On 23 November, Cavalier was at Vergèze between Nîmes and the sea where he held an assembly and council of war. The governor of Nîmes, informed of the presence of Cavalier with a cavalry detachment inside the encircling walls of Vergèze by an agent of the spying priest Terrien of the Vaunage, an ambiguous figure trusted apparently by Cavalier but who for long succeeded in keeping the authorities informed of his movements, ordered out a hundred and forty dragoons and two hundred foot soldiers towards Vergèze. By the time Cavalier's sentinels gave the alert it was too late to retire from the village with the cavalrymen and join the main body of the troop concealed in dense olive groves around. Cavalier gave the order to charge at a gallop down the long main street and force an exit against the dragoons through the single arched gateway that had not been walled up. The intrepidity and success of this movement headed by himself cost an uncertain number of losses on both sides, and Cavalier, heavily outnumbered, retired into the woods with his men while the soldiers, rather than pursue them, pillaged the town and executed a number of randomly chosen inhabitants whose belongings were later seen by Soeur de Mérez on offer for sale in the Nîmes market.

In a regional atmosphere of apparently universal mistrust, hatred and terror an isolated incident—which may seem, as the only recorded example to throw a more sympathetic light on the dark historical reality about it, more isolated than in fact it was—occurred between 22 and 25 November near to Lussan. A young married woman, Madame de Mirmand, issue of a distinguished family of the Languedoc nobility, set out from Uzès with an unarmed escort, contrary to the advice of friends and family, to join her husband at Saint-Ambroix. Although Catholic, she was known for benevolence toward the new converted and evidently felt no distrust of the people of a district where her family held an old respected position. Conscious of her own goodwill, she thought herself safe but was stopped in the wood near Lussan and killed with her female companion and the escort. A sense of outrage quickly spread through the region and reached Cavalier, who with his troop was encamped near Uzès. He immediately determined to find and punish those responsible, whom he, like others, believed to be irregulars of the Camisard movement not subject to group discipline, and he was soon given their identity by local inhabitants equally indignant. Brought before him, the three men were condemned and summarily executed. "If I had but one of them Hangmen, who were in great Numbers with Intendant Basville, I would have made them suffer a more cruel Death than that of being shot," he later wrote.

Jeanne de Mirmand was not the first case of a woman fatally attacked and the reaction to it, both of the Camisards and the people, is enlightening. "She belonged to one of the leading families of the Languedoc," wrote Marcel Pin, "and even if the nobility had almost no effective power any longer, it kept its prestige ... all the new converted condemned the murder ... which could have decided some of them to change their attitude [to the uprising]. Hence Cavalier's sentencing of the murderers." But he added to this somewhat deprecatory analysis the reminder that Jeanne de Mirmand was a believing Catholic though tolerant, and that the Camisards always spared Catholic gentry who had not openly taken part against them. The argument strengthens the theory that for these people, at that time, the uprising would have been sooner over and with less torture, execution, destruction and massacre had the respected local hierarchy with interests in the region been allowed a hand in dealing with it. An entire population of one of the humblest countrysides of France need not have been reduced to the homeless, starving indigence forced on it by the civil service and the military, with the royal approval pencilled on a note among the reflections of Versailles.

"Finy"

The commander of a regiment in the Cévennes during the burning, Colonel de Marcilly, was critical of the policy as being against the king's interests and likely to lead to civil war. He urged that the destruction proposed and enforced by Basville of thirty-one parishes, which Montrevel himself referred to as both "frightful" and useless, be halted. The relations between Basville and Montrevel deteriorated as this disagreement hardened, and the marshal admitted his impotence in countering the Camisards who had an "extreme superiority".[12] But Julien was not to be stopped by the misgivings of a general whose inertia he had come to despise. In continual cévenol downpours since 30 November, turning roads and fields to mud, he completed the destruction of the last communities of Saint-Germain-de-Calberte and Saint-Etienne-Vallée-Française where many inhabitants still waited in hope of reprieve. On 14 December the weather turned fine and Julien wrote to the minister to announce that he had entirely finished the long and painful mission entrusted to him, ending his despatch with the single word, *Finy*.

He wrote contemptuously of the mountain Camisards under Rolland who had never during two months attempted to stop the devastation: "I can say that these rebels are really cowardly to have seen so much of the country burned under their noses ... without daring to show themselves and oppose it." It was reported that some of the dispossessed still found about their former homes were arrested, the men executed on the spot and the women whipped. Monahan suggests the possibility that "the intendant known for his ferocity simply had no stomach for the torture and execution of women."[13] Basville, who had found in Julien the ideal executant of his will, wrote to him, "You have certainly carried out one of the hardest tasks a man could undertake and have perfectly succeeded." Yet this "scorched earth" was at the heart of the kingdom and its ruined inhabitants were subjects of the king; and Bosc recalls that in spite of all evidence to the contrary the king was believed sensitive to the sufferings even of those of his people declared heretic. Ruins are still visible in remote places of the Cévennes, giving body to Bosc's lament: "This land systematically burned and ravaged, without a single house left intact, where a few frightened inhabitants wandered among the ruins like hunted animals in an atmosphere stinking from the acrid smoke of the fires..." And both Colonel de Marcilly and Soeur de Mérez were quick to realize that, as he put it, "the first effect of this razing to the ground is to produce four thousand more rebels."

With the burning of the Cévennes completed, Cavalier's operations in the plain were continued for their own sake, part of a war which was seen, with all its frequent brutality, as holy and in need of no justification. There is also a sense appearing from the pace and audacity of his activity that he was by now regarding himself as a professional soldier whose calling was the training and command of men in battle. The "baker's boy" had found his metier in the excitement of action and there could be no return to the life of his father's fields. A Catholic carter who had seen army service was captured and later released by Cavalier's troop; he described his observation of the men, of the leader's habit of life and his appearance. The troop was composed of two hundred horseman, eighteen hundred foot soldiers and thirty mules for the transport of baggage. Cavalier dined at a table with one of his officers and was served by a cook and valet; he was neatly dressed in a coat of Holland with silver buttons and in chamois breeches adorned with silver braid. His sword was of rich workmanship. If Rolland in the mystery of his mountain forests had fantasies of noble titles, Cavalier evidently cultivated a more worldly reality equally remote from his origins. Wherever he passed from one encounter to another a summary martial law was applied, with executions of traitors and informers and sometimes more indiscriminate massacres, but at this stage the purpose was less the destruction of religious buildings than seeking occasions of battle. He carried off victories at Aubais in the Vaunage, at Tornac near Anduze in the battle of the Madeleine at a site once again sanctified by a victory of the Resistance over the retreating German army in 1944, and at Corbès in the foothills with many of his new recruits armed only with slings and stones. With his fast-moving troop he was so much master of the roads between Nîmes and Montpellier and the cévenol fringe that the post to Paris could only travel with a powerful escort and no individual without Huguenot credentials was safe. To make matters worse, the *Camisards blancs* took advantage of the disorders to pillage, steal and murder without fear. Montrevel was now criticized on all sides, as Marcel Pin summed up: "Unintelligent and pretentious, the marshal lacked the two qualities of his unfortunate predecessor, courage, and activity." Bosc was still more scathing: "If (Montrevel) avoided the Camisards because instinctively he feared them, as a great lord he looked down from the height of his self-conceit on this peasant rabble that dared to measure itself against a Marshal of France." In the shadows, Basville awaited one last ineptitude of the marshal that could be his downfall.

Julien's claim that the work was *finy* proved delusory in face of the pitiful determination of the Cévenols to return to their native surroundings under the protection of Camisard groups in the locality, hoping to recover something of what they had left behind, feeding themselves with chestnuts and sheltering under blackened, roofless walls. A second operation of radical purging of the villages and farms of parishes adjacent to those destroyed by Julien was set on foot in order to starve out the Camisard groups in the hills, under the command of an officer who was to prove as ruthless and apparently fired by hatred of the Huguenots as he had been. This was brigadier Planque, born, said Cavalier, in Montpellier of good family but a bigoted papist who "put every Protestant to the Sword he met, tho' there was no Resistance ... without sparing Women or Children ... this brave Champion used all his endeavours, not to meet with us, and like Don Quixote, took often the wandring Clouds, for Troops of Camisards who fled from him." On 12 January 1704 at Saint-André-de-Valborgne in the process of "visiting parishes in detail", five hundred starving inhabitants were herded into the church; thirty chosen at random were taken out and executed as they left the building. The bodies of the rest were thrown, living or dead, into the icy water of the Gardon, carried downstream, and fired on from the bank by the soldiers. Survivors of this and other villages were ordered down into the defended towns of the foothills while the army proceeded to devastate farms and hamlets, demolish ovens and mills, find and scatter the stores of wheat, wine, and other supplies that either the returning populace or the Camisards might survive on. Antoine Court claimed that Planque killed more than six hundred people in the course of his progress through the still inhabited zone, walling up doors and windows and the entrance to caves.

On 18 January Rolland set a successful ambush at Pont-de-Vallongue and killed a number of soldiers before withdrawing into the forest, but otherwise the army and the brigadier were left to carry on their work untroubled. Chamillart, who by now held a low opinion of Montrevel's performance in a backwater post far beneath his prestige as marshal of France, asked Julien for advice. Julien gave it with *une extrème joie*. The sole solution to his mind was a complete, systematic depopulation of the entire Cévennes, leaving only Catholics in occupation; the others should be allowed to die at sea. Julien's opinion never varied and he held to it firmly. The history of the uprising in the Cévennes is often a stark demonstration of the workings of the military mind, obtuse, inflexible, and angry. The character of the commanding general who helped bring it to an end, de Villars, was more that of a diplomat than a soldier though his reward was promotion to the ultimate rank of marshal of France.

Julien, as if to offer further proof of the army mentality, on 13 January invested the fortified hill town of Lussan which he regarded as a stronghold occupying a central position of the first importance in the region of Uzès, and whose inhabitants he mistrusted. On arrival with three hundred foot soldiers and seventy dragoons he had the gates closed and assembled young and old in the courtyard of the château, arrested forty-six young men of the village and sent them under guard to Nîmes. He destroyed the mills, bread ovens and food stores before moving on to the surrounding villages where by this time he found only children and old people. Wherever he went, he was told that the men were away in the fields and distant pastures, but by the rigour of his methods he left terror behind him to cut the Camisards of Cavalier from their base of supply. An unintended result naturally was that the houses and farms of Catholics were left as the rebels' only source of provisions, and attacks on them became more frequent, ubiquitous, and repeated.

In mid-February an independent uprising was attempted, and brutally crushed by Julien, in the Vivarais. None of the cévenol leaders or groups were involved and the men of the Vivarais were inexperienced in face of a powerful army commander of large forces and ruthless methods against the civilian population on which any guerrilla band must depend. In analysing the defeat of the Vivarais, Bosc described the cévenol techniques that succeeded best: "They had acquired over time an extraordinary flexibility of movement which could get them under shelter on the least alert. Above all, they knew how to avoid combat when all the conditions for success seemed not present ... the insurgents of the Vivarais ... instead of exhausting the royal troops by snaring them in places difficult of access, breaking them up into small groups and decimating them in ambushes ... preferred to risk fighting on open ground without knowing the strength of the adversary." It is evident that Bosc was describing the methods of Rolland, not of Cavalier; and his analysis raises the question whether, had Cavalier joined forces with Rolland in the hills rather than operate as he did in the plain where eventually the army was bound to crush his relatively modest troop by huge numerical superiority, the uprising might have continued longer and gained more for the cévenol people. However, by 1704 the mountain bands were finding greater and greater difficulty in providing for themselves in a devastated country; the addition to their numbers of Cavalier's eighteen hundred foot soldiers and two hundred horsemen would have led to the rapid break-up of the Camisard army due to starvation and lack of the powder and shot manufactured by Cavalier in the caves of Euzet. The war developed in the only way it could, its end in either amnesty or defeat was ineluctable, and it is to the credit of Cavalier's intelligence that he was the first to realize this.

His most spectacular successes, however, still lay ahead. Meanwhile, in Julien's absence in the Vivarais, Cavalier, in the words of the Catholic historian Louvreleuil, "far from hiding like those of the mountains, carried off terrible strokes of boldness close to Nîmes", attacking villages and executing suspects wherever he went, and sending a message to Montrevel to announce that he would "employ the arms of the Eternal to exterminate Catholics" and burn the mills supplying flour to the city. As the military operations in the Cévennes foothills relentlessly continued, the pace and violence of Cavalier's reprisals grew in proportion. On 28 February the duc d'Uzès was arrested by a Camisard band on his way to Montpellier, and released when his identity was known. Others, less well born, were not so lucky as individual murder turned to massacre. Between 29 February of this leap year and 1 March more than sixty Catholics were massacred at Beaucaire, a hundred and thirty-four in Montrevel's account.

Marcel Pin admits that of the different troops of Camisards, Cavalier's appeared the most cruel since those in the Cévennes worked among a principally Protestant population, whereas in the plain Catholics were the majority. And these terrorized people, with Bishop Fléchier at their head, demanded to know what the army was doing to protect them. Pin gave the answer: the troops of the king excelled at pillage, at the massacre of unarmed country people, the rape of girls ... fighting fanatical partisans who aimed straight was less to their taste. Cavalier, Bosc concluded, decided to neutralize the opposition by terror and succeeded in emptying the countryside as the Cévennes were emptied; by his intelligence of the situation he so imposed on the army as to fix it in place, hidden behind the ramparts of citadels at his approach. The extraordinary result was that the young baker's boy held a marshal of France and his army in check and controlled by his movements, "which cannot be," Basville wrote to Chamillart, "since he is a young man of hardly twenty, son of a peasant."

To soothe their self-esteem the authorities insisted on the occult existence of a directing consistory behind the successes of a troop containing neither gentlemen nor trained officers; this belief endured until well after the last stirrings of the uprising and was never substantiated further than by the advent from time to time of some more or less suspect emissary from London or Amsterdam, intriguing, spying and arbitrarily distributing small amounts of unaccounted money with no credible prospect of more. The ineffectiveness under Montrevel of an army believed by many Catholics to prefer the life of barracks in towns to the dangers of hills, rivers and woods, drove the cadets de la croix to their own vengeances and terrors, justified and encouraged by the Church hierarchy, by Basville and even by the king himself who agreed in principle to the "reprisals" as long as no specific order was given that they be generalized.[14] The reprisals took a horrific turn in villages and towns where the Catholics were in the majority, such as Bagnols-sur-Cèze where on 22 February *cadets* attacked the new converted in a frenzy of murder, mutilation, infanticide and rape of wounded or dying women. On the road between Bagnols and Barjac on the same day a militia group arrested three young cévenol women, raped them, then filled their vaginas with gunpowder and lit it. These men were eventually brought to trial due to the confession of one of them, and Antoine Court, recounting the event, stated that he was given the details by eyewitnesses and inhabitants of Montclus from where the five men came. In the name of religion life and pain were made insignificant as candle flame stifled in sectarian darkness.

For several days at the end of the month both army and Camisards were blocked wherever they found themselves by unprecedented continuous downpours and flooding of the rivers. Montrevel, isolated in Sommières without forage for his horses, believed that the Camisards could be trapped in the nearby Vaunage; nightly ambushes were set on the few open paths into the surrounding hills but once again no Camisards appeared. Cavalier was on higher ground near to the Gardon north of Nîmes; on 8 March he attacked a troop of *cadets* which had occupied and pillaged the village of Garrigues, killing seven of them, pursuing the others to the walled village of Boucoiran and repeating the operation two days later at Saint-Chaptes seven kilometres away. Montrevel, who reached Nîmes as the waters receded, took the decision to attack the Camisards, now localized in the area close to the Gardon and to the fortified villages between Nîmes, Uzès and Alais, with all the troops he could find. On the 13th he received the intelligence that the rebels were at Castelnau-Valence sixteen kilometres from his headquarters at Uzès, and that their numbers were reduced to three hundred and fifty against his five hundred elite men from the marine regiment and a hundred dragoons.

The pugnacious but not highly intelligent colonel de la Jonquière was put in command of this formation which promptly set off in the direction of Castelnau, found that the Camisard force had moved on, and fell back on Moussac where the soldiers spent the night allegedly pillaging and drinking while Cavalier and his troop were at nearby Cruviers-Lascours. On the 14th at dawn, Cavalier resumed his northward march having become prudent enough to avoid direct battle faced by a much larger force; as he wrote in his memoir, "two swords are longer than one". At Cruviers the army executed three women suspected of prophecy, then followed the traces left by the retreating Camisards in the wet ground. At nine o'clock they were sighted close to Martignargues on a small scrub-covered hill; to the military, the terrain was favourable and the moment long awaited of a direct confrontation on open ground with the principal adversary had come. Meanwhile Cavalier, implored by the terrified population of every village he passed to protect them, turned to face la Jonquière and his six hundred well-armed men, first ordering any of his troop unwilling to fight to retire; sixty did so, leaving him with two hundred and ninety whom he exhorted, "Brothers, let us redouble our prayers and arm ourselves with faith, we will be the victors and none of us will lose our life!" He placed his men in the familiar U-shape, cavalry forward and hidden among the trees to the left, sixty foot soldiers lying prone among the gorse bushes to the right and forward also of the main line, with himself in the centre and partly sheltered in a ravine. An officer familiar with Cavalier's tactical method advised caution, but la Jonquière, relying on his far greater numbers, marched directly towards him, the cavalry with drawn sabres preceding the infantry. Cavalier's orders were that no shot be fired until the army was well advanced into the trap and had fired first, then his cavalry, until now invisible, would move forward from the trees and open fire during the three or four minutes of the adversary reloading, at the same moment as the main troop confronting them and the Camisards risen from among the gorse bushes on the right. The result was a hail of shot at short distance under which the dragoons, fired on from several directions, turned their horses uncontrollably and fell back across the lines of men behind them, preventing them in the panic of the onslaught from reloading. The Camisards now charged into their midst and completed the rout. The officers stood firm but their men from élite regiments ran in the direction of the river where those who were not massacred on the bank were drowned in the flood; the officers, mostly noblemen, stood firm and were killed fighting, their bodies stripped of uniforms, their pockets emptied of jewellery and gold coins.

Cavalier appropriated the horse of la Jonquière who was wounded but escaped to Boucoiran, one of the few who succeeded in swimming across the Gardon. A witness reported that the river water, at the weir of Portal, was turned to blood. The estimate of the royal troops killed was three hundred and fifty soldiers and twenty-two officers; of the Camisards, twelve were wounded of whom two later died. Cavalier's prophecy was fulfilled in a victory which some commentators have suggested was at least in part due to the soldiers' drinking of the night before, while others, including the general de La Lande sent by Montrevel to review the site of the battle, concluded it was so complete that only a professional officer with experience of high command in the field and twelve hundred men could possibly have organized it. The Camisards carried off their substantial booty to the caves at Euzet while the inhabitants of Martignargues, Lascours and other villages were driven forth to bury the dead.

The news of this resounding victory against the most highly reputed royal regiments spread terror in the region so that other troops dare not move except in force. At Versailles the systematic denigration of Montrevel by Basville, who was tired of his inactivity and dalliance with provincial women, was finally and decisively capped by reports of this disastrous military humiliation. "His majesty is very angry at this sad event," Chamillart wrote to the marshal who, nevertheless, kept the king's affection; he was transferred to the Guyenne where nothing was happening or would happen to disturb him, and de Villars, diplomatic, intelligent and active was appointed to the Languedoc in his place. Notification of these decisions reached Montrevel on 31 March with the king's reproach that he should have personally confronted the Camisards rather than send la Jonquière, a subordinate officer of whose military career nothing more was heard and who claimed that his orders had been badly executed on the ground, to do the work in his place. The spread of blame was taking its usual downward, diluted course.

The victory of Martignargues was the uprising's culmination and also that of Cavalier's career. The tactic used there was the same as at Lussan, Vagnas and elsewhere and depended to a great extent on the choice of terrain giving a possibility of concealment on the flanks, and on the discipline of the Camisard troops which in turn depended on their conviction that the fight was in the name of God through his prophet. Cavalier's fulfilled promise that no life would be lost among his men added enormously to his prestige and was soon known among the civilian population and in the opposing army. Many historians, including even Bosc, seem to have shared in some degree the disbelief of the authorities that so inexperienced and untrained a leader, from so unprivileged a background, could have carried off such a victory by his own gifts; Marcel Pin, on the contrary, asserted in a balanced judgement that Cavalier owed the success to his merits alone: "He had learned to choose his ground, to hide and protect his men, and to wait for the favourable moment. The day before, faced with adversaries less tired from the night's excesses, his victory might have been less decisive." As it was, he was henceforth regarded by his officers and followers, by the population and the army with a fearful and admiring awe. Villars, when he heard an account of this battle, compared Cavalier to the young Julius Caesar. Level-headed though he was, it would be understandable if this proof of his military gifts gave him, for a time which proved crucial, a potent self-confidence sapping his usual prudence and caution.

Notes

1 Charles-Joseph de La Baume, *Relation historique de la révolte des camisards*: 169
2 Henri Bosc, vol. 1: 716 note 46
3 Ibid: 756-7
4 Archives du Département de l'Hérault: C 186
5 Bosc: vol. 1: 803
6 Agnès de La Gorce, *Camisards et dragons du roi*: 215-16
7 Archives de la Guerre, vol. 1708, folio 77
8 Marcel Pin, *Jean Cavalier*: 249
9 Archives de la Guerre, vol. 1701, A1 folio 41
10 Bosc, vol. 2: 348-9
11 Ibid: 451-2
12 Ibid: 546-7
13 W. Gregory Monahan, "Prophétesses et rebelles", in *Les Camisards et leur mémoire*: 78
14 Archives de la Guerre, vol. 1796, folio 53

de Villars, 'the Child of Fortune': Pierre Imbert Drevet, 1714 (Wikimedia Commons)

Chapter Seven
Louis-Hector de Villars

Nages

The resilience of Camisard foot troops covering distances of two or three days' ride in their worn-out boots, after bloody battles and permanent alerts, created scenarios sometimes hard to credit. From Martignargues Cavalier's men passed through the woods to Euzet where they deposited in the caves an arsenal of captured weapons, guns, swords, pistols, bayonets and shot to equip new recruits, and by 20 March were in the Vaunage again, demolishing village fortifications erected by the army, and in the vicinity of Nîmes where a number of Catholics unwise enough to go to their fields were murdered. The Camisards controlled the roads and captured convoys of provisions, money, and post. Commerce in the city was immobilized and the two dragoon regiments stationed nearby were not enough to arrest the movement of Camisard cavalry which was in growing numbers as horses were requisitioned or stolen in the Camargue. During these days, after the victory of Martignargues, young riders from the plain or the mountains had the freedom of the roads and woods and an exhilarating belief, with Cavalier, in their invincibility as long as the word of God was safely delivered to them and faithfully observed. But it was the whispered message of a country priest that was to be their undoing.

The *curé* Terrien of Montpezat in the Vaunage had exchanged letters with Cavalier earlier in the year about the motives of the uprising and its aims. Cavalier apparently trusted him since no attempt was ever made to attack his presbytery, the authorities assumed some confidence existed between them, and a Protestant figure who came to play a significant part in what followed, the baron d'Aigaliers, described him as a "perfectly honest man". He was, however, a spy and informer with a network of spies working for him while he allowed Cavalier, and perhaps others, to believe him disinterested and charitable, a rare Christian free of hatred and opposed to persecution of those who disagreed with him. This mistaken belief was the primary cause of the Camisards' defeat at the battle of Nages.

Contradictory accounts of Cavalier's state of mind in these first weeks of April refer less to the reality, as far as it can be guessed, than to the *parti pris* or bias of the writers and their beliefs. To set against the supposed arrogance and inflated confidence of Cavalier in his favoured arena of the Vaunage, is his cautious placing of twelve hundred men in the bois de Lens adjoining it while he waited to see how the enormous weight of the army outnumbering him would be manoeuvred during the period of transfer of the military command from Montrevel to Villars. But any assumption he may have made of Montrevel's continuing passivity during this period was wrong; the marshal was determined, as his own words afterwards showed, to avenge the humiliations of Martignargues and of his dismissal from the command in Languedoc by a victory of numbers over the peasant troop which had so far eluded him.

On 14 April Terrien informed the marshal of Cavalier's presence in the bois de Lens, and on the night of the 15th that his force would sleep at Caveirac, under cover of old olive groves and vineyards in the centre of the Vaunage plateau. Montrevel publicly announced that he was going to Montpellier to bid farewell to Basville, and that he had ordered the Nîmes garrison eastward to Beaucaire. On the 16th he left Nîmes in the westerly direction of Montpellier with his usual large and visible retinue ensuring that the Camisard scouts would see him pass, then doubled back through the woods to emerge unseen at Calvisson while on his orders the garrisons of Nîmes, Sommières and Lunel, with a regiment of dragoons totalling more than three thousand men, prepared to surround and close the Vaunage plateau and its adjoining woods. Cavalier, splendidly dressed in captured uniform and riding la Jonquière's magnificent horse, perhaps nursed a project of invading Nîmes from Caveirac with his troop of a thousand, now confidently marching in ranks by road from village to village, the men also uniformed and better armed than ever before. Cavalier's imprudence on this fateful day was certainly a result of excessive audacity bred of his spectacular victory at Martignargues, and he has always been blamed by Huguenots for what followed, his character denigrated and his successes, far exceeding those of any other Camisard leader, retrospectively belittled as the action of Rolland was magnified.

After a morning's work of three unsuccessful assaults on the garrison of Caveirac with loss of several men, the Camisards camped on the hill between Boissières and Nages. A siesta was authorized, two sentries posted and Cavalier endeavoured but failed to keep awake. The sentries' vigilance, too, was relaxed and the first dragoons, riding along the crest, came on the Camisards by surprise at one thirty in the afternoon. The Camisards retired in good order in the direction of Boissières where further progress was blocked by the remainder of the dragoons from Nîmes; they then turned about and headed for the "sacred hill" above Nages, site of a prehistoric fortified town and now occupied by Montrevel's forces in hiding among the trees. The Camisards could only take refuge in the village of Nages at the foot of the hill, a trap where they were attacked by the encircling army from every side. "The Mareschal had taken possession of all the Hills and Avenues thereabout ... he having posted a strong Detachment of Dragoons and Grenadiers, at the Foot of those Hills and Roads. After having examined into the Posture of our Enemies, we expected nothing but Death," Cavalier wrote.

A fierce struggle followed in which Cavalier and his companions succeeded in forcing the barrage with heavy losses, only to find other battalions newly arrived and waiting for them. In their struggle to cross the valley and reach the woods where escape lay, Cavalier's infantry was largely destroyed; with his eleven-year-old brother Pierre and the remains of his cavalry he fought his way to the bank of the Rhosny stream which runs in a deep ditch through the centre of the Vaunage, and crossed it within sight of the sheltering bois de Lens where other surviving remnants of the force gathered piecemeal to find one another. The battle raged from one thirty to eight at night when the last Camisards disappeared into the forest with time to distance themselves from their pursuers during the hours of darkness. Some four hundred of his men were killed, according to Cavalier, six hundred in Basville's account. In the words of the Commandant Blachère, "The revolt had suffered irreparable losses in money, arms, ammunition and above all in men formed to combat." De Villars, newly appointed and arrived in the province, said of Cavalier, "This leader acted on this day in a manner that amazed everyone. He comported himself in the most thorny and delicate circumstances as any great general would have done." The last word on the battle of Nages was perhaps that of general de La Lande to the minister: "In the thirty-three years of my service I have seen nothing like this war. These rebels who have become hardened fight desperately like people with no fear of death and who in dying count on being martyrs." Montrevel, his wounded pride somewhat soothed, wrote to the king, "I have the honour to inform your Majesty that I leave to make my way to the Guienne having been happy enough to destroy entirely the troop of Cavalier and Catinat, strengthened by a large part of the youth of the Cévennes ... I succeeded in my plan of surrounding them..."

Cavalier recorded that "I lost in that unfortunate Day more Men than I ever had done at once ... thus Mareschal Montrevel (to make use of his expressions) took leave of his Friends." Cavalier remained hidden in the bois de Lens for two days, attempting to reform the men left to him, and to assess his position. His great advantage had always been to be informed where the enemy was, to elude combat when the odds were against him and fight when they were more even. Now the country was a desert of ruins and corpses and the remaining peasants had turned less welcoming to a revolt that had lasted two years and brought disaster to their livelihood. Deprived of his sources of information, Cavalier felt lost and discouraged: "Our Friend's Love grew cold, and their Purses empty..." With his band of now more or less unarmed men including the wounded, he made his way across country to Euzet and his cave of reserves where a number of others came to join them. On the 19th he wrote to reassure his father and brother who were imprisoned at Alais: "I take up the pen to inform you of my health which is very good thank God as is that of my little brother though we found ourselves in a terrible combat..."

Meanwhile, lieutenant-general de La Lande had been sent into the high Cévennes to hunt down the bands of Rolland and Jouani, reported to be sheltered at Branoux some kilometres into the hills from Alais. When La Lande reached it, Rolland had disappeared, leaving the inhabitants to fend for themselves. The soldiers were let loose and two hundred subjects of the king massacred; systematic pillaging of defenceless villages and executions without process followed, while Rolland, as before, kept out of sight. None of his historic and contemporary admirers have ever attempted an explanation or defence of Rolland's conduct during the destruction of the Cévennes, greatly surprising to adversaries who expected that a band of armed men would make some effort to protect the civilian population, women, children and old people who were often their own families. The conclusion seems to be that the placing of Rolland on a historical pedestal is for other reasons connected, probably, to the notional idealization of martyrdom in a cause which to many Protestants and opponents of social conformity is still alive.

On 19 April La Lande's information led him with two and a half thousand men to Cavalier and his band of two hundred and fifty near Euzet. The Camisards were again heavily defeated but Cavalier escaped to the bois d'Euzet where the narrow opening to his caves, a slit in the rock, was deeply hidden in the evergreen wilderness of oak scrub and limestone outcrops. La Lande, by threats of instant hanging, induced an old woman who was known by her neighbours to take provisions to the cave to disclose its whereabouts. For Cavalier what followed was an even greater disaster than the defeat at Nages. The army destroyed the supplies, the medication and the weapons in the caves and killed the wounded men, perhaps as many as thirty, where they lay in the underground hospital. The most fatal loss, Cavalier claimed, was his "Powder Mills" from which he supplied his own force and Rolland's: "Before, I had always some Shift to set myself up again, but then had none at all." La Lande claimed in a report to Basville to have killed two hundred and sixty rebels, but Julien, strict on detail, put the figure at ten and stated that more than a hundred and fifty were still in the locality.

It has been pointed out that had Cavalier's troop been eliminated by the two battles at Nages and Euzet, as La Lande's figure suggested, there would have been no need for the authorities to negotiate a peace later with its leader, however prominent he had become.[1] On 20 April the triumphant soldiers marched into Alais with the forks, axes and swords captured at Euzet and "carrying gaily, threaded on their bayonets like kidneys on a skewer, their victims' ears".[2] On the same day, twenty-three Camisards for the first time since the start of the revolt surrendered and handed in their arms at Ganges. Although the war continued in increasingly attenuated form, the double defeat suffered by its chief leader marked the end of the uprising's most active period, and the threshold of the phase of negotiation. Realistic about the irreparable character of his losses, Cavalier "had probably reached the critical moment when human reason is given more weight than the divine".[3]

The Child of Fortune

This was Saint-Simon's name for maréchal de Villars, thought by critics of the Duke of Marlborough to be the best general in Europe. Villars' charm and apparent open-mindedness outweighed the faults pinned down by Saint-Simon, arrogance and avidity; his luck was legendary, his father had been a diplomatist and he himself had served on diplomatic missions to Vienna and Munich. On his appointment to the Languedoc he made a careful study of the record of events, held conversations with whoever at Versailles had witnessed them and concluded that the ecclesiastics of the province were ultimately the cause of disorders which only appeasement could bring to an end. On his journey down the Rhône from Lyon to Beaucaire he assured the Protestant baron d'Aigaliers who accompanied him, having been presented by Chamillart as a man knowing the region and its problems, that he would "always have two ears to listen to both parties"; and his last words to the king on leaving Versailles were that he would act in a different manner to that of his predecessors and "try to end the misfortunes by gentleness where severity is not only unnecessary but entirely unsuccessful". Even Basville seemed to believe that Villars might be the "liquidator of the insurrection" though not by Julien's preferred choice of method, expressed to the marshal at their first meeting on the river, of genocidal extermination. Villars listened, said little and disembarked at Beaucaire where the official, military and noble dignitaries lined up to greet him with a copy of the prophecy by Nostradamus that the general who entered the Languedoc at Beaucaire would dispel the insurgents and re-establish calm in the province. "Since the great prophets are for me," Villars wrote to the minister, "I can hope to have the advantage over all the little prophets of the Camisards."

D'Aigaliers was from a new converted family of the old provincial gentry, compelled to live with their Protestant convictions in hypocritical subservience to a Catholic hierarchy with influence at court and who hated them. In his father's lifetime he preferred to go into exile in Geneva but his wife was arrested and imprisoned in a convent. On his father's death he was authorized to return to France and take possession of his inheritance but condemned to live as a Catholic while remaining secretly Huguenot, a compromise that antagonized the Camisards and their prophets. D'Aigaliers, like many others, was convinced that the king was ignorant of the sufferings of his subjects in the Languedoc, and he conceived the project of travelling to Versailles to enlighten and touch the heart of a monarch who, like his minister, was in fact perfectly well informed of them. The baron proposed to Chamillart to enter into contact with the Camisard leaders and negotiate an amnesty followed by the creation of a regiment formed from their number, to be called the régiment Villars with—a vital detail—himself at its head.

The king's reaction to this was mistrustful, and d'Aigaliers was refused an audience but sent back to his native province with Villars who would henceforth oversee his activities, suspect to both government and insurgents. Although a man of religious beliefs for which, in the end, he sacrificed himself, his intervention as a Huguenot nobleman with right of access to both parties was not disinterested and was often disingenuous. In particular his dealings with Jean Cavalier were damaging to Cavalier, to d'Aigaliers himself and to the rump of intransigent Camisards who would never lay down their arms unless the Edict of Nantes was re-established, a totally unrealistic condition. He intervened without the support of any remaining respected feudal structure, and was the only member of the class of *notables*, bourgeois or noble, to attempt an active part in bringing the tragedy to an end. He appeared to both sides, perhaps undeservedly, as less a negotiator of goodwill than a self-serving broker whose delusions of usefulness were the by-product of religious obstinacy and caste presumption. Nevertheless, in the early days of Villars' command, the marshal trusted him enough to keep him nearby and even to speak well of him to the king, who was more inclined to believe him a spy of the new converted than a "zealous and faithful subject".

The personalities of Villars and Basville were in sharp contrast but each was a friend of Madame de Maintenon, and both knew they must cooperate to resolve the crisis in the interest of their careers and standing at court. The marshal wanted a dukedom and an army, the intendant feared the disgrace of failure. Villars' religion was tolerant and relatively enlightened, that of Basville narrow and aggressive; in other words, the degree of religious conviction was high in Basville and modest in Villars who believed in diplomacy, persuasion and flexibility, while Basville's aim was to crush the uprising completely. He disapproved of the marshal's liberal tendencies but was wise enough to collaborate loyally with a commander whose fame and influence were far greater than his. Both were courtiers urbane enough to avoid open rivalry, though the divergence of their views was immediately known and no amount of urbanity would disguise Basville's dislike and distrust of d'Aigaliers, of his presence at the marshal's side, and of all he proposed.

Villars' first gesture, possibly suggested by d'Aigaliers, on his arrival at Nîmes was to order the demolition of the gibbets so plentifully used on the Esplanade under Basville's system of summary justice; his next was to release some of the hundreds of prisoners held in the fort without trial and on no serious charge, while others found more culpable were deported from Arles to the islands of Quebec which few would reach alive. At Sommières on 24 April Villars assembled and addressed the new converted of the district, disavowing the clergy and their excesses and suggesting a less severe policy towards the Huguenots who could, he said, pray to God in their homes in the manner they wished. This was taken by some in his audiences, as he repeated the address in towns around the province, to authorize Protestant services in private houses, a concession to which the king would never agree. But Villars felt he had arrived in the Languedoc at the opportune moment, with the rebellion showing signs of weakening after the catastrophe of Nages; at Sommières he learned that thirty or more Camisards had surrendered their arms, and as the days went by, more and more in small groups across the region submitted to the authorities, hoping for pardon as the marshal promised. "This must be an effect of my sermons," he wrote to the minister. Meanwhile, Cavalier was reported to be in the woods near Anduze with two hundred men, and Rolland with as many in the mountains; by the 27th Cavalier was again in the Vaunage and alarming Bishop Fléchier who wrote from Nîmes that "a great troop of these rebels having been destroyed one thought it to be the end. One was wrong..."

Under the influence of the marshal, nonetheless, a change of attitude to the Camisards began to appear and a way was opened toward the negotiation that Basville had till now always strenuously opposed.[4] On the 23rd Villars wrote to the minister, "Monsieur de Basville is sounding out Cavalier," through the intermediary of a farmer, Lacombe, for whom Cavalier had worked as a boy and who may have been related to him. After a first aborted attempt, Lacombe was sent back by Villars to find out what were Cavalier's conditions for a surrender, and prompted Cavalier to write to the marshal at the end of the month. The letter repeated the same claims as before—freedom of conscience and liberation of prisoners and galley-slaves—but added, for the first time, the suggestion that amnestied Camisards leave the kingdom with the king's permission.

An Oratorian priest at Pézenas, Father Girard, wrote a contemporary chronicle of the last phase of the uprising and said of Cavalier that "he saw himself, with his skill and genius, absolute chief of a large number of rebels. He knew that he was spoken of throughout France ... he could enlarge his troop as much as he wished ... all this engendered in so young a man an extreme pride ... but finally stunned by his recent losses and wearied by all the murders he had bloodied his hands with, he began to show himself more tractable." This is the nearest to an understanding of the state of mind of Cavalier after Nages to be found in contemporary accounts, and those that came later would be more rather than less distorted by preferential bias. But the evidence accumulated by Marcel Pin could argue that Girard was right to suggest a change of mentality or perception in Cavalier, and this would also accord with his apparent understanding of the history and of the histrionic element in his own part in it. Although the vengeful Madame du Noyer asserted that Cavalier had been ordered in trance to lay down his arms,[5] it is probable that by the end of the uprising he no longer received the voice of the Spirit, and to the anger of many former Camisards, notably Marion, he kept silent afterwards about what they saw as an essential feature of Camisard resistance.

Villars attempted by three attacks in different places with two thousand men to dislodge Cavalier and his three hundred, not all armed or trained, from the hills above Euzet and out into the plain, but each time Cavalier mysteriously disappeared. On 9 and 10 May he preached to an assembly of three thousand near Aigremont and the marshal sent detachments from Sommières and Nîmes to encircle the Camisards who again eluded them. Villars grasped the impossibility of crushing the rebels by running after them while search and revolt continued indefinitely, and he decided finally to engage Cavalier directly and if necessary to meet him.

The Labyrinth of Negotiation

The course of negotiations that brought the uprising to a halt, and then carried it into a process of slow local attrition, did not show Cavalier to advantage and his own conduct in them laid him open to accusations of conceit, naivety, ambition, duplicity and self-delusion. Sorrow for the loss of lives including many of those closest to him was perhaps not comforted by the same intense religious fervour felt by many of his companions; he wrote of "the Prisons full of poor Protestants, and the Country reduced to a Desart; all which dreadful Ideas, gave me a great deal of Uneasiness, and the more, that the Succours, which had been promised me for two Years before from England, did not come." The promise of succour, however, still held fast in the mind of Rolland and the difference between them on this point was crucial to their differences on the negotiation and its consequences.

Villars' relative openness to a peaceful process encouraged two prospective negotiators to take the initiative, the ruthless general de La Lande and the baron d'Aigaliers, both of them motivated by hopes of advancement if they succeeded. La Lande overtook the baron by sending a letter to Cavalier inviting him, with guarantees of safe conduct, to a meeting which was agreed for 12 May, on the summit of a hump-backed bridge over a broad stream between Alais and Vézenobres. Cavalier believed La Lande to be an "honest man", and there is no good reason to think him wrong; he brought with him to the meeting Cavalier's young brother Pierre taken prisoner at Euzet and handed him over, also with a letter from their father. The brothers embraced with much emotion. A year earlier, when Montrevel offered an amnesty, the Spirit had advised Cavalier, "My child, I tell you that great propositions will be made to you; don't believe them." This time, he seems not to have consulted the Spirit but trusted himself "entirely in Providence". La Lande asked what were Cavalier's demands and at once made clear that the first of them, freedom of conscience, would never be granted by the king. The second, liberation of prisoners, seems not to have been discussed since it was on the third, permission to leave the country, that attention was focussed.

At La Lande's dictation, Cavalier wrote a letter of submission to the king, to be taken to Villars humbly requesting that he and four hundred followers be permitted to leave the kingdom and that Huguenots who had attended assemblies be pardoned; he added the request that those leaving be allowed to sell their property, and that the same pardon and authorization be given to the troops of Rolland and other leaders. Cavalier claimed to have communicated to the others the terms of this letter but Antoine Court accused him of not doing so; as often in a relatively undocumented history it cannot be known which version is true. As they were separating, La Lande, who was a marquis, made an inept gesture that showed his misunderstanding of the mentality of the rebels he was dealing with; telling Cavalier's men to drink the king's health he tossed onto the ground a purse which split open and threw out a quantity of gold coins. There was a muttering of anger and no one came forward to pick them up. After the general had ridden off Cavalier ordered that the coins be taken to Lacombe and offered to the poor of Vézénobres.

His conversation with La Lande left Cavalier silent and sad, according to his friend and admirer Bonbonnoux: "What were their deliberations? That's what we never thoroughly knew. Cavalier made a mystery of it." And he equally reported nothing to Rolland of the outcome of the discussion; Bosc, misinterpreting the request in a footnote to the signed letter that Rolland and his troop be also permitted to leave the country, accused Cavalier of guaranteeing their submission without their agreement and so prejudicing the later chances of a settlement. But no guarantee can be read into the wording of the letter,[6] and what ambiguity there may be would not be enough to prejudice an agreement between former companions in arms both seeking peaceful resolution.

Rolland's later resentment had other sources than a simple failure of information about the talks with La Lande. Villars recommended to the king the terms of Cavalier's letter, suggested tolerance as perhaps only a marshal of France could dare to do, and put forward the proposal that Cavalier and his troop enter the royal service in a regiment where they could be left to pray to God in their own way and not be compelled to Catholic observances. A truce was agreed until the king's answer to this was received; when it came it stated coldly that Villars' proposal was not to the king's taste though the rest of Cavalier's prayer was allowed in principle: "I see nothing in the writing of Cavalier that cannot be allowed him and those who found themselves in this revolt." These comforting sentiments did not outlast the first relief at a prospect of bringing the sedition to an end, the balance of force being seen to shift as Camisard solidarity broke up.

During this time d'Aigaliers, dismayed to find that La Lande had stolen a march on him, determined to correct the situation in his own favour and in doing so effectively aborted the delicate agreement in process of birth between the authorities and the Camisards. None of the Catholic commanders who had faced Cavalier had succeeded in destroying him in the field; the Protestant gentleman with his limited but tenacious ambitions and precedence of rank in the regional hierarchy set about it in a different way. The day after Cavalier's conference on the bridge with La Lande, d'Aigaliers persuaded him to another with himself. "Cavalier came to see me ... I put it to him that a vile subject could never bargain with his legitimate sovereign, but that being only a poor peasant without education he could have known no better. Thereupon he wrote to the marshal de Villars." Religious arguments were used by this Protestant *notable* with motives both private and doctrinal to induce Cavalier, perceived as the principal leader of the insurgents, to throw away the advantage of his position after his meeting with La Lande, a soldier with whom he had a more equal understanding despite their official difference in rank. Philippe Joutard offers a simple, perhaps too simple, explanation for this surprising reversal: "Having come out of the prophetic climate the former baker's boy felt his social inferiority. He felt himself a villein or serf faced with his lord and the irresistible force of hierarchy led him to forget what he had always said and even what he had succeeded in safeguarding the day before."

If the analysis, however regrettable, is correct, it supports the argument that a less emasculated local class of *notables* might from the beginning have dealt with the insurgency more peaceably than the army and the civil service controlled from the bureaux of Versailles. The Protestant *notables* of whom d'Aigaliers claimed to act as spokesman were unanimously opposed to Camisard violence, believed that to rise against the king was to invite divine malediction, and that submission to the royal clemency, however delusory, was a sacred duty. Yet if these right-thinking Protestants had had their way, the heroic idealism of the Cévenols would have been still-born and French Protestantism deprived of perhaps the most admirable chapter in its history. Bosc goes so far as to claim that "without the young rebels, the Protestant faith would have been wiped out of the Kingdom."

Cavalier yielded to the baron's arguments, his officers were called, lectured in the same way and required to agree to the terms of a new letter to the marshal dictated by d'Aigaliers, free of any conditions and begging the king's forgiveness "following the example of the divinity of which he is the living image on earth". Armed with the letter which might, if all went well, earn him the place of colonel of the régiment Villars, d'Aigaliers hurried to Nîmes to deliver it to the marshal, and with it the fatal binding of Cavalier to a submission which he appeared to have agreed not only on his own behalf but also that of the leaders in the Cévennes whom he had not consulted. Marcel Pin rightly pointed out that Cavalier had reason to think the conditions of his first letter had been agreed by the king. The new element in the second letter was his offer to the marshal to serve under his orders in the regiment which, in common with d'Aigaliers, it was his ambition to form. The baron's self-serving intervention in the peace-seeking had the effect of throwing into the shadows what might have been obtained: "By his fault," wrote Bosc, "the Camisard revolt which had forced the greatest king in the world and the most absolute of monarchies to come to terms with peasants in revolt, suddenly came to an end." But if, as he added, Cavalier was later bitterly to regret the loss of advantage of his first discussion with La Lande, and if he was now reduced to being an instrument in the hands of the authorities, his later actions and career show that a motive of his apparent surrender to d'Aigalier's wishes was the hope of new life in the profession of arms which, against all probability, the baker's boy had made his own.

On 13 May Rolland, still ignorant of the details of Cavalier's conversations, organized one of the most successful of the many ambushes in the high Cévennes, praised by later admirers possibly concerned to bypass criticism of his inactivity during the months of burnings. With the troops of Jouani and Castanet as well as his own he trapped in a valley leading to the Plan de Fontmort an army contingent returning to the mountains from Alais. Some followers claimed that this was a military force of several hundred men but Blachère argued that Rolland would never have attacked a purely military detachment and that this was in fact, as others claimed, a mule train carrying arms, ammunition and, above all, money. More than a hundred and twenty soldiers died in the ambush, including several officers, and the Camisards led the laden mules away with their booty. Bosc contrasted the tactics of Rolland with those of Cavalier: "If (Rolland) did not have the gifts of a true head of an army, at least he was clever enough to make up for his lack of military science with peasant cunning and his perfect knowledge of the country ... he preferred to surprise the enemy rather than to attack him openly." Rolland's victory at Fontmort, described by Bosc as "a masterpiece of the genre", demonstrates that he and the other leaders could have continued a guerrilla war in the mountains for months, perhaps years, with the foreign help they hoped for.

The "masterpiece" came at a delicate moment for negotiations already under way; Basville and Villars decided to delay informing the court, and Cavalier, learning by a message from Rolland on the 14th of his success and fearing that the authorities could take it as a challenge during the agreed truce, wrote to the marshal with his regrets, at the same time advising Rolland of the armistice which Rolland and the other leaders then accepted. But this, due to Cavalier's failure, for reasons that have never been clear, to keep Rolland informed earlier was the start of misunderstanding and mistrust between the leaders undermining all later attempts to agree a united front and an equal shared advantage from the possibility of peace.

The marshal and the intendant, pleased with the results of d'Aigalier's negotiation which was taken as supplanting that of La Lande, ordered him to return to Cavalier, now at Tornac, and invite him to a meeting to be held at Nîmes. Cavalier later admitted that "A Man of greater Experience than I was, would perhaps have acted with more Caution on this critical Occasion, and would Probably have avoided to treat with the Mareschal Personaly ... but my Youth and Unexperience gave me Confidence, and ... there were none about me much Wiser than my self, or more practised in Affairs of this Nature that I could confide in." The rumour that Cavalier was to meet the intendant and the marshal on the outskirts of the town caused a growing effervescence in the Nîmes population. Accompanied by his young brother, by Daniel Guy and Catinat his lieutenants and by d'Aigaliers, he approached the gate of the Madeleine. "Every artisan closed his shop to run and see Cavalier arrive ... and the walls were packed with people," wrote Soeur de Mérez. Catholics and Protestants joined in a festival atmosphere in the hope of restoring the idea of peace, though it was many blood-stained years since that had reigned. As Cavalier rode across the Esplanade where the gibbets and wheels had stood, women pressed forward to touch his coat and priests were seen to tremble in horror from a distance.[7]

The meeting took place in a convent garden outside the western walls with troops of both sides ranged in disciplined order. Cavalier, this young man of the people who had terrorized the country all around and been obeyed like a god by his constantly replenished and growing troop of men, was splendidly dressed in captured uniform and finery, and adorned with items of jewellery, an emerald ring, gold watch, snuff box; his appearance caused a great stir, described by de Mérez: "His face is very good-looking, one would say eighteen years old and we are assured he is only twenty-one ... he had such an air of sweetness that one would never have thought him capable of all the crimes he committed." The conversation was held in a quiet corner of the garden near the resurgent spring called the fountain of Nemausus, between only Basville, Villars and Cavalier, leaving no written record. Cavalier laid his pistols on the ground at Villars' feet and the marshal commanded an orderly to replace them in their holsters. Following the formalities of *politesse*, observers from far off saw an apparently animated exchange with gesturing and raised voices; Cavalier remembered that Basville, who hated insubordination and had hoped for two years to capture, interrogate, torture and execute him on the wheel, became repeatedly angry at this meeting on equal terms, and was only calmed by the marshal's reminder that he, the commander-in-chief, was Cavalier's interlocutor. But Basville's letter to Chamillart after the meeting somewhat qualifies Cavalier's account: "He ... seemed to me have a good mind and great assurance. Looking at him one wonders how he could have so strongly imposed himself as to become absolute master of such a great number of villains."

The discussion, led by Villars, centred around the formation of a regiment in his name and in which the Camisards could serve as an alternative to emigration. Cavalier claimed that three thousand Camisards would follow him, a figure doubted by Basville who, however, was particularly concerned to get Cavalier away from the region where his authority and fame might at any time spark another revolt. In Cavalier's account Villars promised that the king would allow the men liberty of conscience and the right of assembly although he knew well that the king would not. In the letters of Basville and Villars to the minister and to the king there was no mention that liberty of conscience had been raised. Bosc concluded in favour of Cavalier: "He undoubtedly had the courage to speak out and it was probably this that provoked the intendant's anger ... Villars must have promised a relative freedom of conscience, limited to Cavalier and his troop, a spoken answer that tied him to nothing..." It was an answer whose right value Cavalier recognized, the fine words of the marshal "not inspiring in me any great confidence". He was authorized to assemble his men and others at Calvisson in the Vaunage while the king's reply was awaited, and Basville stated that Cavalier declared he could answer for Rolland and the other chiefs. This rash claim, whether or not made, was repeated by Villars in announcing to the king Cavalier's guarantee of the submission of the other leaders, and that all troops would be assembled by 1 June to put themselves at the king's disposition. Villars by many accounts promised, or induced Cavalier to believe that he promised, a rank of lieutenant-colonel in the regiment to be created, and Cavalier was guided in all his actions until he left France by the desire for this promotion.

Much of the discredit too easily thrown at Cavalier's memoirs derives from his publication in them of the text of an alleged treaty between himself, Basville, and Villars, signed by them all in the garden outside the walls of Nîmes and guaranteeing the cévenol claims of freedom of conscience, liberation of prisoners and the right to worship, although none of them was later granted. Antoine Court concluded that Cavalier's alleged treaty was imagined or made up afterwards, and others have followed him. Bosc, however, was not convinced that Cavalier had invented the treaty but that it was probably the text first presented by him to La Lande on the bridge, and of which La Lande wrote to the minister, "I reduced his demands which at first were exorbitant." That twenty years later Cavalier included this text in his memoir is explained, though not vindicated, by his desire to defend himself against the accusations of abandoning the cause and betraying his companions in arms brought by Marion and others in London in 1708.

But in the days after the meeting, Cavalier's officers, even the faithful Bonbonnoux, and many of his followers came to feel that the only outcome of all the negotiation, and of the amnesty, had been to the sole advantage of his ambition and that the aims of the uprising, the fate of the galley slaves and prisoners, the cause of freedom of conscience and assembly, the cause of faith itself had been abandoned by a leader not empowered to speak for them all. The marshal always denied promising the Camisards these freedoms; nevertheless under his authority during the following days at Calvisson a huge crowd celebrated publicly and freely the Protestant services long refused them, and this certainty in the mist of historical ambiguity surrounding a conference without witnesses must testify to some verbal consent or approval exchanged between Villars and Cavalier on the vital questions at the heart of the cévenol revolt. If so, Cavalier's account of his part in the negotiation must be credited with it. It is certain, too, that he was the first and for long the only Camisard to realize that the uprising was defeated, would gain nothing more and could only continue at the cost of lives, of villages, homes and fields, and of the destruction of the country that gave the Cévenols their name and identity. If in the widening split between Rolland and Cavalier during the following days Rolland appeared to the majority of Camisards, and since then to Huguenot posterity, as the intransigent leader inviting martyrdom by remaining true to their ideals, and as the steadfast champion of their demands, a reasoned judgement on Cavalier must still be that it was he who had understood the realities and worked to save lives including his own. The mythology attached to the Huguenot tradition celebrated at the *Assembleés du Désert* of the mas Soubeyran could illustrate T. S. Eliot's line that "human kind cannot bear very much reality".

The atmosphere at Calvisson would certainly support this. As many as fifteen thousand Protestant worshippers streamed into the village from Nîmes, Sommières, Alais and the region of Uzès, and others followed over the next ten days to a total estimated at forty thousand with continual psalm singing, preaching, walking on coals, practice of religious cult forbidden since 1685 and convulsive manifestations of trance and prophecy in the belief that the terms of the Edict of Nantes would be restored. Cavalier, acclaimed by the crowds, preached once but was reported to distance himself after the first day from the collective enthusiasm which he knew was built on a sense of sublime illusion, though he did not yet say so. It was not until his meeting with Rolland on 24 May, probably at the mas Soubeyran, that he disclosed the truth about the peace negotiation and its outcome. By then the royal answer of the 18th had been received, possibly on the 23rd, pronouncing the king's willingness to pardon rebels who surrendered and to allow an unspecified number of Camisard soldiers to leave the kingdom by 1 June. No formation of a regiment was mentioned and the marshal was ordered to ensure that Cavalier left the province, at the head of his men, by a specified route to the Spanish frontier and then to Portugal.

To those who prayed and wept, chanted, prophesied and opened their conscience to the Spirit in unbridled enthusiasm, the king's letter addressed nothing but royal cant, cruel in the context of what had been done to them and their families: "I cannot (even within the principles that have long served me as a rule to my conduct toward those who have remained in the Protestant religion) publicly authorize them in their errors."[8] This was the message that had to be delivered to Rolland whose pride was already upset by Montrevel's evident choice of Cavalier as spokesman for the Camisard army. Rolland's reaction, then and later, was revealing. He grew violently angry, then temporized and finally dug in his heels. "You should die of shame to have betrayed your side. I will never accept such a peace unless the liberty of conscience is entirely and for ever re-established," he shouted at Cavalier. Lacombe who was present warned Rolland that if he refused the peace he would be the cause of the loss of many families, and even of the Cévennes itself, but Rolland replied that he had been given no consideration; added to his known jealousy of Cavalier's military success this was a factor in the rupture between them and understood by the authorities whose emissary had made separate contact with Rolland and who wrote on the 27th that "He was half won over. What prevented him from being entirely so, a painful subject for him, is seeing Seigneur Cavalier ... receive preference over him ... he says everywhere that he used to command him and could not now obey him. It is a delicate question of honour." And Basville wrote on the 17th to the minister, "it seemed that from professional jealousy (Rolland) wanted a separate treaty", an impression repeated in a letter on the 28th, and corroborated by the later violent, though transient, attack on Rolland by Ravanel who accused him of planning to betray the cause in the same way as Cavalier.

At this moment in the Camisard drama of contending forces, where subjective and religious motives were inseparable, a potent new element came into play. This was brought to the Cévennes by an emissary of the Allies, Tobie Rocayrol, a bankrupted silk merchant from Lyon who had taken refuge as a Protestant in Geneva and courageously returned to the Cévennes on a mission to encourage the Camisards not to make peace, arriving in Nîmes on the 25th. Whether before this the Allies took Rolland to be the commander-in-chief of the Camisard troops is not sure, but by the time of Rocayrol's arrival their intelligence had certainly informed them of Cavalier's negotiation, and Rolland had written on the 22nd to Richard Hill, the English government's representative in Turin, "Rest assured that even if the king agrees to all our demands we will do nothing without your agreement ... and on your advice, and that we will hold up the troops here as long as we can." This makes it evident that Rolland intended to reject the terms of Cavalier's negotiation before he knew what they were, that he had been for some time in negotiation with the Allies, and that he kept Cavalier in the dark about these positions. His anger therefore seems in part to have been factitious, his refusal of the peace fortified by the prospect of foreign intervention and money. It also suggests that the two principal Camisard leaders were mutually suspicious and that Cavalier probably believed Rolland would be adamant in refusal and beyond persuasion.

Rocayrol, relying on Rolland's letter of the 22nd, entered into contact with him on the 26th with the news that an Anglo-Dutch fleet of forty-six ships had entered the Mediterranean and that two English frigates were ready to attempt a landing on the beaches near Aigues-Mortes with five hundred men and supplies of arms and ammunition. Rolland's first action was to send express messages to two of Cavalier's chief officers, Ravanel and Catinat at Calvisson, giving this information and urging them to reject their leader and join him in the Cévennes. Ravanel must have been chosen by Cavalier as his principal lieutenant for his ferocity and not for pliancy, and Catinat had been a notably vengeful and ruthless campaigner with his cavalry troop committing a variety of atrocities. Bosc described the character of Ravanel as uncouth, irascible as he was aggressive, and with his crudeness the incarnation of the fanatical type. He was reported to have an open festering sabre-wound on his arm which he liked to display before disinfecting it with eau-de-vie, of which he would drink the blood-stained remains. His religious faith was strict, violent and uncompromising, and until now he had been totally loyal to his leader and fought by his side with fierce gallantry. But he was made suspicious and angry by Cavalier's distant attitude toward the religious manifestations of Calvisson and the apparent turning of his back on prophecy and inspiration, and the resulting fury aroused a terrible reaction against the leader who had for Ravanel epitomized the Camisard resistance. "He separated himself from Cavalier with as great force as he had attached himself."[9] The militia captain Berlie who was with the Camisards during the days at Calvisson and observed them closely stated that "Ravanel, in command in Cavalier's absence and urged on, so they say, by Rolland, began to instil in the troop sentiments very different from those they had when Cavalier left them."

On the 26th Cavalier, who was received at Alais with the same fascinated attention as at Nîmes, organized an assembly beyond the Gardon which some of the people of Alais crossed with water to their waist in order to attend; on the same day Rolland summoned another, below the walls of the town. The clash between the two commanders was made public and unmistakable.

During the night of the 27th an emissary from Rolland arrived at Calvisson announcing that the Queen of England implored the Camisard forces to accept no terms of surrender such as Cavalier would recommend, because help in arms and men was on the way. Ravanel and some other officers decided to lead a revolt the next day to refuse whatever terms were offered short of their full demands. When Cavalier arrived they asked to know the conditions of surrender and were told that they would depart on the 31st for Portugal in scarlet uniform. The Camisards in growing numbers joined Ravanel and Catinat in their refusal and a violent altercation followed in which Cavalier attempted to regain control of his men. Ravanel was heard to roar in the streets in his wild voice, "Let those who love God and his religion follow us! Let us join Rolland! We are betrayed by our enemies." He led those who would follow him out of Calvisson as Cavalier made a last appeal, which went unheard. "Forgetting suddenly that Cavalier had commanded us and that we obeyed him almost like God himself, we turned our back on him," Bonbonnoux wrote in his *Mémoires*.

Humiliated and sad, Cavalier left Calvisson with fifty faithful Camisards including Daniel Guy and Salomon Couderc; the following day he met Ravanel and the troop that had abandoned him in the bois de Ners and made a final unsuccessful attempt to rally them. "It was here," Bonbonnoux wrote, "that I saw for the last time this commander for whom I have always felt the greatest respect." Cavalier in his *Mémoires* gave an account of the events at Calvisson which Bosc stated to be falsified in the interests of his reputation and to conceal the humiliation he had suffered. However, Cavalier's claim that the peace was refused because parents or relations of the Camisards had not been released is confirmed by Basville who wrote to the minister on the 30th: "The pretext of these madmen (*furieux*) was that the prisoners had not been liberated and that before leaving they wanted their relations and friends to have freedom to pray to God in the desert."[10] On the 29th Villars issued a threatening ordinance making explicit the refusal of liberty of conscience and assembly and that the king's pardon was all that could be hoped for; on the same day he wrote to Cavalier in harsh terms: "I tell you for the last time that the prisoners will be freed ... and that you can take with you whoever is in reach ... for the rest, they can either serve the king or leave the kingdom ... If God abandons your people to the point of refusing the king's goodness I will shortly make them die either with weapons or of famine in the woods." And he at once ended the truce and sent out detachments with orders to find and encircle the obdurate rebels in the Cévennes.

La Lande, however, succeeded in obtaining an extension of the truce to 5 June, believing that Rolland could still be brought round. "Cavalier is in good faith and has kept his promises ... he has done marvels," Basville wrote to the minister, and Villars was later reported as saying that foreign emissaries had made use of Rolland's vanity to which Basville added, again to the minister, that (Rolland) "apparently wanted to go on for a time enjoying the pleasure of being the chief, now that Cavalier no longer is". Rolland's great success at Fontmort had made him more exigent and aggressive; recognizing this, La Lande and d'Aigaliers forgot their differences and enlisted the services of local *notables* to meet Rolland and persuade him to halt the insurrection before the measures "of extreme rigour" were put into effect and the country was ruined, but Rolland threatened to have these deputies shot if they showed themselves in his camp.

At this stage of the insurgency's slow ending, the authorities in the province had a double concern which reappeared from time to time afterwards. One was that a new Cavalier might spring up to lead the rebels, and later came the fear of Cavalier's return to do so himself; the other was the recurrent fear of an Allied landing of troops to join the Camisard force and continue the war, although surrenders of small groups continued throughout these months in towns or countryside. "We must take them separately and wait for them to give up one by one and do retail what we hoped to do wholesale," wrote Basville in commercial language. Villars, meanwhile, hoped to keep Cavalier with him perhaps to guard him from temptation, and the marshal of France's esteem for the baker's boy grew the better he knew him: he, "a peasant from the lowest order and aged twenty-two ... disposed his troops for action as well as any very competent officer could." Chamillart believed that Cavalier might reveal to Villars details of the supposed secret consistory, the sources of the Camisards' supplies and the caches of their arms, but Cavalier, as Bosc concedes despite his criticisms, never betrayed friend or secret, and the marshal did not press him.

While surrenders continued, a number of communities—Alais, Anduze, Saint-Jean-du-Gard and many others—sent delegates to a meeting at Durfort to put together a joint appeal to Rolland and those with him to allow peace in the Cévennes and let refugee peasants return to their destroyed land and homes. Reciprocal mounting anger was the result, with Ravanel threatening to take his men to pillage the property of any who refused to sustain them, and Rolland complaining that the authorities had dealt only with Cavalier who was his subordinate and whose "inspirations" came from himself whereas his, Rolland's, were directly from God. Villars sent d'Aigaliers, and authorized Cavalier to make a last approach to the intransigents, and Rolland's mother also appealed to him to surrender: "you won't kill me because I am your mother, but I won't leave you until you give our country peace." The truce, extended to the evening of the 5th, was running out as Rolland sent a more subservient letter to the marshal begging a further delay of a month and swearing fidelity to the king in an obvious attempt to gain time. On the 5th he heard from an agent of the Allies that a convoy of money was on the way. The delay was refused but the marshal held back while Cavalier and d'Aigaliers went to meet Rolland for the last time. Cavalier had the impression, observing Rolland and Ravanel, that Rolland was no longer free to move on his own and that he was treated as suspect by his own supporters. Ravanel, in a trance and speaking for the Spirit, accused Cavalier of treason and Rolland of having let himself be corrupted; in an atmosphere of rising verbal violence and threat that could quickly become physical, Rolland concluded that the "Spirit did not want him to surrender". It is hardly surprising that on the 7th and before the expiry of the last extension of the truce, Villars lost patience, decided to act rapidly and firmly, and set his troops on the move.

Villars believed that Rolland was Ravanel's prisoner and impotent to decide for himself, and without doubt Ravanel terrorized his fellows by prophecies and threats. Basville's belief, since he received in early June a message from Jouani in the high Cévennes that he was ready to discuss surrender, was that the remaining Camisards were weakened and shaken, wanted to give up but were held back by hope of outside aid, and that Rolland had to be helped. La Lande equally believed in an imminent surrender and hesitated to march against the Camisard groups in spite of the marshal's orders, writing to the minister on the 12th that "the more I examine ... the genius of the people, the more I see that they must be taken gently and the troubles ended by negotiation."

Basville merely regretted that it would cost "more blood" to bring the revolt to an end, though he was at no time frugal in the amount shed on his orders.

The optimism of the authorities was based on their opinion that Cavalier had been the principal adversary, and that the movement could not long survive his departure which should happen as soon as possible, though Villars wrote to the minister on the 16th that this was delayed because Camisards giving up their arms day by day were asking to join their former leader. On the 14th Villars wrote to the king: "When I arrived in the Languedoc there were continual massacres which thank God have ceased. We have the principal and most capable of the rebel chiefs in our hands ... and we hope to see all the rest follow." The optimism proved mistaken; Rolland and Jouani, when subsidies finally reached them, were able to continue their stubborn, cunning and elusive resistance for a long time after Cavalier had marched away with his remaining followers, and many Camisards in the deserted forests and secret caves of the Cévennes preferred martyrdom, whether in skirmishes or on the scaffold, to the loss of ideals for which they had sacrificed their families, fields and homes.

On 9 June Cavalier was informed by Villars of the king's order that he and the remnant of his troop go to the eastern frontier, to the octagonal, prison-camp like enclosure built by Vauban at Neuf-Brisach, and await orders for their attachment to the army of the Rhine in formations and under command yet to be decided. Cavalier's ambition of a colonel's brevet receded as his numbers fell, now reduced to a company, not a regiment. In Nîmes he was followed everywhere by a crowd filled with curiosity and admiration, but he went under escort until on the 14th he was ordered to Vallabrègues, an island in the Rhône, with his ninety men: "They put us under a Guard much stronger than we were, so that we seemed to be their Prisoners." Men unlocked from forts and prisons were allowed to join him but for galley slaves he could obtain only an unsecured promise of their release once he arrived at Brisach.

Villars had understood by the evasiveness of the minister's replies that the hope of a regiment in his name was a lost one, and taking pity on Cavalier's disappointment he sent him on his way to the Rhine as a "lieutenant-colonel without brevet". Cavalier had become an encumbrance, thanks largely to the crowds who surrounded him wherever he went. His troop on departure numbered a hundred and twenty of whom twenty were mounted and all were armed; the order of route, signed by the king, stated that once arrived at Brisach the Camisards "will withdraw from the kingdom", implying that they would be free to do so although when the time came this freedom appeared as insecure as any other in the king's realm. On 21 June Cavalier left Nîmes surrounded by a large crowd accompanying him on the road for three quarters of a mile to say their farewell; on the 26th he left his native province, never to return.

Rolland

On 17 June Villars issued an ordinance threatening the arrest of fathers and mothers of Camisards refusing to submit, and on the 22nd a number of men from Rolland's troop asked the conditions for doing so. Villars well understood that the only way to bring religious peace to the region was the reestablishment of the Edict of Nantes, a simple measure which, said Bosc, "only a tolerant monarch less infatuated with pride than Louis XIV" would have taken, but the marshal knew that Vauban, a marshal of genius like himself, had incurred royal disgrace in 1688 by defending liberty of conscience; and he knew also that even if he suggested it, such a freedom would never during the reign be granted. On the 23rd the marshal was visited by one of the chief inhabitants of Mialet, a friend of Rolland but unnamed in the records, who informed him that there were now three sorts of Camisards: the discouraged who wanted to give up, the fanatics who would continue the struggle, and other individuals "without religion but used to licentiousness ... to being fed by peasants ... and to doing nothing but steal and live in debauchery." The informant advised that he would only defeat the rebels by exterminating the third group and that once those of the first had surrendered, the declared enemies left would be destroyed by the country itself, and this, although it would cost time and suffering, was what happened.

The phantom hope of foreign intervention was occasionally revived by some news of coastal movement. On 24 June a mixed force of mercenaries, deserters and adventurers set sail from Villefranche with the project of disembarking in the Golfe du Lion near Sète. Richard

Hill wrote to the duke of Marlborough describing this as "a desperate attempt"; the Allied emissary Rocayrol had informed Rolland on 26 May that this expedition would shortly sail and Rolland replied that he could send down fifteen thousand men to the coast, though his numbers were then perhaps eight or nine hundred and diminishing as piecemeal surrenders cut them back. In the event, he and the other leaders in the Cévennes kept their distance in the mountains. "Their absence at the decisive moment rendered this attempt at a landing uncertain at the least," Bosc said. On the 25th a strong wind got up and increased the next day with mountainous waves flooding smaller vessels able to approach the shore and making the landing impossible, and on the 29th the fleet withdrew; after this fiasco the impetus drained away from any movement of the Allies to come to the rescue of the Camisards. Marlborough himself wrote that no one "could be more concerned for doing good to the Sevenois than I am, but I am sure the methods we have hitherto toke will do them no good."

Cavalier wrote many years later in despair at the failure of the governments at war with France at the time of the revolt to intervene effectively: "Being Masters of the Sea, they might easily have sent us Succours, at least some Arms and Money: for had they sent us but twenty thousand Pounds Sterling, we would soon have made up a Body of fifty thousand Men, but ... they look'd on this War, as a sudden Blaze which soon vanishes away ... the Allies wou'd have saved some Millions and a great deal of Blood ... but 'tis difficult to discover the Policy of Princes."[11] This was not the problem with Louis XIV's policies regarding religion, which were perfectly clear and immovable. For what reason d'Aigaliers chose at this point to go to Versailles and attempt to advance the Camisard claim is inscrutable; possibly no more than private ambition of profit by drawing attention to himself and continuing, if possible, the role he had played to such damaging effect with Cavalier. Villars suspected that Rolland and d'Aigaliers were somehow complicit and in contact with the secret consistory of Basville's imagination; from both sides, exaggeration and fantasy echoed and distorted the reality of the conflict and its possible resolution.

D'Aigaliers obtained nothing at Versailles but the award of a pension for his services which was never paid, and a promise of general amnesty and release of prisoners but not of the *galériens*, Christians of the wrong persuasion whose punishment continued at the king's pleasure. On the 27th Villars received the visit of a "new man", an agent who told him that Rolland still intended to give himself up and waited only for the moment when he could bring the greatest number of his followers with him. Marcel Pin's opinion was that Rocayrol may have suggested this course and that Rolland followed his advice, though "the wily cévenol peasant never had any intention of surrendering and until his death continued the playacting ... between the marshal and Rolland, it was the sheep-gelder who always managed to fool the former ambassador of the king of France."[12] But it was only the marshal's patience that was deceived, and not for long.

Cavalier was now at Mâcon with his troop, where d'Aigaliers arrived on 9 July on his return journey to the Languedoc. Cavalier greeted him with due politeness but rightly suspecting he had been sent by the minister to extract or to pass information gave nothing away and said that what he had to impart would be for the king alone. The baron's usefulness and even his nuisance value were running out. The only information he was able to pass to the minister from Mâcon appeared to be that the Camisards enjoyed the tolerant sympathy of a population largely Catholic, many of them attending the public Protestant prayer services out of curiosity and perhaps in silent admiration; Cavalier's renown preceded him and his ambition now was to reach Versailles and, if possible, convey to the king the aspirations of the cévenol Huguenots, apparently still believing him ignorant of them. Bosc suggests also that Cavalier calculated he might yet obtain a regimental command by making revelations to the minister, but this suggestion contradicts the recognized fact that he never betrayed any man or secret. More plausible is the likelihood that Cavalier hoped to be allowed to return to the Languedoc, negotiate again with Rolland and the other leaders and help to bring about a peaceful end to the tragedy of the people.

He arrived in Paris on 15 July and next day was civilly received by Chamillart, surprised to see this young man, almost still a boy with an expression of gentleness, who had for so long held the king's armies at bay. Cavalier's claim to have had an interview with the king has been generally discredited but not disproved, and the claim interpreted as his attempt to redeem his reputation from the criticism that he had won nothing from the authorities by betrayal of the cause. It seems likely only that he was stationed on a stairway to watch the sovereign pass from one ceremonial occasion to another. Voltaire's story that the king looked at him silently and shrugged his shoulders is taken from an account by Madame du Noyer without authentic source, and fits badly with the concession made by Saint-Simon that Louis XIV, however essentially disdainful, was always polite.

Chamillart saw Cavalier a second time, not at court where according to Saint-Simon there was "a scandalous concourse of people come to see Cavalier wherever he went", but at his country house. A pension was awarded with an immediate advance, the only payment ever made, but no concession to the religious claims of the Huguenots, and no promise of a colonelcy unless d'Aigaliers succeeded in raising a regiment in which Cavalier could serve. For the present, he was told to return to Mâcon and await the order to lead his men to Brisach. This reached him on 6 August, with Chamillart's announcement to him that d'Aigaliers had failed in the Languedoc. On the 16th, Cavalier and his troop with a company of archers set off from Mâcon to the fortress of Brisach where, he became convinced, it was the government's intention to keep him prisoner for life. "I determined to quit the Kingdom the first Opportunity, which soon offered..."

The Allies' concern was to encourage the remaining Camisards to continue their guerrilla tactics after Cavalier's departure, although this purpose seems to have come from a subsidiary level since no concerted military effort to reach the Languedoc and exploit the Camisard resistance materialized. Tobie Rocayrol was sent, at a wage of one gold *louis* per day, to convince the Camisards that help was on the way. Cavalier's former troop was now dispersed, some joining other troops, some surrendering, the majority returning home, leaving Rolland as undisputed chief though with the threatening shadow of Ravanel at his shoulder, and Rocayrol's mission was frustrated at the outset by the loss to the Camisards of the most capable of their leaders. "They don't even try to fight," Rocayrol wrote, "it is a constant truth that they do no harm except to those who harm them." To the question why, in that case, the authorities continued to hunt them down, it can only be answered that the possibility of foreign invasion, never more than a chimera, misled both sides into a long struggle with unnecessary mortality and civilian misery. Mazel expressed the dilemma in a few words: "Our poor troops diminished from day to day and those who remained constantly urged us to accept the offers made us, that it was necessary to temporise and that a bad agreement was better than total destruction. But reasonable as that was, we could not resolve to give up so good a cause which had cost so much bloodshed ... and was commanded by God."

For as long as there were guerrilla bands in the mountains the authorities would ally them, in their heads, with a phantom force sailing to disembark on the sands of Aigues-Mortes or Sète. Rocayrol's visit reinforced Rolland's unpredictable and sometimes capricious course of action, or inaction. When the baron d'Aigaliers, fresh from Versailles, endeavoured to reach Rolland a few days after Rocayrol a meeting was arranged at Durfort at which d'Aigaliers spoke to and attempted to mollify the assembled Camisard leaders and men. Rolland answered that he had given his body and his life to God and would never abandon the Cévennes, and continued in the same vein until d'Aigaliers interrupted him. The image left is of Rolland pressing forward on the road to martyrdom with hesitant step and by disingenuous means, a combination that has earned for him a place in the heart of all cévenol Protestants as the ultimate crafty but heroic resistant. "He is an altogether brutal animal who doesn't reason," wrote Basville to the minister.

As Cavalier's troop dissolved in piecemeal surrender, Rolland retired with his into the remotest part of the high Cévennes where it was impossible to reach them and from which they scarcely emerged. "He only keeps going by cleverly and carefully hiding himself," the marshal wrote. An exception was an attack on Le Pont-de-Montvert, with the aim of seizing provisions, on 19 July, easily repulsed with the loss to the Camisards of twelve killed and thirty wounded. Villars understood, with the help of intercepted letters from Richard Hill, that Rolland had refused Cavalier's example less from principle than in hope of enlarging the war with foreign aid and men. The failure of this to reach the Languedoc left the remaining Camisards in a pitiful state, without provisions or ammunition, and in hiding from one mountain cave to another: "Our condition grew from day to day sadder and more desolate,"

Bonbonnoux wrote. After the failure of d'Aigaliers' meeting with Rolland, another nobleman, the marquis de Ganges, made an indirect approach to him with the approval of Villars who believed Rolland to be in need of help, offering safe passage to Geneva for himself, his followers and his young wife the demoiselle de Cornély; there was also the promise of a comfortable pension to be paid by the French Resident in Switzerland. Rolland refused this, the last attempt to manoeuvre him into submission, with a letter notable for the firmness of his attachment to his religious cause and for the apparent continuing belief (shared with Cavalier) that if the king learnt of the wretchedness of his cévenol subjects he would accord them the liberty they wanted.

The authorities were reduced to reliance on betrayal as the only means of capturing the elusive leader, lying low in forest caves like an eel among rocks, who now personified the rebellion. Basville's first move was to release from detention Cathérine and Marthe de Cornély of whom the second was the lover of Rolland's chief lieutenant, his scribe and companion Malhier, the intendant admitting in chill bureaucrat's terms that "the desire that Rolland may have to see her could contribute to his capture". An informer was recruited, one Malarte, a smallholder from near Uzès and said to be related to Rolland, who undertook to watch the movements of the Cornély sisters. He reported on 13 August that they were installed in the château de Castelnau, a fortified building belonging to an absent Protestant family, and that Rolland and Malhier were to join them that night. The two men arrived at nine on horseback and tethered their animals to a tree, guarded by two of Rolland's troop. Before dawn Malarte rode off to Uzès to alert the officer commanding the garrison who put a detachment of dragoons on the road to Castelnau. The sleeping sentry on the tower awoke to see it already encircled and gave the alarm. Rolland, who had narrowly escaped an identical trap at the château de Prades near Lasalle by leaping in his underclothes from a first floor window, now was able with Malhier to ride out of the courtyard and toward the woods where safety lay, but was shot dead fifty metres from the building in a sunken track where dragoons were posted. Malhier, less fortunate, was captured and taken to Nîmes to be broken on the wheel while Rolland's corpse was embalmed, tried, condemned and ceremonially burned at the stake.

The betrayal, hunting down and killing of Rolland was emblematic of the final defeat of the uprising, although this had not yet fully come, but already the mood of the beleaguered Camisards was melancholic since Cavalier's disappearance, which can be seen as deeper in its consequences than the more dramatic and idealized fate of Pierre Laporte, enshrined in the Huguenot calendar as Rolland, most resolute of Camisard leaders.

Penultimate

Bonbonnoux wrote of Rolland's death that "it made a great revolution in our affairs. Many who would otherwise have continued for a long time benefited from the king's amnesty, put themselves into the enemy's hands and laid down their arms." Another consequence was a growth of mistrust among the Camisards because Rolland had been betrayed by a relative, and because now no chief had the authority to rally and unify the remaining rebel groups. Marion stated that after Rolland's death his troop dispersed and Ravanel took the remains of Cavalier's men down into the plain where they were accustomed to operate. Rolland's captured companions, and notably Malhier, were executed with extravagantly drawn out horror on the Esplanade at Nîmes on 16 August before a huge crowd. Villars, though triumphant at what he saw as the impending collapse of the uprising, was offended: "As for the cruelty of their death ... I leave it to the bishops to decide what their religion requires, but ... I think it better for the king's service to discontinue this practice; the prompter the death the better, and the more decent." On the 18th, Bishop Fléchier who had watched the executions wrote to a Spanish colleague, "There is nothing so useful, important and necessary as to teach Christians of our day to die well."

The Cornély sisters, whose marital or non-marital status as mistresses was much discussed by Protestant historians anxious either to show their heroes' humanity or to acquit them of sin, were captured on 14 August; on 3 November Basville allowed them to leave France for Switzerland, showing clemency to these well-born girls that was not extended to the women of the people who were often condemned to be whipped in public, and sometimes hanged. The two sisters had no more use as bait and the Camisard faction was breaking up. On 20 September Basville recorded that five hundred and thirty Camisards had surrendered in a month, of whom a hundred and thirty had emigrated to Switzerland and the rest returned home. By November, almost all the remaining rebel leaders, Castanet, Jouani, Catinat, Salomon Couderc, with their followers, had surrendered and only the ungovernable Ravanel with Bonbonnoux and twenty men remained at large, starving, penniless, and without supplies of ammunition or medication. After the failure of his last attempts to negotiate a settlement, d'Aigaliers, self-seeking and sometimes guileless, was distrusted on both sides, by the government as a faithful Protestant, and by the Camisards as an emissary known to be hostile to the violence that was their last resort. On 18 August Chamillart notified Villars and Basville of the king's decision to send d'Aigaliers out of the kingdom with a pension which, despite Villars' three attempts to have it paid, never reached the exile who was at one moment in his homeless decline reduced to eating his horses.

On 25 August Cavalier learned of Rolland's death and wrote to the minister from Ornans near the frontier, expressing his satisfaction at the news and offering to return to the Languedoc to help bring the remaining rebels back to "the quality of faithful subjects". One explanation of this apparent volte-face from Cavalier's former loyalties, which has earned him as much condemnation from the Huguenots as his later service in the English army, could be that Rolland's disappearance removed the chief obstacle in the way of his desire to save lives in a struggle he knew to be lost; another may have been to throw a smokescreen over his own movements now that he had taken the decision to avoid Brisach and cross into Switzerland at the first opportunity. On the 26th he warned his ninety-five men, all armed, of his intention to steal away that night without attacking their escort of twenty archers. The Camisards unanimously approved, a barrel of wine was supplied to the archers, at three in the morning the refugees entered Montbéliard, a town allied to the Swiss Cantons, and were at Lausanne on the 30th. "This rascal has taken in so many clever people he must be very clever himself," wrote Soeur de Mérez, while the court, the intendant and the marshal all breathed a sigh of relief at the departure of Cavalier, the only leader capable of assembling an organized opposition to the government in the Languedoc.

At the invitation of Richard Hill, Cavalier travelled to Turin where Hill presented him to Victor Amadeus, duke of Savoy who commissioned him as colonel of infantry, commanding for the moment only the troop he had brought over from France. Cavalier, although he pursued his military career in the Allied armies, played no further part in the uprising in his native Cévennes. The marshal wrote to Julien that "the revolt has never been so near to ending, but while there are still armed men one cannot call it entirely finished." On 23 September d'Aigaliers with a troop of thirty-six, of whom half were not rebels, arrived in Geneva. He never understood, said Bosc, that "In those pitiless years one could only remain a Protestant in hiding or by fighting, not in claiming to be at the same time on the side of the king." Secrecy was to remain the condition of survival for those who waited, as the generations passed, for freedom of conscience to be restored in their country.

Notes

1 Frank Puaux, in Jean Cavalier, *Mémoires sur la guerre des Camisards:* 173
2 Marcel Pin, *Jean Cavalier:* 340
3 André Ducasse, *La Guerre des Camisards:* 154
4 Henri Bosc, *La Guerre des Cévennes,* vol. 3: 428
5 Madame du Noyer, *Lettres historiques et galantes:* 293
6 Bosc, vol. 3: 469, 473
7 Pin: 364-5
8 Archives de la Guerre, vol. 1731, folio 115
9 Bosc, vol. 3: 578
10 Archives de la Guerre, vol. 1799, folio 186
11 Jean Cavalier, *Memoirs of the wars of the Cevennes:* 174-5
12 Pin: 390

'God put it into my heart to make a hole in the wall.' Abraham Mazel, prisoner in the Tour de Constance (EmDee/Wikimedia Commons)

Chapter Eight
Huguenot Survival

Historiography

No written record of their actions was kept at the time by any of the Camisards, many of whom were illiterate or nearly so. The accounts of Cavalier, Marion, Bonbonnoux and Mazel were all written later and depended entirely on memory that could be both inaccurate and tendentious. Rolland wrote nothing; letters sent out in his name were put on paper for him by his aide César Malplach acting as his secretary. Therefore the first contemporary written records were the work of Catholics—letters and reports to Chamillart by Basville, by the marshals and generals in the field, and his replies—or the correspondence of fluent, educated and deeply prejudiced ecclesiastics such as Bishop Fléchier of Nîmes or the garrulous and erratically informed Soeur de Mérez whose source within the walls of her convent was necessarily the hearsay she solicited and passed on. Camisard atrocities were reported with outrage while a blind eye was turned to those authorized by the government. The humble origins of the Camisard men and their leaders created a presumption against them of guilt in the reigning climate of royal idolatry and centralized power. When one adversary in a bloody civil conflict is in power and keeps the record and the other is made up of those down the social scale who in Michelet's phrase "have no history", for a time only an authorised version and its backing of official documents are heard and seen.

Even Huguenots who had left France to escape persecution considered obedience to the king and idolization of his person to be incumbent on Protestants as on Catholics, and from their Alpine security they loudly condemned the cévenol insurgents, and viewed their pretensions to prophecy with horror. But prophecy was, as I hope to have shown, an instrument, however histrionic, of disciplinary control in war at least as much as an article of faith. As time passed between the events of the uprising and the accounts of those who wrote about them, the claims to inspiration by the Holy Spirit came to be seen by writers as less significant and much less natural a cause than was an explosive response of the oppressed to their tormentors. As Voltaire put it, the Camisards "acted like wild beasts, but their young and their females had been taken and they tore to pieces the hunters who came after them."

As news of the insurrection and of the humiliations suffered by the army spread through Europe reports began to appear in the press of capitals where French military reverses were welcome: the *Gazettes* of Amsterdam, Berne and Brussels, the *Mercure Historique* among others, and in the English press, uncensored, prolific and not usually very well-informed. The first history to be published, however, was by Louvreleul the *curé* of Saint-Germain-de-Calberte, whose parish lay at the heart of the Camisard country. Appearing in 1703, two thousand copies of his chronicle were sold within four months and a new version was produced the following year and soon translated into Italian and English.

The focus at this stage was on *prophétisme*, fanaticism and their nature; Louvreleul believed them due to demonic possession and his opinion was probably followed by many Catholics as the war went on and their anger grew. However, another priest, the abbé de Brueys who was a former Protestant with the pugnacity of the convert, claimed in his *Histoire du fanatisme de notre temps* of 1709 that fanaticism was a melancholy or mental illness, but also argued that the practice of prophecy was not a spontaneous explosion of collective madness but a prepared operation led by exiled Huguenots cooperating with the enemies of France. Voltaire wrote at some length on the insurrection and on Protestantism in general, and with distaste for what he considered Huguenot pedantry and republicanism; "those psalms ... which charmed the court of François II were no longer made for the populace under Louis XIV." With regard to atrocities, Voltaire shifted his position; in the first edition of *Le Siècle de Louis XIV* he declared that the king "made war on these wretches as they deserved", but toward the end of his life, when he was taking an interest in the continuing persecution of Protestants, he amended the sentence to become: "he made war on these wretches with a barbarism surpassing their own". As

Montaigne had said, "It is setting a high value on one's opinions to have a man cooked alive for them." And Montesquieu claimed to establish a link between monarchy and Catholicism, and between Protestantism and republicanism, a connection which at the time of the Revolution seemed vindicated by events.

In 1705 a vivid and immediate account of the insurrection as experienced in Nîmes was completed but circulated only in the form of written copies until a printed edition was issued in 1874. This was the *Relation historique de la révolte des camisards* by Charles-Joseph de La Baume, a Nîmois judge who had presided over many of the trials and inquisitions under torture of Huguenot captives, had pronounced many death sentences and watched over the executions that followed. By definition, his attitude was that of a judge, the enemy of disorder applying laws he accepted, and though his point of view was Catholic he cannot often be attacked for exclusive partiality. La Baume was an eye witness to Cavalier's reception in Nîmes, to his interview (from a distance) with Villars and Basville in the gardens, and to the great Protestant gathering that followed at Calvisson. His account of these events, and his view of the war supported by the daily experience of a judge in practice, make his *Relation historique* a unique element in its detailed chronicle of the incidents of the war and the interrogation and trial of captives, if not of their historical evaluation. He wrote as a lawyer trained to weigh selected evidence no matter how obtained, and mercy may not generally stand high among forensic attributes.

The first historian to attempt a historical evaluation was Antoine Court, whose work took many years to prepare and write, and many more to find a publisher, a feat achieved at last in 1760. Living in Lausanne until his death, Court accumulated a vast archive of material on the war and above all of accounts by surviving participants. Court's chief merit lies in the collection of evidence which without him would have disappeared. Hostile to Camisard violence, he emphasized the chain of brutality where atrocities on one side answered those on the other, and concluded that the initial responsibility for the war lay with the clergy and the authorities behind them. Philippe Joutard in his historiographical study *La légende des Camisards* judged that while the work of Court cannot be compared to that of Gibbon, it marked a date in French historiography which otherwise had to wait until the second half of the nineteenth century to see a systematic connection between erudition and the human aspect of history. But Court's voice remained an isolated one until a translation of an essay, by an unnamed author, from the *Foreign Quarterly Review* of February 1830 appeared in the *Revue britannique* in 1834. This seems to have been the first work in which the Camisards appear as heroes worthy of mention, "a vision that introduces the historiographic revolution of the following years".[1] The author gave as full an account of the events of the war and its causes as could be drawn from readings of Louvreleul, Brueys, Court and *Le Théatre sacré des Cévennes* by M. Misson, published in London in 1707 and translated as *A Cry from the Desert*. "These men were barbarous and implacable," the author wrote of the Camisards. "How could they be anything else? ... Those who speak with horror of the bloody executions attributed to them say nothing of the many edicts that reduced them to despair and forced them to defend themselves." And he went on to praise their courage and their victory in forcing the great king to deal with them as "equal to equal".

Napoléon Peyrat and Jules Michelet followed eloquently in the process of rehabilitation of the Camisards about whom they both wrote with the empathy of passionate historians of Protestant family origins, and with this increasingly romantic view came a fixed preference for Rolland the undefeated in the fight against despotism, a hero for nineteenth-century rebellion, over Cavalier the negotiator, converted to rational discretion, who ended his life in the service of the English army. Through the century the opposing religious camps and their literary spokesmen produced rival views, both fictional and historical, of the uprising in a process described by Philippe Joutard as "the golden legend against the black".

The writer who most exemplified the difference between historical allegiance and narrative sympathies was Balzac, who fully approved the religious policy of Louis XIV and the Catholic monarchy as a fundamental principle of order, but nevertheless felt a great admiration for Cavalier, comparing him to the young Bonaparte, and evidently recognizing in the career of the baker's boy the story of a "Balzacian character", opposed to society or using it to satisfy ambition, at war with the powers of the day before joining them, and finding his genius in action on the battlefield with his life as the stake.

In the twentieth century much attention has again been focused on the prophetic and inspirational phenomenon. Charles Bost after the First World War concluded that the "inspired were mentally or nervously sick". He wrote that "the prophets worked on minds that a calmer preaching would have left luke-warm." Emmanuel Le Roy Ladurie proposed another psychoanalytical explanation: "Protestant asceticism ... is carried to the point of extreme exaltation in the Cévennes ... accompanied by grandiose phenomena of convulsive hysteria ... in the Freudian scheme, sexual repression logically ends in hysterical situations." In both writers it may seem that aetiological interest has outweighed historical concern. This was corrected by Henri Bosc in the publication, in 1985 for the tricentenary of the Revocation of the Edict of Nantes, of his encyclopaedic work *La Guerre des Cévennes* in six volumes, exhaustive, as readable as Gibbon, supported by scholarship never yet challenged, and balanced and compassionate. Bosc was a pastor who gave his life to the Camisard history and whose thesis—the contents of volume V—was applauded as a masterpiece and unanimously received by the jury of the Institut de France on its presentation in 1973. Bosc waited twelve years to find a publisher brave enough to produce an edition of the four thousand pages of *La Guerre des Cévennes*, which long made superfluous any other detailed and full-scale history.

Scholarly effort on the Camisards continues however, notably in the work of Jean-Paul Chabrol, Philippe Joutard and Patrick Cabanel; a symposium, *Les Camisards et leur mémoire*, was held at Le Pont-de-Montvert three hundred years after the assassination of du Chayla and was attended by a great audience of teachers and students of a history that has also fascinated novelists such as Jean-Pierre Chabrol and André Chamson. The marseillais director René Allio contributed to the tradition of a living legend, supported by the continuing oral witness of cévenol families whose forebears have often not moved from their rebuilt stone houses in the valleys and the fringes of the forest and who honour the memory of a *galérien* among their ancestors, in his 1972 film *Les Camisards*, austere and tragic as the first European guerrilla war itself of which survivors, stubborn witnesses of ongoing memory, continue to offer evidence through their descendants. And in one or other of these still unmodernized houses may yet be unearthed hidden papers to light up some corner of the struggle like those discovered by Marcel Pin, the biographer of Cavalier, in which he found "the sand that had dried the ink in 1703".

End of a Revolt

Patrick Cabanel describes in his *Histoire des protestants en France* how the walls of his home in the Cévennes still showed, like many others, the black scars of the great burnings: "One is struck by the modernity of this destruction..." The displaced population remained crushed into camps for more than a year before being authorized in September 1704 to go home and rebuild what they could find among the ruins, while groups of the last resistants continued to give themselves up in hope of amnesty. Villars saw clearly, and warned the court, that even if the revolt was declining no change of spirit could be expected, but this intelligent appreciation did not hamper his pursuit of a policy of extreme severity against those who would not accept the terms of surrender and pardon offered. La Lande set these out for Marion to consider: "that no one would be molested for their religion, no one would be forced to attend mass. All could serve God in their own houses, with the Bible and Protestant books; but there would be no more singing out loud of psalms."

On 13 September the last encounter that could be called a battle rather than a skirmish took place at Saint-Bénézet on the Gardon, close to Cavalier's birthplace. The Camisards under Ravanel were attacked in the wood where they were sheltering, driven across the river where they met at once another army contingent, driven back over the river and trapped by forces advancing on them on both sides. The survivors crossed the river a third time near Ribaute and a few succeeded in reaching the woods of Bagard, trackless, impenetrable and out of sight. Ravanel had apparently not learned from his superior Cavalier the elements of strategy which, it is true, Cavalier himself had neglected at Nages. But Ravanel's survival among the dead at Saint-Bénézet had none of Cavalier's bravura in the crossing of the Rhosny in the Vaunage. Ravanel escaped by feigning death among the bodies of his followers, and he was accused by many in the Huguenot camp of having saved his own life at the expense of others. His intransigence was to be the cause of many unnecessary deaths in the months to come and appears as the last, toxic fruit of "enthusiasm" as defined by Locke: "a strong and firm persuasion ... of any truths wrought in the mind extraordinarily by god himself and influences coming immediately from him". History seems not to lack examples.

The defeat at Saint-Bénézet was followed by the surrender of Catinat and Castanet, both allowed to depart with their followers to Geneva. Marion described the dilemma of the remaining leaders and the pitiful condition of their men making it evident that the revolt was near its end: "We had no inspirations either ordering or forbidding us to lay down our arms ... our poor troop diminished day by day and those who remained constantly urged us to accept the proposals made to us ... but we could not decide to abandon so good a cause, which had cost so much blood..." To encircle and trap the last small bands of starving men, methodical beats of sections of forest were organized while it was made known that Basville favoured allowing those who surrendered to return home. On 30 September, Salomon Couderc and Jouani with forty men, fifty guns and, some believed, two cannons made from the bronze of church bells, gave themselves up to La Lande, but the government refused Basville's advice to give them permission to return home, the king being convinced, rightly, that they remained dangerous and were better expelled from the kingdom. Jouani became an officer in the royal army and departed to fight in Spain though forbidden to return to France without permission from the government. On 8 October Marion, Mazel, La Rose and eighty followers surrendered at Saint-Jean-du-Gard, marching in to beating drums and watched by a population moved at the sight of this last parade of haggard, disease-ridden, heroic resistants.

On 27 October Villars issued a new ordinance forbidding assemblies, which he believed were always the starting point of disturbance, and the necessity for this order is the proof that assemblies, in spite of the fierce punishment of those caught and the misery of the people in a year of failed harvest, continued to be held as they always had been. Bonbonnoux gave an account of the few Camisards still on the run who would stop to kneel in the snow and pray, as if prayer in public gathering and intercourse with God were worth all the pains of the wheel or stake awaiting them. On 7 November five of Ravanel's men surrendered, leaving him with no more than eleven, and reported him to be ill and with a maimed arm. On the 14th Villars informed the minister that the cévenol communities, infuriated by the continuing resistance, were now driving away the Camisards who appeared at their doors, just as Catinat was reported to be back in France with new promises from Queen Anne of rescue for rebels holding on in the mountains. This delusory project would suggest that Allied intelligence, through dubious agents such as Flotard, about affairs in the Languedoc and the condition and numbers of the surviving rebels hiding in caves was far less accurate than the information delivered to Chamillart and Basville by their spy networks. Meanwhile, the army counted on denunciations by peasants, an encouraging development expected to lead, as it soon did, to effective betrayals.

The first of these was by two brothers Bourguet, Camisards from the beginning, who led the authorities to hiding places of their friends and houses of secret sympathizers. Money was found in the room of a neighbour of the Bourguet at Corbès and he was arrested. "It is an excellent thing to see these people accuse one another as they very rarely do," Villars wrote to the minister, and Marion described one of the brothers "running here and there leading detachments wherever our poor brothers hid, pursuing them like a devil incarnate..." Over Christmas a number of arrests were made and on the 26th Basville reported the discovery of two powder-making installations in the high Cévennes. "So disappeared, at this end of 1704, the last rebels driven by despair and exhaustion into a dead-end. Denunciations finally ruined the revolt ... but, in this traumatised country, the population, urban as well as rural, remained Protestant at heart."[2]

Only Ravanel, Bonbonnoux, Claris, who had walked on fire, and Abraham Mazel remained at large. Mazel was captured at the end of the year and thanks to the intervention of a priest whose life he had spared, was condemned only to prison in the Tour de Constance at Aigues-Mortes. The States General of the Languedoc voted large financial rewards for this result to the marshal and his wife and Villars was recalled to Versailles in mid-January, elevated to duke and given the chief command of the armies on the eastern frontier. Michelet wrote that "he returned glorious from a peace which he hadn't made ... the Languedoc remained crushed but not pacified, and Berwick, the bastard of James II had to be sent there." To his credit, Villars had above all understood that the *curés* needed to be taught humanity and kept in their place; before leaving the province he wrote to the Bishop of Alais, "Your priests should be looked to ... consider how the zeal of the wisest and most saintly of the bishops has to be moderated." A beneficial consequence of the war in the Cévennes was a tempering of the influence on everyday life of an intolerant and undisciplined element in the Catholic clergy.

Castanet, who had returned to the Vivarais to call assemblies and preach out his sacred mission, was captured near Barjac on 15 March; under torture he revealed only that the Allies and the exiles planned an invasion of the Cévennes by land or sea, and that he and Catinat had come to distribute subsidy to potential rebels. On the 26th Castanet was executed on the wheel at Montpellier before twelve thousand people with full ceremony. "Castanet made a very beautiful death," Marion wrote from London in his memoirs, but his revelations reignited the suspicions of Basville and others that the Camisards and their leaders who had been allowed to emigrate, most particularly Cavalier, were awaiting the moment for a return, backed by a well-equipped foreign army, to revive the uprising.

In fact, the Bourbon marquis de Miremont was secretly organizing the most audacious conspiracy he had yet conceived. The last exhausted Camisards, if they could be found, were to see the arrival of the aid they had expected for two years. Marion, returned from Geneva, would with the remaining leaders attempt to buy arms and ammunition with some of the money frugally doled out from England, and create formations of the faithful willing to risk their lives. But the money supposedly sent was still not reaching the men in the forests and in their disappointment they put together an extravagant scheme which would be their undoing; Basville and the Duke of Berwick, the bishops and judges were to be captured and simultaneous attacks in the principal towns would end in the slaughter of the garrisons and the arrest of the governors. Basville would be executed and the others embarked on a ship to England. A continuous flow of instructions came meanwhile from Miremont and the agents of the Allies but without money for acquiring arms as if the remaining insurgents were being driven headlong into a wall by intent.

According to Marion's account of this conspiracy of l es enfants de dieu, the bankers and other leading citizens and merchants of Nîmes were giving encouragement, and promises of support, to a group of defeated plotters some of whom were guided by inspiration and others by despair. These personnes considérables, Marion claimed, would throw off the mask as soon as the marquis de Miremont arrived at the frontier of the province. The battle cry was to be "Long live the king without Jesuits, and freedom of conscience!" A meeting of all the leaders was called at Montpellier where they were to sign receipts for the money still in the hands of agents, a fatal precaution by remote authorities with no knowledge of the immediate dangers; Ravanel and Catinat were at Nîmes, Marion and Claris near Saint-Jean-du-Gard where they remained. In the citadel at Montpellier were held on suspicion a number of new converted prisoners with some of whom the almoner, the abbé de Massillan, had established relations of trust. He had the confidence also of Basville who placed him where he was in order to pass on information gathered in the secrecy of the confessional, an example of the ruthless hypocrisy of Church and state acting together. One of the prisoners, Chevalier, confessed to Massillan that a conspiracy was about to explode on 25 April and that the leaders were in the town. He refused to say more, and Basville ordered the gates of the town closed on the 17th and 18th while a systematic search was made by night in the houses of suspects. A large number of arrests followed and incriminating documents found which enabled Basville and Berwick to decapitate at a single blow the plot of the enfants de dieu, an adventure of naivety in which Miremont the ambitious politician of royal blood attempted to use the peasant survivors of persecution and war. Torture and fear soon led the authorities to the house in Nîmes where the long-sought Ravanel was discovered, while Catinat was arrested at one of the city gates. They were executed in the flames on the Esplanade next day before a great crowd and a powerful military presence in case of disturbance, with the sound of drums to drown the chanting of their psalms as they burned.

Other arrests and executions by fire and wheel, two hundred according to Voltaire, of gardeners, millers, carters, farmers and merchants followed in an atmosphere of terror, spying and denunciations which left the citizens "petrified with horror",[3] though not all of them. The charity of Soeur de Mérez was not strained: "We see a terrible scene, but what was prepared by these scoundrels for tomorrow has led us to great actions of thanks to the Lord ... all seems pacified." Bosc, among others, suspected that the plot had been allowed by the authorities to ripen and grow in order to capture the remaining Camisards and as many as possible among the civilian population who still favoured them. "The whole plot of the *enfants de dieu* smells of machination and trap."[4] Moreover, it is hard to believe that Nîmois bankers and businessmen would have been foolhardy enough to risk their lives in a heavily policed and militarized city by encouraging, and still less joining, the desperate insurrection of an unstructured band of failed rebels planning to overthrow the state; and if they had, it would not have been necessary to rely on subsidies, never received, from foreign governments through undependable agents some of whom might have been spies.

Basville and Berwick both solicited the king for a reward to the abbé de Massillan, betrayer of the secret of the confessional but "zealous, discreet and virtuous".[5] On 13 May Chamillart wrote to Berwick that for the future it would be better that he and Basville moderate the extreme ferocity of the condemnations which had sickened the people of Nîmes, even the Catholics, and from the 16th there were no further public executions. A consequence of the failure of the plot was to discredit Miremont and his ally La Bourlie, marquis de Guiscard, in the eyes of the Allied governments, and permanently to erode their belief in the military possibilities of insurrection in the Languedoc. The Camisards had never received help from saviours over the water, some like Rolland had continued the fight in a belief that help would come; and the few remaining were now abandoned.

Marion, who had stayed away from the conspiracy of the *enfants de dieu*, was among those few still living as hunted animals in the mountain forests. At the beginning of July he decided to give himself up, hoping, although he had returned to France without permission, to benefit from the renewed offer of amnesty announced by Berwick after the bloodbath of the Nîmes executions. He was detained for some weeks in comfortable conditions while Basville decided whether more useful information could be extracted from him by torture, or by passing him over the frontier into Switzerland where he might join the squadron of spies enrolled by the French government. Choosing the second course, Basville overlooked the objection that Marion was an *inspiré* whose every action was dictated by the inner voice; and not long after his return to Geneva he left for London, pursuing to the end of his life a fantasy of general European conversion. Before Marion was conducted to the frontier with his companion La Valette, who surrendered at the same time, they were visited in their confinement by Massillan the almoner—a visit that suggests an attempt to enrol them in a network of spies—and were told of the dramatic escape of Mazel from the Tour de Constance.

The Tour de Constance is an immense circular moated tower within the outer defences of the fortress of Aigues-Mortes containing three superimposed, vaulted prison chambers lit only by long slit windows through six-metre walls. Mazel was imprisoned with thirty-two other men in the topmost room, the Salle des Chevaliers, while the captive Huguenot women, some of them to remain in the tower for more than thirty years, were in the *salle* below. The only exit was by three barred doors down a guarded spiral staircase in the thickness of the walls; water came from a rain reservoir on the roof, and food, *le pain du roi*, was raised by a rope passing through a circular, well-like opening in the centre of the floor. There was no sanitation, but the Tour de Constance was a merciful place of incarceration compared to many of the other prisons in France where captives died of dysentery, or by being trampled to death by other captives in blind, airless dungeons.

Mazel, imprisoned since January, had been inspired from the beginning to organize an escape which required at least the complicity of all the others; "God put it into my heart to make a hole in the wall," he recorded, and his fellow-prisoners were evidently as convinced as he by the inspiration. An iron cramp securing two stones was removed from the wall, sharpened with a hammer and anvil of cannon balls, and used to enlarge one of the slit windows. A rope was made of bed-clothes, a bar of wood attached to the bottom end and the top tied to the cramp re-embedded in stone on each side of the opening. Mazel was the first to go down, thirty metres astride the wooden bar, on the night of 24 July, three years to the day after the assassination at Le Pont-de-Montvert where he had struck the first blow; he was followed by seventeen others before the alarm was given. Together they swam the moat and escaladed the outer wall, then ran over a bridge of the canal joining Aigues-Mortes to the sea and vanished into the darkness of the surrounding leech-infested marshes where they hid for twenty-four hours before separating. Three were captured, eight gave themselves up, Mazel was amnestied and allowed to depart for Geneva with Marion and La Valette, and the rest disappeared into the Cévennes to lead the life without escape of hunted refugees in a land turned inhospitable.

Geneva, Cavalier, and the Allied Nations

Marion's first action on arrival in the Swiss capital, where his companions saw a *temple* and a *pasteur* for the first time, was to issue a bitter diatribe attacking those pastors who had fled France after the Revocation, leaving their flocks to persecution and ultimately to martyrdom. "They have flown from kingdom to kingdom, not because of the persecution ... but to find that fat land where peace and abundance reign." Since martyrdom was the aim of rebels who would not accept the pardon offered to them, Marion's accusation seems like the outburst of a man suffering a sense of neglect. His next angry response was to the failure of the Allied agents, particularly of Richard Hill, English envoy to Victor Amadeus of Savoy, to supply the cash subsidy required by these veteran penniless immigrants. "You maintain at Lausanne the Camisards who left France ... and even give high pay to people who call themselves Camisards who are the deserters of France..." This appears to refer to Richard Hill's support of Cavalier and the award to him of four hundred gold *louis* on behalf of Queen Anne.[6]

In action, the Camisards were bonded together; later, when the outcome of action was part of history, jealousies appeared and their focus was chiefly on Cavalier who paid the price both for his successes and his defeat. Marion's written attacks in London on Cavalier's record and character, which contributed to the later criticism by Antoine Court and Napoléon Peyrat, have the accumulated anger of envy. "So soon as M. Cavaliers arrived I carried him to our camp and his Royal Highness received him very well. He gave him a commission to be colonel in his service," Hill wrote.[7] Cavalier left Lausanne for Turin and the court of Savoy on 20 September with seventy of his men, leaving the others in Switzerland where the diverse groups of Camisards soon made themselves unpopular. Prophetic manifestation was particularly disliked in Geneva and the rough manners of peasants added to occasional lawlessness due to penury made these refugees still more unwelcome in an orderly Calvinist society; some of the Camisards crossed the frontiers to join armies in Germany, others went on the long journey by foot to Poland or Holland. Those in Switzerland became increasingly a social responsibility no one wanted, while the failure of the conspiracy of the *enfants de dieu* resulted in disillusionment in the military and diplomatic circles of the Allied nations, as well as among the Camisards seeing the disappearance of their last hope of a return to the Languedoc. Attacks on priests in Catholic areas began to occur, with robbery of items of value in presbyteries. It was logical, said Bosc, that certain of these "displaced heroes and unemployed combatants" for whom death was now the only other way out should be tempted to renew their guerrilla activities or to rejoin Cavalier and enrol with him.[8] The crushing of the revolt in the Cévennes left a vacant space in the military possibilities of the Languedoc into which the ambitious Miremont, the undisciplined La Bourlie and other agents looking for gain would not be long in seeking a way; and this was presented to them by the development of an Allied plan to equip a fleet.

Cavalier was disappointed in his effort to raise a regiment in Savoy, and decided to make his way to Holland without authorization of the duke. Arriving at the end of December, he was extremely well received by diplomats and soldiers and feted in the society of the curious.

The Duke of Marlborough wrote to him on 22 February, "I cannot sufficiently praise your zeal for your poor brethren in France ... the Queen, I assure you, is sensible of it." He wasted no time in putting up his plan of action. Since the road to the Languedoc was now closed by French forces at the Swiss and Savoyard frontiers, he advocated an invasion from Spain, a plan which coincided with that adopted by the Dutch States General. The English government ordered the raising of four regiments. Cavalier was commissioned as colonel and Miremont as lieutenant-general commanding. Exiled Camisards from Switzerland and Germany hurried to Holland to serve under the famous colonel in hopes of returning to their native land. England and Holland began the process of bargaining on the financing, equipping, ordering and manning of the expeditionary force and the fleet destined to carry it. Miremont wanted overall command and was enraged to find that this had been given to Lord Galway, who as marquis de Ruvigny had taken exile in Ireland, while La Bourlie was equally indignant at being placed under the orders of Lord Peterborough. Miremont resigned his commission and La Bourlie crossed to London to remonstrate with the Duke of Marlborough, their umbrageous and cloistered behaviour at the outset of a complex international military operation seeming to strangely foreshadow that of Gaullists in London in the Second World War.

Cavalier disembarked in England with his regiment on 31 July and was interviewed by the Lord Treasurer Godolphin to whom he explained that on the arrival of an expeditionary Protestant force in Catalonia the Protestants of the Languedoc would rise again as one man. Godolphin declared that Cavalier's plan accorded perfectly with that of the Queen and her ministers. Miremont and La Bourlie, however, favoured a landing at La Rochelle on the Atlantic coast, much closer to Paris and not in mountainous country; the decision went against them and La Bourlie, as unwilling as Miremont to serve under Galway's orders, incited a mutiny among his men; three regiments of exiled troops were broken and reformed, their officers dismissed and La Bourlie was ordered to leave the fleet.

Sailing on 24 August from Portsmouth, the ships were driven by a storm onto the Devon coast where they anchored until finally making sail for Lisbon at the beginning of November. Between seven and eight thousand men were carried in three hundred vessels; at Lisbon the King of Portugal had oranges and lemons distributed against scurvy and the army rested until the end of the year, with visits to the vineyards of the Tagus, before setting out to pass through the Straits of Gibraltar and head northward to Barcelona, key to the Languedoc across the frontier and held by the King of Spain and the Bourbon comte de Toulouse. "This departure from Lisbon," said Bosc on a note of grudging admiration for the lad from Anduze, "marked for Cavalier a new starting point; a march on Catalonia with another march towards the Cévennes in view." He had accepted the presence in his regiment of an equal proportion of officers from the nobility with those from the ranks of his companions: "This mixture seemed hard to the gentry, associated with and even subordinate to officers recruited from the plough ... but it honours the cévenol shepherd who, becoming a colonel, blushed neither for his origins nor for his companions."[9]

The raising of the siege of Barcelona seemed to open the road toward the Languedoc although the French army commanded by the Duke of Berwick remained beyond the frontier in the Roussillon. On 13 January the Allied army, of which the English element including Cavalier's regiment numbered no more than five thousand men, had disembarked in the province of Valencia and begun to make its way northward, joined by reinforcements as it went. At the same time Berwick was massing a Franco-Spanish army of thirty-two thousand to face them. The Allied army, of whom many and particularly the English recently arrived were sick with dysentery, marched toward the plain at Almansa, where Berwick was encamped, on the night of 24 to 25 April. The encounter finally began at three in the afternoon. By six the murderous battle was won by Berwick's army, with massive losses on both sides and the almost complete destruction of Galway's infantry including the regiment of Cavalier and his Camisards who were reported to have fought like lions. Cavalier himself received serious wounds in a dozen places and his life was saved by an English officer whose name is not known. The hope of reaching Roussillon and the Languedoc to reawaken the cévenol revolt was extinguished by this victory of a mainly French army commanded by an English prince, bastard son of James II by a sister of the Duke of Marlborough, over a predominantly English army commanded by a French marquis who in exile had been decorated with an Irish earldom.

The defeat of Almansa caused the Allies to turn their attention elsewhere and a plan was formed, and a fleet and army assembled, for an invasion through Provence, a natural point of entry into France for Victor Amadeus who was joined by Cavalier, partially recovered from his multiple wounds. His presence with the Savoyards brought back the familiar fears that he was the only figure able to raise a serious revolt in the Languedoc if the invasion were to reach it. On 5 August Chamillart wrote to Basville: "There is no doubt that Cavalier ... now with the army commanded by the duke of Savoy who treats him with every kind of flattery and has him to eat at his table, will try every means to penetrate into the country where he is known," and the Prince of Monaco attempted unsuccessfully to have him arrested in Menton. But the invasion of Provence and the siege of Toulon were repelled by prompt action of the French, and the Duke of Savoy withdrew from the coast and returned to Piedmont; the fleet sailed away and the Allied hope of reaching the Cévennes finally collapsed. Bosc wrote of Cavalier's despair on finding that his part in the action of war and in the cévenol uprising, though not his military career, was at an end.

Salomon Couderc, one of du Chayla's assassins, returned to his homeland from authorized exile, was captured and burnt after refusing under torture to give names of his companions in France. One by one, those of the Camisard refugees, isolated and weakened by privation, who refused to surrender and leave the country, return to their homes or serve in the royal armies were caught like starving animals in the forest beats and executed. Others, abandoned by the population, were betrayed and their progressive disappearance left only a few followers in the deepest hiding-places. "Our home was the forest, the mountains, the valleys, the most deserted and remote places, sometimes the lair of rocks and caves ... I could say like Jacob ... 'the ground was my bed, the air was its roof and the sky my covering'," Bonbonnoux wrote. But before their disappearance the Camisards took care, and great risks, to punish those who had betrayed their friends; at Mialet, they executed Bourguet from Corbès, at Durfort, the traitor Salles, and at Monoblet,

Martin, who had led the royal troops to places of assembly. "In this way," wrote Court in a notable understatement, "they taught respect to informers and traitors."

Abraham Mazel

In London, Mazel seems to have kept away from the proselytizing activities and public show of the French Prophets. Although he was devout, utterly committed to Camisard beliefs and frequently inspired, it may be that the prophets' pilgrimage of conversion across Europe interested him less than the rule of faith in his native Cévennes and the fate of his remaining comrades. Bosc was certain that the chief motive of Cavalier's visit to London with his friend and lieutenant Daniel Guy in February to March 1708 was to make contact with Mazel and incite him, with the support of Miremont, to leave England and accept the task of raising a revolt in the Vivarais, Cavalier being shadowed wherever he went by Chamillart's spies and too well-known for secrecy. Mandated by Miremont as official emissary for this expedition, Mazel, with Daniel Guy and Cavalier's secretary Antoine Dupont, left London for Geneva on 25 August. In early spring of 1709 the three men passed the frontier, armed with pistols and a sword between them and approached the Rhône near Valence, crossing it to the western side on the night of 4 April. On 12 May Mazel issued a manifesto demanding the restoration of the Edict of Nantes, and began the process of recruiting and inflaming his followers with prophecy and preaching. By 20 June they were reported to Basville to number between three and four hundred.

The first encounter was on 22 June when the Swiss element in the royal army turned tail and fled; Mazel was wounded and this small Camisard victory was followed by a movement of six thousand troops toward the River Ardèche and into the Vivarais to prevent the rebels from entering the Cévennes. On 8 July the last battle of the Camisard War took place on the steep mountainside of Leyrisse; hugely outnumbered, the rebels knelt in prayer in the open as the military approached, then marched toward them and opened fire first. The rumour that Cavalier was present and in command was disproved by the evidence of this tactical blunder; the soldiers attacked with bayonets before their opponents could reload and in spite of fierce resistance the battle was soon over. The army was said to have lost fifty men and as many wounded; Antoine Laporte was killed with at least sixty of his companions; Mazel, whose wound had prevented him from fighting, escaped with Guy to re-form the survivors; guerrilla revolt had become a way of life and martyrdom its last purpose.

On 1 September Mazel and Guy, with a few companions, after weeks in hiding and harassed by hostile peasants both Catholic and Protestant, were located thanks to an informer in a nearby village at Gilhac. The troops encircled them, they escaped into the night but Guy was shot dead as he ran. His body was exposed on a wheel at Vernoux and left to rot. One after the other the rest, at least forty according to Antoine Court, were recognized, betrayed and delivered for execution. Court, then a boy of fourteen, was present at an assembly where he saw, and never forgot, Mazel the "prophet", hunted, hirsute and bloodied. Mazel was near Uzès in November and was joined by his old companion Claris, the last Camisard leader at large in the Cévennes, whose presence may have been to each of them some solace in the long shadow of mortality that had taken almost all of their leading Camisard comrades; Basville, contrary to earlier practice, made no offer of amnesty to either of them or to their troop of fifteen men. Whatever the hopelessness of their plight, starving, wounded without medication, short of ammunition and rejected now by the population like infected rats, despair was never part of their experience; the elaborate tortures awaiting the captured, or the quick death given to the luckier, neither frightened them nor shook their absolute certainties. It can be said of religion that it may make the last pains endurable, and the courage of the Camisards dying on the wheel is the example.

At this point, far too late to serve any of its intended purpose, a fleet of English ships anchored in the Golfe du Lion and a landing was made at Sète; Agde was briefly captured before the invading force was driven back to its ships by French troops present in the Languedoc in great numbers and moving swiftly. Any hope of an Allied intervention from the sea was cut off at source and the trickle of money reaching the small band of still active rebels dried up. On 14 October Claris and Mazel took refuge in a farm near Uzès, where they were found; Mazel, the first and last of the Camisards, was killed, and Claris, attempting to escape once again, was captured. On 25 October Pierre Claris was executed on the wheel at Montpellier; Basville wrote after his interrogation, "he died with great firmness, although he was only a mason, and I found in him far more intelligence than I would have expected, with a talent for speaking and for moving the people."

The disappearance of the last of the resistants marked the end of the war in the Cévennes. A few survivors, lost and despised,[10] remained abroad but the fire of the Camisard uprising would not be relit. However, on 25 August 1715 as Louis XIV lay dying at Versailles, "his flesh decaying and gangrenous, the first synod of the *Églises du Désert* was held in a quarry not far from Nîmes ... heresy was being reborn everywhere."[11]

Travelling Prophets

The French Prophets in London and their followers were pursuing not martyrdom but missionary apotheosis. Disappointed by the scepticism of an English audience which they had courted, they began to receive intimations through Élie Marion from the Spirit that it was time to move on. Frontiers of language and regulation seemed to mean little to them and in many countries of northern Europe there was already a Huguenot exile presence. Further south were unreformed populations and the capitals of infamy. On 14 July the four missionaries, Jean Allut, Charles Portalès, Nicolas Fatio and Élie Marion, left London for Harwich.

They reached Berlin, where there were many French Protestants in exile and an active French culture, on the 23rd; they were promptly attacked in court by the Calvinist consistory as they had been in London and were ordered to quit Berlin by sunset and the kingdom within three days. They stayed a fortnight in Leipzig and on 1 September Marion announced imminent persecutions against the city before leaving with his companions to make their way by stages towards Vienna. Each onward move was made on the instructions of the Spirit, and in each town they visited the reception was as it had been in Berlin; the inspired itinerary was as prudence dictated. On 20 October they reached Catholic Vienna where many more and virulent prophetic warnings were uttered before a hurried departure for Holland. Three of the missionaries re-embarked for London, leaving Fatio in Rotterdam, and arrived there on 4 December. The outcome of the tour appeared discouraging but the imperious apocalyptic mission was not long put off; another embarkation from Harwich to Holland was taken on 9 June 1712, with Stockholm as the destination. Marion was convinced that the Spirit had orders to be passed through his voice to Charles XII of Sweden, seen by the visionaries as the Lion of the North who with the Great Bird of the East, the caliph, would sweep Europe with the fire of religion.

The king was not in Stockholm but in the northern part of the Ottoman Empire and the Spirit ordered Marion to lead the group of missionaries to the Levant to find him, "for I have a message to give him from the great king who anointed him". In Danzig the four missionaries were arrested by officers of the King of Poland as suspected spies from Sweden. They were held in various prisons for eight months in conditions of hardship and privation until liberated on 5 May 1713 with none of their possessions returned, including passports. Marion fell ill with violent fevers during the imprisonment and never returned to health; the journey continued through Germany, where new passports and a supply of money were obtained with the help of resident Huguenots, to the Danube where they embarked for Belgrade to cross the Ottoman Empire: "You will not have to stay long in the town I am sending you to, I mean Constantinople. But I will do great things there."

What these were to be never transpired; in Constantinople help was sought and obtained from the English ambassador and care was taken, no doubt on his advice, to avoid prophecy in public. The stay was brief and the journey resumed at the beginning of September under the ambassador's protection and in an English ship towards Italy, with Rome as its ultimate destination. Marion, growing weaker, no longer spoke with the Spirit's voice. On 3 October the ship landed at Livorno, famous for religious tolerance thanks to its cosmopolitanism. On 23 November three of the missionaries set off for Rome, leaving Marion "ill to extremity" in Livorno where he died on the 29th; they reached the end of their mission's trajectory on 3 December. Although they were now at the heart of Catholicism, "Babylon and the great prostitute personified",[12] the prophets were sparing of threats of cataclysm as issued in Vienna and Leipzig; prison in Poland had perhaps taught discretion. On 10 December the three started the return journey to London after eighteen months of a pilgrimage which, viewed in a perspective of Camisard exploits in the Cévennes, of the daring of Cavalier, the heroic obduracy of Rolland, the faith of the tortured and executed, seems a saddening delusion of men with no homeland and no place to find in the daily reality of other men and women.

Colonel Cavalier's Progress

After the battle of Almansa Jean Cavalier saw no more action in the field. His career was that of an officer of special talents for which the times were unsuited, and around the Allied military headquarters in Holland he was only one among many half-pay officers senior to him and from higher social backgrounds, though he was the only hero in their ranks. His usefulness as potential leader of revolt in the Languedoc ended with the Allies' failure to mount an invasion and his presence and demands for a regimental command became an encumbrance. After a series of deferrals and disappointments, Cavalier decided to try his chance in England. In London, the activities of the French Prophets and the resulting disturbances of the peace were not helpful in his search for employment. As Pin wrote, Cavalier had been the most famous of the "inspired" but now understood that his crises of inspiration were not of divine origin; he had become a regular army officer and an orthodox Protestant, distancing himself from prophecy in the hope that the authorities in England would see his successes as due only to military capacity—which no one doubted. However, from the moment that he no longer wished to return to conspire in the Languedoc but to mount a regiment with himself in command, his status diminished. The English government had abandoned thoughts of invasion, was not raising regiments, and Cavalier was given a modest pension but no new commission. He, the prodigious guerrilla warrior, joined the ranks of unneeded half-pay officers whose warlike ambitions, if they had them, were never likely to be met.

Cavalier had both financial and marital difficulties and in the hope of resolving both he accepted, in 1713, a position in Portarlington in

Ireland where the marquis de Ruvigny, become Lord Galway, had been rewarded by William III with an estate confiscated from a family that had chosen to follow the deposed James II. At Portarlington, where French was still the language of the majority of the citizens in 1820, a failed English colony under the previous owner was replaced with a largely French settlement including a number of Huguenot officers and men to form a garrison, and in this static, mostly unemployed and inglorious company Cavalier spent the next thirteen years. He married in 1723 and spent much of his time writing the *Mémoires sur la guerre des Camisards*, often criticized, not always unjustly, for inaccuracy and false claims, which was first published in English in Dublin in 1726. The emphasis on his own exploits was clearly intended to impress his superior officers with his military ability and potential usefulness, and in 1735 he was promoted brigadier general. Three years later, he became lieutenant governor of the isle of Jersey, and major general in 1739. In Jersey the shepherd boy of Ribaute, the baker's lad of Anduze, led the life of a *grand seigneur*, though without, apparently, domestic happiness. His estranged wife, daughter of a French aristocrat, came to Jersey in 1739 to beg forgiveness, though it is not known for what, and was turned away. If Cavalier found consolation in the island, few would begrudge it him. In 1740 he travelled to London where he fell ill; he died in Chelsea on 17 May. Pin stated that he left considerable debts, but the mixed fame of the daring Camisard, with his great gifts and commonplace faults, left the Huguenots of the Cévennes and of the diaspora still more in debt to him in memory.

Protestants of France

The Camisard War ended, as it had to, with the defeat of the weakest: the great king had won a victory over a fraction of his people. The villages and farms of the high Cévennes were destroyed, between ten and twenty thousand of the civilian population had died and four thousand Camisards were killed in action. The population was allowed by degrees to return to rebuild their homes and lives; between 1720 and 1750 there was a slow regrowth to relative prosperity in subsistence-farming communities so poor that they were exempted from tax for several decades. The *temples* everywhere remained razed to the ground and were not rebuilt until after 1820; the Edict of Nantes was never restored but lived on in memory, and still more in imagination, as the free ideal under which French people could keep respect for their conscience.

In the first aftermath of the uprising it could have seemed that the revolt, the death roll and the suffering had been for nothing, and some Protestants of the *refuge* believed that the cause of the reform was set back by the violence of the Camisards and the phenomenon of prophecy. These two aspects of the uprising have been, on the one hand, the cause of its ill-repute among early historians; but on the other, they are integrally part of its survival in the zone of legend lying between memory and myth, which accounts for the continuing passion aroused by the drama and the actors in it, and to a considerable extent for the resilience of Protestantism in France, with the panache and heroism of the Camisards borrowed to light up a sober Calvinist scenery while the shadow of their violence is muted. Cavalier, despised by orthodox Huguenot historians for his denial of the *prophétisme* they rejected, began with time to be restored to esteem as some of the emphasis of admiration shifted from martyrdom to prowess.

The second and yet more significant result of the war was indirectly to ease the restoration of Protestantism in the eighteenth century, largely through the work of Antoine Court, by forcing prudence in repression on the authorities: "It took 60,000 soldiers to defeat the Camisards ... The revolt left so fearsome a memory that magistrates in the Languedoc no longer dared to act as ferociously as Basville ... the Protestants were stronger because they were more feared."[13] Moreover, Philippe Joutard points out that most of the men who helped Court in the peaceful reorganization of the Church of the *Désert* after 1715 were former Camisards. It has also been argued that the humiliations suffered by the army and by its marshals in the Cévennes, and the demonstration that in Voltaire's words "it is easier to lead 100,000 men to war than to force submission on the minds of the convinced", were the first undermining of absolute monarchy. "The king, the state, even the pope, all were damaged by the persecutions against the Huguenots. Why? Because after such a breaking-point there was nothing inviolable left in France."

Patrick Cabanel went further: "Was there by this war on the Protestants the first loss of the sacred aura of power and of the law ...and can it be seen as one of the sources of the French Revolution and the execution of the king?"[14]

Modern historians give the Camisard uprising much of the credit for the survival of French Protestantism through the eighteenth century until the Revolution: "The fear of reigniting such a war was a powerful element of dissuasion to the authorities. The persecution continued but never with the intensity it had before ... for once and for some time, fear had changed camps."[15] The laws of repression remained in force but were not applied except occasionally to make examples. The bishops were made to temper their anger and the priests to learn discretion. The most striking illustration was the holding of an assembly by Antoine Court on the outskirts of Uzès in September 1744, attended by seven thousand people and left undisturbed by the authorities despite the bishop's complaint that he could hear the chanting of psalms from his garden.

The opinion of the enlightened, and particularly that of Voltaire leading them, moved with the tide as the century progressed so that the Revolution was prepared for the concept of liberty of conscience. The last execution of a Protestant on the wheel was that of Jean Calas, by a gross miscarriage of justice, in 1762 at Toulouse. The case was taken up by Voltaire whose *Traité sur la tolérance* was read all over Europe, and led to the rehabilitation of Calas in 1765: "Paris and all Europe are moved to pity and demand justice..." By 1789 the cause for which the Camisards had fought was won in all but name. Rabaut Saint-Etienne, a Protestant pastor from Nîmes, formerly in hiding but elected in 1790 as first president of the National Assembly and second personage in the state after the king, declared to the Assembly, "It is not tolerance I ask for, it is what you demand for yourselves, liberty, equality of rights." This step was taken by the Constituent Assembly on 24 December 1789, decreeing at last that every citizen be free to "practise the cult to which he is attached". The Edict of Nantes was no longer needed.

The Camisards who took refuge in Switzerland were not far from the homeland, and their descendants were able to keep the frame of a cévenol identity with their exiled nationality. Others who went to the Protestant German regions and to Holland were integrated into the Huguenot communities already living there, and from 1685 onwards thirteen thousand went from Holland to South Africa where they were progressively absorbed into the Dutch Afrikaner community, became *voortrekkers* in the great Dutch exodus and trek to the Transvaal and the Orange Free State, and later fought against the English in the Boer War; in the middle of the twentieth century it was calculated that a quarter of a million white South Africans were of Huguenot descent and many South African family names are of French origin. The exiles in England were joined by a small number of Camisard refugees; some of these travelled to America with Huguenot companions in groups totalling three thousand settlers, and although no French churches lasted more than a generation in the English colonies, many Americans of Huguenot descent, whether Camisard or not, attend the annual remembrance at the mas Soubeyran. In England a Huguenot Society devoted to historical and genealogical research was founded in 1885, but the great Huguenot religious community of seventeenth-century London was before long absorbed into the Anglican Church and probably the many English people with Huguenot blood feel the connection as interesting but remote.

The consequences for France and French society of the persecution of an identified minority of the population by the rest have been much discussed by historians; the certainty is that they were damaging. Warren Scoville in *The Persecution of Huguenots and French Economic Development 1680-1720* asked, "How can one estimate the harm wrought by distorting and perverting the moral decency and character of Frenchmen who actively participated ... or who passively witnessed the acts of cruelty?" Edgar Quinet in 1845 had answered part of the question: "The persecutions that the Catholics made the Protestants suffer, corrupted the former." Cabanel, whose authority in French Protestant history is unquestioned, asks if the nation had inflicted on itself a wound "of which it still today carries the trace ... without ceasing to feel the effects."[16]

Emmanuel Le Roy Ladurie states that in the struggle in the Cévennes the resistants took the ethical and political character they still have—

"rigid moralism, resistance to arbitrary power and to persecution, and defence of individual liberties". The historic Camisards' real claim to enduring reverence is that they held fast to that single right of men chained to the oar, of women shut in the Tour de Constance, of victims on the scaffold, of refugees across frontiers, of cautious families in hiding under their own roof—free exercise of thought in the quiet of their minds.

Notes

1   Philippe Joutard, *La légende des Camisards*: 173
2   Henri Bosc, vol. 4: 596, 620
3   Ibid, vol. 5: 183
4   Ibid: 185
5   Ibid: 206
6   David Agnew, *Protestant Exiles from France in the Reign of Louis XIV*, vol. 2: 62
7   Ibid: 61
8   Bosc, vol. 5: 398
9   Napoléon Peyrat, *Histoire des pasteurs du Désert*, vol. 2: 331-2
10 André Ducasse, *La guerre des camisards*: 221
11 Ibid
12 Jean-Paul Chabrol, *Élie Marion le vagabond de Dieu*: 202
13 Charles Bost, *Histoire des protestants de France*: 138
14 Patrick Cabanel, *Histoire des protestants en France xvi-xxi siècle*: 785
15 Philippe Joutard, *Les Camisards*: 218-19
16 Cabanel: 787

Bibliography

Agnew, David, *Protestant Exiles from France in the Reign of Louis XIV*, 3 vols. (London: 1871)

d'Aigaliers, baron, *Souvenirs de la guerre des camisards* (Lausanne: 1866)

Ascoli, Georges, "L'Affaire des prophètes français à Londres" in *Revue du XVIIIe siècle*, I (1916)

Basville, Nicolas de Lamoignon de, *Mémoires pour servir à l'histoire du Languedoc* (Amsterdam: 1736)

Blachère, Commandant Louis, *La Guerre des Cévennes* (Alès: 1970)

Bonbonnoux, Jacques, *Mémoires* (Montpellier: 1983)

Bonnemère, Eugène, *Les Dragonnades* (Nîmes: 1996)

Bosc, Henri, *La Guerre des Cévennes, 1702-1710*, 6 vols. (Montpellier: 1985-93)

Bost, Charles, *Histoire des protestants de France* (Neuilly: 1924)

Braudel, Fernand, *The Identity of France*, vol. I (London: 1988)

Brueys, David-Augustin de, *Histoire du fanatisme de notre temps* (Utrecht: 1737)

Cabanel, Patrick and Joutard, Philippe (eds.), *Les Camisards et leur mémoire 1702-2002* (Montpellier: 2002)

Cabanel, Patrick, *Histoire des Cévennes* (Paris: 1998)

Cabanel, Patrick, *Histoire des protestants en France xvi-xxi siècle* (Paris: 2012)

Cavalier, Jean, *Memoirs of the Wars of the Cevennes* (London: 1727)

Chabrol, Jean-Paul, *Abraham Mazel le dernier camisard* (Nîmes: 2009)

Chabrol, Jean-Paul, *Élie Marion le vagabond de Dieu* (Montpellier: 1999)

Chabrol, Jean-Paul, *Jean Cavalier (1681-1740), une mémoire lacérée* (Nîmes: 2010)

Chabrol, Jean-Paul, *Rolland l'insoumis* (Nîmes: 2012)

Chamson, André, *Castanet le Camisard de l'Aigoual* (Paris: 1979)

Court, Antoine, *Histoire des troubles des Cévennes ou de la guerre des camisards* (Montpellier: 2002)

Crouzet, Denis, La nuit de la Saint-Barthélemy: un rêve perdu de la renaissance (Paris:1994)

Cunningham, R.N., *Peter Antony Motteux 1663-1718* (Oxford: 1933)

de La Baume, Charles-Joseph, *Relation historique de la révolte des camisards* (Montpellier: 2004)

Defoe, Daniel, *Review of the State of the English Nation* (London: 1708)

De Mérez, Soeur, "Mémoire et journal", in *Chroniques du Languedoc* (1874)

Ducasse, André, *La Guerre des Camisards* (Paris: 1962)

Fléchier, Esprit, *Lettres choisies de l'évêque de Nîmes* (Paris: 1752)

Gorce, Agnès de la, *Camisards et dragons du roi* (Paris: 1950)

Jouanna, Arlette, *La Saint-Barthélemy, les mystères d'un crime d'état* (Paris: 2007)

Joutard, Philippe (ed.), *Journaux Camisards, 1700-1715* (Paris: 1965)

Joutard, Philippe, *Les Camisards* (Paris: 1976)

Joutard, Philippe, *La légende des Camisards* (Paris: 1977)

Jurieu, Pierre, *Lettres pastorales addressées aux fidèles de France* (Rotterdam: 1686-1688)

Knox R. A., *Enthusiasm* (Oxford: 1950)

Lacy, John, preface to *A Cry from the Desart* (sic), English translation of Misson, François Maximilien, *Le Théatre sacré des Cévennes* (London, 1707)

Lavisse, Ernest, *Louis XIV* (Paris: 1989)

BIBLIOGRAPHY

Le Roy Ladurie, Emmanuel, *The Peasants of Languedoc* (London: 1976)
Le Roy Ladurie, Emmanuel, *Histoire du Languedoc* (Paris: 1962)
Locke, John, (ed.) John Lough, *Locke's Travels in France 1675-9* (Cambridge: 1953)
Louvreleul, Jean-Baptiste, *The History of the Rise and Downfall of the Camisars* (London: 1709)
Marion, Élie, *Avertissements prophétiques* (London: 1707)
Mazel, Abraham, *Relation, in Journaux camisards, 1700-1715* (ed.) Philippe Joutard (Paris: 1965)
Michelet, Jules, *De la Révocation de l'Edit de Nantes à la Guerre des Cévennes* (Montpellier: 1985)
Michelet, Jules, *Louis XIV et la Révocation de l'Edit de Nantes* (Paris: 1985)
Mingaud, J, *Troubles des Cévennes à l'occasion de la guerre des camisards, éd. du Journal*
Misson, François Maximilien, *Le Théâtre sacré des Cévennes* (Paris: 1847)
Monahan, W. Gregory, *Let God Arise: The War and Rebellion of the Camisards* (Oxford: 2014)
Mouysset, Henry, *Les premiers Camisards* (Montpellier: 2010)
Noyer, Madame du, *Lettres historiques et galantes* (London: 1757)
Noyer, Madame du, *Mémoires*, 4 vols. (Cologne: 1710)
Peyrat, Napoléon, *Histoire des pasteurs du Désert*, 2 vols. (Valence: 1842)
Pin, Marcel, *Chez les Camisards* (Alès: 1938)
Pin, Marcel, *Jean Cavalier* (Nîmes: 1936)
Poujol, Robert, *Basville roi solitaire du Languedoc 1685-1718* (Montpellier: 1992)
Puaux, Frank (ed.) *Jean Cavalier, mémoires sur la guerre des Camisards* (Paris: 1918)
Randall, Catharine, *From a Far Country: Camisards and Huguenots in the Atlantic World* (London: 2011)
Rolland, Pierre, *Dictionnaire des Camisards* (Montpellier: 1995)
Saint-Simon, duc de, *Mémoires* (Paris: 1856)
Schwartz, Hillel, *Knaves, Fools, Madmen, and that Subtile Effluvium: A Study of the Opposition to the French Prophets in England* (Florida: 1978)
Schwartz, Hillel, *The French Prophets: The History of a Millenarian Group in Eighteenth-Century England* (London: 1980)
Shaftesbury, Lord, *A Letter Concerning Enthusiasm* (1708)
Tournier, Gaston, *Le baron de Salgas* (Musée du Désert: 1941)
Treasure, Geoffrey, *Louis XIV* (London: 2001)
Treasure, Geoffrey, *The Huguenots* (London: 2013)
Vidal, Grégoire, *Lettres et Rapports sur la Guerre des Camisards* (Montpellier: 1988)
Villars, Maréchal, *Mémoires* (Paris: 1884-1904)
Voltaire, *Le Siècle de Louis XIV* (Paris: 1740)
Voltaire, *Lettres philosophiques* (Lettres anglaises) (Paris: 1999)
Voltaire, *Traité sur la tolérance* (Paris: 1763)

Archives Historique du Ministère de la Guerre, 1702-1707
Archives de la Société de l'Histoire du Protestantisme Français, Paris
Archives du Département de l'Hérault.
Huguenot Library, University College London

Index